The Cycling Year *volume two*

The Cycling Year *volume two*

A record of the 1991 cycle racing season

by:
Phil Liggett
John Wilcockson
Rupert Guinness

off-road correspondent:
Simon Burney

photography:
Graham Watson

SBL Springfield Books Limited

Published by Springfield Books Limited,
Norman Road, Denby Dale, Huddersfield
HD8 8TH West Yorkshire, England

British Library Cataloguing in Publication Data
    The Cycling Year a record of the 1991 cycle racing season
    I Liggett, Phil 796.62

ISBN 1 85688 020 6

Design: Douglas Martin and Shirley Warren
Typesetting: Armitage Typo/Graphics Ltd
Colour reproduction: Colorcraft Ltd, Hong Kong
Printed and bound in England by Butler & Tanner Limited

Acknowledgements

The publishers and contributors are grateful to the following people for supplying additional material for use in this book:

ASL of Lausanne, for the pictures of the Tour de Romandie on pages 48-49

Carpress of Brussels, for the maps of Het Volk, Paris-Nice, Tirreno-Adriatico, Milan-San Remo, Tour of Flanders, Ghent-Wevelgem, Paris-Roubaix, Flèche Wallonne, Liège-Bastogne-Liège, Amstel Gold, Vuelta a España, Dauphiné Libéré, Giro d'Italia, Tour of Switzerland, Tour de France, Championship of Zürich, World Championship road circuit, Paris-Brussels, Paris-Tours and Tour of Lombardy

Stewart Clarke of ActionPact, for the picture of Phil Anderson on page 6, and pictures for the Milk Race on page 64 (bottom left), 66 (bottom left) and 67, the Kellogg's Tour of Britain on pages 106-108, the Grundig World Cup series on pages 126-127 and the World Mountain Bike Championships on page 138-139

Julia Ingersoll, for the account of the NORBA series on pages 114-115

Willie Mathews, for the pictures of the NORBA series on pages 114-115

Sergio Penazzo, for the picture of the Giro d'Italia on page 74 (top left)

John Pierce, Photosport International, for the picture of the Nissan Classic on page 134

John Pratt, for the pictures of the Ore-Ida Women's Challenge on pages 82-83

Presse Sports, for the pictures of Criterium International on pages 26-27, Four Days of Dunkirk on pages 46-47, Classique des Alpes on pages 50-51, Dauphiné Libéré on pages 68-69, Championship of Zürich on page 112, Grand Prix de la Liberation on pages 128-129 and Paris-Brussels on page 131

Mike Randolph, for the photographs of the Montreal Grand Prix on pages 140-141

Karen Schulenberg, for the pictures of the Tour du Pont on page 52-57 and the Corestates Championship on page 71

Stuart Walters, for the Milk Race picture on page 66 (top left)

Mark Wohlwender, for the pictures of Stephen Roche on page 27, and the Tour of Switzerland on pages 80-81

Cover pictures:

Front: Miguel Indurain on his way to winning the final time-trial of the 1991 Tour de France

Back: The Giro d'Italia races through the village of Castelrotto, in the Süd Tirol, on its mountainous passage to the summit of the Passo Pordoi on Stage 17

Endpapers: The Banesto team brought its victorious Tour de France to an end with a lap of honour on the Champs Elysées

Frontispiece: The 1991 season was one long success story for Gianni Bugno, Miguel Indurain and Claudio Chiappucci

Contents

Foreword: by Phil Anderson

Change has been the definitive word for the 1991 cycling season.

We have seen the creation of a new hierarchy in the peloton. The Italians continued to dominate the international scene with riders like Gianni Bugno, Claudio Chiappucci and Moreno Argentin, but a wave of new champions joined the elite. Amongst them were Melchor Mauri, Franco Chioccioli and Miguel Indurain, who won the Tours of Spain, Italy and France respectively. And Maurizio Fondriest and Laurent Jalabert entertained us with a close battle for the World Cup.

On the political front, 1991 has seen a whole swag of upheavals. The biggest was the helmet dispute between us – the riders – and the UCI, who tried to make wearing helmets compulsory. Then as the season closed we were all worried about the effect on cycling of the worldwide recession; several major sponsors have pulled out, leaving riders without jobs for 1992.

And of course, 1991 saw my fortunes take a brighter turn with 11 wins (12 if you count a criterium) in my first year with Motorola, after three doldrum years with TVM where I won a total of 15 races. So it is a year I shall certainly not forget.

Bugno, Chiappucci, Chioccioli, Mauri and Indurain led the way in the performance stakes. They are far from being new to the professional scene, proving that perseverance really does pay off! Bugno showed he was a real champion with his victories in the World and Italian Championships and the Clasicá San Sebastian – as well as dominating the the FICP world rankings and finishing second in the Tour. Chiappucci showed his Tour de France second place in 1990 wasn't just a fluke by winning Milan-San Remo, then taking second and third places respectively in the Italian and French Tours. And the manner in which Mauri, Chioccioli and Indurain won the major tours left no room for doubt that the best man won – in all cases, they were easily the strongest in the field.

As for Greg LeMond, champion though he is, 1991 was a year he would sooner forget. Losing the Tour was a blow. Apart from the World Championship road race, it's the only event he looks to and I guess if he can win it, good luck to him. But this year, even though he started the race in better condition than in the previous two years when he won, he didn't make it. It's ironic that he was whipped in the end by Chiappucci – a guy he has had such a publicised feud with since their duel in the 1990 Tour de France.

Is Greg a good example for riders to follow? He is certainly a great rider, but I reckon he is an oddity really. His method of training and racing for one race alone is not for everyone. Few riders can afford to risk saving all their efforts for one race like the Tour. Greg can get away with it because of his status as a three times Tour winner, but like it or not, most riders depend for their contracts on earning enough FICP points to get a good place in the rankings, and that means racing all year round.

It was a year of turmoil in cycling politics. Protests are nothing new in the peloton, but the dispute over the UCI's attempted compulsory helmet ruling pushed our anger to the point of unprecedented solidarity. I am a supporter of wearing helmets, but I believe it should be our choice. We are professionals, and while there are good arguments for juniors, amateurs, and recreational riders being obliged to wear them, I believe we have the experience and maturity to be able to judge for ourselves. It was for *that* reason I and many others joined the series of protests which began at Paris-Nice in March.

An important result of our protest was that it proved – to us, as well as everyone else – that we can bring about change. We do have a say. And now, it is not uncommon to see race organizations, especially in Italy, responding to rider 'go slow' campaigns against bad lighting in tunnels or, in many of the early season races in February and March, for the peloton to protest at racing in conditions of frost, rain and cold fronts which make roads dangerously slippy.

We achieved one of our major 'victories' in the Tour de France, when we demanded the reinstatement in the race of my Swiss team-mate Urs Zimmerman, after he had been eliminated because he did not make the transfer from St Herblain to Pau by the official plane but – because he does not like flying – went by car instead.

But the real test for the new, stronger peloton might come from another direction altogether. The worldwide economic recession has caused many sponsors to pull out of cycling. Weinmann, Histor and Toshiba have announced that they will not continue in 1992, and that means a lot of good riders have no jobs next year. The recession has also seen the market value of riders drop from what it was three or four years ago, when the English-speaking riders were the driving force behind the wage increases. Sponsors have less money to spend and now, after the wage boom of the eighties, salaries have levelled off a lot.

Another factor in this levelling-off is that some riders, currently still on huge wages, are not producing the results they should; they're not giving their sponsors value for money. Hence the current emphasis on FICP points to determine a rider's worth. Without points, contractual security is hard to get. Some of the big names are finding this out already; Sean Kelly and Laurent Fignon are two who – because of poor seasons – found themselves with contractual problems.

But, as *The Cycling Year* shows, the 1991 season proved that there is still plenty to be excited about and that in periods of change – competitive, political or economic – winning is still the highest card any rider can play.

Phil Anderson

World Cyclo-cross Championships: 2-3 February

Professional: 3 February

After the race was over, in the freezing cold of the Gieten forest in the north-east corner of Holland, the talk was not so much of the victorious Czech Radomir Simunek claiming an eastern bloc 'first' with his win, but more of how Adri Van der Poel came to lose a rainbow jersey by a single place for the fourth year running. With the race coming down to a three-man road sprint along the 250m finishing straight, the partisan home crowd were in no doubt as to the outcome: hadn't their man won Holland's only road classic, the Amstel Gold Race, in a sprint finish the previous year?

Simunek had been forced to ride on the front for most of the last lap, with Van der Poel happy to shadow his every move and Bruno Lebras of France – seemingly content to hang on to the break and assure himself of a medal – making up the trio. So it was Simunek who led out the sprint; the Dutchman came up to his right shoulder, but Simunek kicked again: his sights were set on another rainbow jersey to accompany those he had

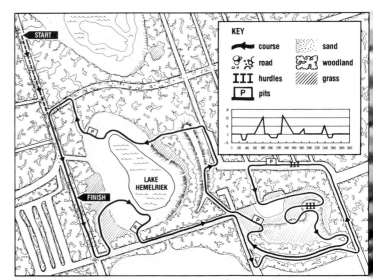

Gieten, Holland: 3km

Adri Van der Poel leads Radomir Simunek and Roger Honegger on the main run-up

won as a junior in 1980 and amateur in 1983 and 1984.

The race had started a little over 64 minutes earlier, with a frantic dash down the same road that later formed the finishing straight, and then into the first of the stretches of deep sand skirting the lake. With the Worlds course rendered super-fast by the freezing temperatures – in marked contrast to baking heat of the previous two years – most riders were concentrating on hanging on to their place in the lineout as long as possible and hoping the man in front would not leave a gap: too much effort spent closing these gaps would tell later in the race.

It was a leading group of ten men who first put daylight between themselves and the rest during this first lap. The break included the full quota of Dutch riders, who had raced their national championships over

exactly the same course just three weekends previously, and whose frozen tyre marks were still in evidence. Swiss rider Roger Honegger was in an aggressive mood, and although he would have preferred a softer, slower course, it was his constant attacks that reduced the front group to eight men. Then, with just three and a half laps to go, Van der Poel attacked, splitting the group in half. Simunek countered immediately, his style effortless and face expressionless; Lebras got across; and for nearly half a lap Honegger yo-yoed, just a few seconds adrift, his earlier efforts now costing him dearly. Finally the string snapped, and with Lebras hanging on for grim death it was down to the last lap and whether Van der Poel was fresh enough to attack again, or confident enough to leave it to the last minute. It seemed he was going to play the waiting game, sitting behind Simunek, and changing at the last pits onto a bike with road tyres in preparation for the sprint. But in the event it was Simunek, his mind

Simunek takes the sprint from a dejected Van der Poel. 'I was hoping Lebras would pass me so I wouldn't have to finish second again!'

Thomas Frischknecht was in a class of his own in the amateur race

Britain's Roger Hammond, seen here tackling the deep sand surrounding the lake, finished a creditable 11th after spending much of the race in the lead group

no doubt returning to the moment in 1990 when he punctured as he chased down eventual winner Henk Baars in the final 500m, who repeated the sprint which had given him his last amateur title in Holland seven years previously.

An interested spectator amongst the crowd of 20,000 who had braved the wintry conditions was Danny De Bie, who had won the event in 1989. His place in the Belgian team seemed assured this year until two weeks before the race, when – sensationally – he was accused of trying to defraud a dope control. Despite his desperate attempts to clear his name, in the end the UCI decided that De Bie should not ride 'on moral grounds', and the Belgians had to make do with cheering on their top man Wim Lambrechts to an eventual fifth place.

Amateur: 2 February

In contrast to the professional race, the amateurs were dominated from start to finish by 20-year-old Swiss star Thomas Frischknecht. After taking the junior title just three years ago in the snow and mud of Hägendorf, Frischknecht showed himself, in the fast, icy conditions of Holland to be a man for all courses.

Fifty-five riders set off on the long road start, and Frischknecht was amongst the leading four, going into the first set of hurdles after only 600m just behind Poland's Wojcliek Kadrynksi, and coming out with a 10m lead. Then he simply put his head down and rode away. He was 10 seconds clear at the end of the first lap,

and 25 seconds clear after two laps: the chasing group which, as in the pro race, contained the whole Dutch team, seemed resigned to fight over the silver and bronze medals. The ten-strong chase group split during the final lap, and it was the Dane, Henrik Djernis, who nipped round Italian Daniele Pontoni on the line to claim second place, 23 seconds behind Frischknecht.

For the Dutch, desperate to win on home ground, there was disappointment: for the Swiss, who have successfully incorporated team work into what is considered an event for individuals, elation.

Junior: 3 February

As a taster for the pro race held later in the day, the junior championships were battled for and won by a strong Czeckoslovakian team. Before the morning was over they had taken the gold and silver medals and placed all four riders in the top six. The winner in the five-up sprint finish was Ondrej Lukes who was three lengths clear of Jiri Pospisil, Jan Ulrich, Vaclav Vetlicka, and Poland's Dariusz Gil. These five broke clear from a ten-man lead group which had dominated the race from lap three.

The lone Pole in the group, Dariusz Gil, attacked repeatedly in an attempt to rid himself of the Czech quartet, but try as he might, their superb team work contained his efforts every time and he had to be content with a bronze medal.

RACE DETAILS

DATES Amateur *Saturday: 2 February* Junior and Professional *Sunday: 3 February*

WEATHER *Dry very cold 5° C, clear skies light easterly wind*

RACE DISTANCE *Professionals: 1 hour,*

9 laps; amateurs: 50 minutes, 7 laps; juniors: 40 minutes, 6 laps.

FIELD *Professional: 32 starters from nine nations; 30 finishers. Amateur: 55 starters from 17 nations; 54 finishers. Junior: 47 starters from 13 nations; 45 finishers.*

COURSE *3km in length, 27m height difference. Road start (off circuit) joins*

finishing straight to give 500m of road before turning onto sandy section and run through pit number 1. Good position leaving road important. One major run-up on steep steps and two runs through deep sand per lap, plus three sets of 40cm high hurdles, totalling six dismounts per lap. Ground hard: frozen sandy soil left rutted by Dutch championships three weeks before.

Track racing: October 90-February 91

During winter, cycling *aficionados* turn their attention indoors for the 1990/91 six-day season where, night after night, into the early hours of every morning and in spite of the cold, a select band of cyclists race their hearts and legs out in one of the sport's most dangerous arenas. Off-saddle attractions − rock'n'roll music and bands, à la carte restaurants in the pit, bars exuding a thick fog of cigarette smoke − vie with the sight of the hard racing on the steep banks of Europe's best-known velodromes − which inevitably claim their victims − that combine in an assault on the senses which makes six-day cycling a unique experience for spectators and competitors alike.

The six-day circuit is no longer the sole domain of the track specialist. Many road racers incorporate a six-day programme in their winter training to prepare for the early season road races in southern France, Spain and Italy. And there is now the incentive of valuable FICP points, as well as an opportunity to earn some extra money.

At first, the influx of roadmen was somewhat resented by the track specialists: they claimed the visiting 'roadies' were earning far more in appearance monies and for their top billing, than the dedicated hard-core six-day racers. But this opinion started to change as the benefits became apparent; the dwindling interest of the crowds has been revived by the attraction of more well-known names from the road racing fraternity. And the competition, motivated by rivalry, FICP points, pride and the need to provide crowd entertainment, has become far harder too.

The 1990/91 season, made up of 11 races, starting with the Dortmund Six in Germany (October 25-30) and finishing at Copenhagen in Denmark from February 1-6 was no exception to the atmospheric event spectators had come to expect. An early highlight was the remarkable comeback of Tony Doyle at the Munich Six in November 8-13. His near-fatal crash at the same event one year before was still etched in everyone's minds. An estimated 100,000 people crammed Munich's futuristic Olympiahalle − the site of the 1972 Olympic Games − to witness Doyle and Clark's winning ride. For British rider Doyle, clearly on sparkling form and fully recovered, it was a triumphant return. After the terrible injuries he sustained in his ugly spill with five others on the fourth night of the 1989 Munich race, many people were impressed that he was racing at all.

Doyle's memories of that fateful night are still vivid today. He crashed when Soviet Marat Ganeev rode into his line as he was about to attack coming off the last bank, sustaining an awesome list of injuries: a broken arm, elbow broken in two places, fractured shoulder, knocked out and in a coma for a week. When the stretcher bearers tried to carry him out to the waiting ambulance, they dropped him on the concrete steps; and then, out in the cold night air, failed to cover his sweat-soaked body with a blanket and he got a lung infection as well.

Ironically, in this season's Munich race, it was on the fourth night that Doyle and Clark made their winning move. For the first three nights they had toyed with the lead; now they attacked and took two laps on the field −

Australia's Danny Clark and Great Britain's Tony Doyle recorded one of the most significant wins of the season at Munich − amazingly their 19th win together and only one year after Doyle's near-fatal crash

One of the surprise sensations of the track season was Olaf Ludwig's stunning victory at Dortmund

Six-day racing is more than just a bike race

The team to beat – Germany's Andreas Kappes and Belgium's Etienne de Wilde

enough to secure the final victory two nights later. 'It was supposed to be a sort of rest night, that Sunday night. But we made it World War Three', said Doyle. 'Winning here after my accident proves how good we are', he added, referring to the Australian/British duo's 19 wins together – the equal highest number by any pair in six-day racing. It was Doyle's 22nd career win; for Clark, the win was his 61st – four short of the third highest number of wins of 65 by the now retired Dutchman Peter Post. 'It [the record] means a lot to me and Danny. But I don't know when I'll be riding with him again. A lot of promoters won't want us together because they believe that when we are, it's a foregone conclusion that we will win.'

Tough opponents for the Doyle/Clarke duo were Germany's Andreas Kappes, the new 'wunderkind' of the circuit, and Belgium's Etienne De Wilde. They became the team to beat on the circuit as Doyle's concerns, about promoters' attitudes to himself and his partner, became a reality. Doyle and Clark did not team up again, although Clark edged closer to Post's record with his win at Copenhagen, which took his career tally to 62. The 40-year-old veteran has declared that the 1991/92 season will 'definitely' be his last so time is running out but he is riding with Doyle again and with the Kappes/De Wilde duo also in the picture, winter cycling fans can look forward to some thrilling encounters.

De Wilde and Kappes scored a hat-trick of wins in Germany at Cologne (December 27-Jan 1), Bremen (January 10-15) and Stuttgart (January 18-23). And for De Wilde, his two other successes came at Grenoble (November 14-19) in France, where he partnered veteran

road racer Gilbert Duclos-Lassalle, and then at Antwerp (January 25-30) in Belgium where he teamed up with world road champion and local hero, Rudy Dhaenens.

De Wilde was understandably sensitive when asked to compare his 1989/90 season with this one: many critics had attributed his seven wins in 89/90 to the absence of Tony Doyle. This time, five wins – with Doyle back – was enough to make him feel justified in claiming the crown as the top six-day racer. When asked about not being able to match his seven wins of 1989/90, he said 'That doesn't mean a thing to me, the only important thing is that I'm proving once more that I'm one of the best. Last year, everybody said that I won because Tony Doyle was out. Doyle is there now, and I am winning again.'

With six-day racing enjoying great popularity in Germany, the opening event in Dortmund saw German six-day rookie, Olaf Ludwig, win with Swiss star Urs Freuler. Ludwig didn't win another race, but he had made his mark, showing an incredible grasp of this style of racing. As Doyle reflected after Ludwig and Freuler fought back on the last night to draw even with the new partnership of Kappes and Clark and then win on the very last sprint: 'Ludwig was just too powerful. He was pulling Freuler around, rather than the other way around.'

For Freuler, his luck had run out; he failed to win another race. In the event he came closest to winning – in his home town of Zürich, Switzerland (November 26-December 2), Freuler and his Swiss team-mate Hans-Rudi Marki were unable to make up the one-lap lead the Italian pair of Pierangelo Bincoletto and Adriano Baffi took on the second night and had to be content with

second place. But even that prize was taken away when Freuler was found positive in a dope test taken on the first night. Later, the moustachioed Swiss claimed that medicine he took to cure a cold had – unknown to him – contained the amphetamines found in his urine test.

After Zürich Kappes and De Wilde brought off their hat-trick of German wins, and waiting for De Wilde were four successive titles when he joined Dhaenens on home soil to win at Ghent. This was the climax of their season, the last remaining event – Cologne – being won by Veggerby and Clark.

For the first time, the six-day calendar incorporated a series of sprint matches between the world's top sprinters. While not competing in the six-day competition, their one on one duels were still a great crowd pleaser. And of those who took part, nobody drew as much support as Germany's reigning world professional sprint champion, Michael Hübner

Massage and rest are two of the most important conditions for survival in a six-day race. Here in his trackside pit Olaf Ludwig lets his soigneur *do the work while he relaxes in between races*

Het Volk: 2 March

Belgium without its cobbled monts (if you're French-speaking) or bergs (if Dutch is your natal Belgian tongue), would be rather like the North York Moors without heather or Colorado without the Rockies. But to every professional rider, the sight of these unpleasant little pimples in deepest Flanders in springtime usually causes the heart to flutter and the legs to complain. And as the field rolled away for the Het Volk classic − the first major event of the 1991 road racing season − the rude Belgian weather was a sharp reminder to most riders, who had been racing in the more temperate climate of the Mediterranean countries since early February, that springtime had barely arrived in northern Europe.

Het Volk has a long history of favouring home riders − only five non-Belgians have won since its inception in 1945. This year saw the fifth of these foreign victories: Andreas Kappes is German and proud of it. After a poor season last year with Toshiba, the 25-year-old started this year well with wins in the Luis Puig Trophy and a stage in the Tour of Valencia; also, he has a good friend and tutor in his Belgian Histor team-mate Etienne De Wilde, with whom he won three six-day races last winter at Cologne, Bremen and Stuttgart, and whom he had helped to win the Grand Prix Wielerrevue three days earlier.

The cold, and poor visibility, dampened the spirits of the peloton during the early part of the race, and it was not until the first of the notable climbs, the Old Kwaremont, that the first serious break was launched, by Australian Phil Anderson, who was quickly joined by Belgian Carlo Bomans (Weinmann) and Dutchman Frans Maassen (Buckler). Anderson, top signing for the new American Motorola team, was flexing the legs which had already carried him to impressive wins in the

Frans Maassen (nearest camera), Carlo Bomans and Phil Anderson (behind) forged the only real breakaway of the day

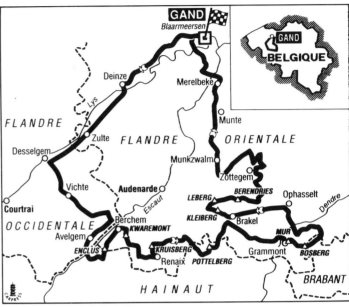

Het Volk, Belgium: 201km

Tour of the Mediterranean and the Tour of Sicily. All three riders were on form, and you have to make hay when the form is there, especially before the rest catch up, so with most of the hills to come and nearly 130km to ride they were away.

Together the three escapers pedalled to a lead of almost four minutes, and with three such strong men well clear the race could have been over, but as the sun tried vainly to push its way through the Flemish fog a spring finally entered the heels of the peloton. An 11-man chase group formed, comprising German Olaf Ludwig (Panasonic), Frenchmen Charly Mottet (RMO) and Laurent Fignon (Toshiba), Dutchmen Eddy Schurer (TVM), John Talen (PDM) and Adri Van der Poel (Tulip) and a Belgian contingent of Edwig Van Hooydonck (Buckler), Etienne De Wilde (Histor),

Anderson's acceleration and the cobblestones of the Old Kwaremont helped split the field one third of the way through the race. Here, Norwegian Atle Pedersen of Tonton Tapis is one of the riders striving to stay in contention

Ronny Van Holen (Tulip), Marc Sergeant (Panasonic) and Johan Museeuw (Lotto). Helped by a closed level crossing that held up the leaders, the chasers caught their prey with 57km to go; six kilometres later, an active main field caught up. With 32km to go the field split at speed, leaving a group of thirty riders out front.

'It wasn't so much an attack as a split,' said Australian Dean Woods, who was caught in the rear group. 'It happened about ten riders up from me. I guess some riders weren't really concentrating.' Also left behind were Anderson, Mottet, Belgian world champion Rudy Dhaenens (Panasonic) and Ireland's Sean Kelly (PDM). In the lead group, which included the formidable sprinters Dutchman Jelle Nijdam (Buckler), Belgian Jan Goessens (Weinmann), as well as Bomans and De Wilde and France's Laurent Jalabert (Toshiba), Belgian champion Claude Criquielion (Lotto) was setting a punishing pace in an attempt to set up a bunch sprint for his team-mate Museeuw. Also in the wind-up to the sprint was Kappes, intending to lead out the sprint for De Wilde, but De Wilde was blocked in the last 400 metres and fell away to finish tenth. 'Suddenly, I found a way through. I felt so strong and I just went.' At the line, Kappes just beat Bomans, who was a metre ahead of Van Hooydonck.

Revelling in his early-season form, Claude Criquielion hauled the leading group towards Ghent at high speed in the hope that Johan Museeuw would reap the benefit in the anticipated bunch sprint

RACE DETAILS

WEATHER *Fog at the start changed to cool mist, with occasional sunny periods.*

COURSE *201km anti-clockwise circuit on the outskirts of Ghent in western Belgium. Route covered 9 'monts', the most notable being the Old Kwaremont (72km), the*

Mur de Grammont (111km), the Bosberg (116km) and the Berendries (148km).

FIELD *190 starters; 101 finished.*

Early part of race uneventful . . . 72km On the Old Kwaremont Anderson, Bomans and Maassen break away, building a maximum lead of 3:45. 11-man chase group

reduces deficit to 1:45 with the help of a closed level crossing . . . 144km the three escapers are finally caught nearing Leberg . . . 150km an active main field catches up and the peloton regroups . . . 167km With 32km to go the field splits and a group of 30 riders gets away. In the sprint Kappes just beats Bomans to the line, with Van Hooydonck third.

Paris-Nice: 10-17 March

The ill-feeling in the peloton against the UCI's hard-shell helmet rule was apparent as soon as the 1991 road season began. The riders were not disputing the safety value of helmets − in fact support for their use had been growing rapidly − but were very unhappy about the UCI's refusal to accept that heat, particularly in the mountains, made wearing them uncomfortable. Also, they were incensed that the UCI had made the wearing of helmets compulsory, thereby taking away every professional cyclist's right to choose for himself. The debate cast a shadow over many of the early season competitions in Spain, France and Italy, and came to a head during the first major stage race in the calendar − Paris-Nice. Unfortunately for the organisers, the 41st edition is likely to be remembered not as one of cycling's most exciting athletic confrontations, but for the riders' stage seven defiance of the helmet rule.

In spite of the discontent that dominated the peloton, however, the race produced some remarkable competitive feats. Foremost amongst these was the performance of Switzerland's Tony Rominger (Toshiba), who relinquished the opportunity to convert his two-year domination of Tirreno-Adriatico into a hat-trick in order to take part in the 'Race to the Sun'. His gamble

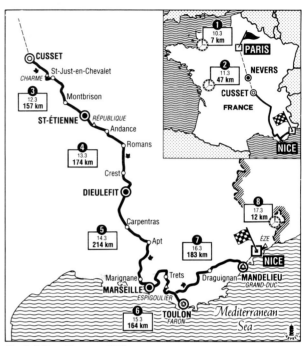

Paris-Nice, France: 957km

paid off; the overall victor, he spent every day but two in the leader's white jersey and won four stages.

And while Rominger and Toshiba tied up the overall race very early with their 0:56 team time trial win over PDM at Nevers − their team headquarters − there were admirable stage victories by Germany's Andreas Kappes (Histor) on stage three, Soviet second-year professional Viktor Klimov (Seur) on stage four, Dutchman Jean-Paul Van Poppel (PDM) on stage five, and German Uwe Ampler (Histor) on stage seven.

Even within each day's racing, impressive helpings of bravado were served up, with Irishman Sean Kelly (PDM) typically prominent. But his hopes of increasing his record seven wins here to eight were dashed when he broke his right collar-bone in a crash on stage three with two team-mates − Belgian Jos Van Aert and Irishman Martin Earley. The cause was a Toshiba feed bag which got caught up in Van Aert's wheel, bringing him down and causing similar fates to befall the two Irishmen who were following his wheel. Astonishingly, Kelly managed to finish the stage and move up to eighth place overall, but the end result was withdrawal from the race that night and a three-week spell off the bicycle which cast a blight over his ambitions for the spring classics.

Stage five to Marseille gave us a convincing reminder that not everyone believed Rominger had victory in the bag. An 11-man break got away, led by the Motorola work-horses Phil Anderson of Australia and Sean Yates of Great Britain, and had other riders been tempted to contribute to the duo's effort it might have changed the course of the race. But others didn't, and apart from taking 0:31 off Rominger the only result of their aggression was to put Toshiba's Pascal Lance of France into 'caretaker leadership' − he too was in the break and easily surpassed his overnight 0:04 margin on Rominger.

Then on stage six Greg LeMond kept his promise to

Andreas Kappes was an easy winner of the uphill dash at St Etienne for Stage 3

attack 'some time': no-one who witnessed it will forget the sight of him bolting away at the bottom of a steep, short descent just 32km into the stage to Mont Faron, and then taking four others – America's Ron Kiefel (Motorola), Belgium's Michel Vermote (RMO), Italy's Emmanuele Bombini (Gatorade) and Denmark's Per Pedersen (Amaya) – on a 120km trek over three mountain passes and to the foot of the Mont Faron finish where they were caught. This day contained other notable incidents, such as Lance's nasty crash at 83.5km, which almost rendered him unconscious and in need of immediate transfer to hospital. His cracked hard-shell helmet indicated the nature of the impact, and also what injuries he might have sustained (rather than the concussion that was eventually diagnosed) had he not been wearing it. Lance's misfortune, and Rominger's brilliant ride to win the stage to Mont Faron, saw the lanky dark-haired Swiss back in white.

It was an event on this stage that put a match to the highly combustible tension over the UCI helmet ruling and thrust aside all competitive interest in the race. As Frenchman Francis Moreau (Tonton Tapis) began his assault on the Faron – under the typically hot Mediterranean sun – he took off his helmet. This infraction earned him automatic disqualification; it also jeopardised the future of the race.

Rumours had been rife that a rider's protest was planned – for the opening World Cup classic, Milan-San Remo, a week later. Moreau's disqualification, for an infringement of the rule in precisely those circumstances under which the riders were most concerned to keep their right to decide for themselves, brought the protest

Viktor Klimov became the first Soviet cyclist to win a stage of Paris-Nice at Dieulefit. Here, the Seur professional leads TVM's Rob Harmeling in the latter stages of their forceful break

Anderson and Yates gave their all in an attempt to wrest the race from Tony Rominger on Stage 5. Yet the efforts of the Australian leader of the Motorola team (seen here leading Pascal Lance, with Yates obscured) came to nothing

An historic moment: on the outskirts of Toulon, protesting riders clash with race officials over the helmet rule. LeMond, Roche, Criquielion, Fignon, Duclos-Lassalle and Madiot are seen here presenting their points of view to race organisers

Tony Rominger's acceleration to the summit of Mont Faron virtually assured him of overall victory. Here, the Swiss rider still has France's Roland Le Clerc for company, but with a kilometre to go the Amaya rider is about to find himself left behind

plans into immediate operation. Overnight, Frenchman Marc Madiot (RMO) telephoned every team leader, rallying support for a protest the next day – stage seven from Toulon to Mandelieu – and that support was just as promptly forthcoming. Leading the hard-line tactics with Madiot were LeMond, Irishman Stephen Roche (Tonton Tapis) and Frenchmen Laurent Fignon (Castorama) and Gilbert Duclos-Lassalle (Z), whose forthright remarks about FICP president Hein Verbruggen had no doubt raised the emotional temperature of the dispute.

So it was a bare-headed peloton which, under the ominous scrutiny of UCI commissaires, rode through the neutral zone to the start proper outside Toulon. When they reached the start line, the race was halted and the riders were warned that their actions were illegal. A 15-minute stand-off between riders and officials ended with the riders deciding for themselves whether or not to wear helmets: when the race set off again, three-quarters of the riders still had bare heads.

News of the protest, which was repeated during Sunday's final and rain-sodden time trial stage to the Col d'Eze near Nice, quickly travelled to Italy, where Tirreno-Adriatico was now six days old, and similar action was taken by the peloton. At Paris-Nice, where the 'sun' everyone had been racing towards still seemed to be a long way away, the only UCI response was to declare every result provisional pending the UCI committee's finding on a race jury report to be submitted the following week. For the time being, even if Rominger's well-deserved victory was officially only 'provisional', the riders were in the ascendant.

Greg LeMond's daring 120km break was a refreshing sideshow to the main business of the race

Stephen Roche's effort on his favourite time trial course fell just over a second short of earning him first place

RACE DETAILS

WEATHER *Rain on stages one and eight, otherwise sunny and fine.*

FIELD: *One less than original 120 starters. 15 teams of eight riders per team.*

STAGE 1 – 6.5km individual time trial, Fontenay-sous-Bois, Paris *Marie and Rominger, with officially equal winning times of 8:29.67, share lead for stage two. Rominger is 1000th/second slower, but race rules discount margins of less than 100th/second.*

STAGE 2 – 47km team time trial, Nevers *Toshiba win by 0:56 from PDM, with Castorama third at 1:07 and Motorola fourth at 1:11. Toshiba's win gives Rominger overall lead, 1:06 ahead of nearest rival, Dutchman John Van den Akker (PDM).*

STAGE 3 – Cusset-Saint Etienne, 157km . . . 61km *17-man break is made on descent of Col de la Charme (45km) and Col de St Thomas (55km), including Rominger, Kelly, Fignon. Break never works and is soon caught on the flat . . . 90km Kelly crashes at feed station . . . 101km Frenchman Patrice Esnault (RMO) attacks, getting 0:34 lead before being caught 10km from finish . . . 157km Kappes wins bunch sprint on steep uphill finish from Vermote and Van Poppel. Rominger keeps lead with 10th place.*

STAGE 4 – Saint Etienne-Dieulefit, 174km . . . 95km *Dutchman Rob Harmeling (TVM) attacks alone at feed station (95km) . . . 124km Klimov counter-chases with 50 km to go, bridging 3:00 deficit within 10km . . . 173km Klimov attacks Harmeling and wins stage, his first professional victory, by 0:06 from Harmeling and 0:22 from peloton. Rominger, in the bunch, is still race leader.*

STAGE 5 – Dieulefit-Marseille, 214km . . . 154km *11-man break forms, including Anderson, Yates, Lance, Van Poppel, and Ronan Pensec (Seur) of France. Anderson, Yates, and sometimes Pensec, are only ones to work. Anderson tries to cut his 1:33 deficit on Rominger, in the peloton. They get as much as 1:50 lead . . . 214km Van Poppel wins stage in sprint from breakaways, 0:31 clear of the peloton. Lance, previously third overall, takes race lead at 0:04. Rominger drops to second at 0:27.*

STAGE 6 – Marseille-Toulon, 164km . . . 32km *LeMond attacks at bottom of short descent, taking with him Kiefel, Vermote, Bombini, and Pedersen. Break gets up to 5:20 lead as it passes the Col de L'Espigoulier (100km) before chase starts . . . 83km Race leader Lance crashes and abandons . . . 158km Break caught by peloton and immediately Rominger attacks on 6km climb to Mont Faron finish. Rominger wins stage, defeating Amaya team-mates Frenchman Roland Le Clerc and Spanish champion Laudelino Cubino by 0:23. American Andy Hampsten (Motorola) is ninth at 0:46 on the stage*

and moves up to sixth place overall at 2:29. Roche, eighth at 0:32, is also eighth overall at 2:38. Rominger retakes overall lead.

STAGE 7 – Toulon-Mandelieu, 183km . . . 84km *Duclos-Lassalle dictates race pace with his attack at start line. Peloton regroups after first hours see many attacks fail . . . 115km Breakaway of Earley, Vermote, Frenchmen Robert Forest (Z) and Jean-Claude Bagot (Castorama) and Italy's Giorgio Furlan (Ariostea) gains 1:14 on peloton by 123km . . . 162km Vermote dropped as race passes Lac de St Gassien . . . 165km Peloton closing in as Earley attacks near summit of Tanneron climb, 18km from finish; he is caught 800m from the line. Ampler wins from Frenchman Eric Caritoux (RMO) and Belgian champion Claude Criquielion (Lotto-Superclub) at 0:03. Rominger fourth at 0:08 with six others, including Roche (eighth) and Hampsten (tenth). Rominger's overall lead is 2:01 on Criquielion (fourth), 2:29 on Hampsten (seventh), 2:38 on Roche (eighth). French Toshiba team-mates, Martial Gayant and Laurent Jalabert, are second and third overall at 1:20 and 1:21 respectively.*

STAGE 8 – 12km mountain time trial, Col d'Eze, Nice *Rominger, last to start, wins stage in 24:09.19 to win overall. Roche, four times winner of the stage, is second at 1:19 and finishes fourth overall at 2:39. Hampsten is third at 0:12 (fifth overall at 2:41), and Anderson is sixth at 0:42 (11th overall at 4:20).*

Tirreno-Adriatico: 13-20 March

The compulsory helmet dispute was not confined to Paris-Nice. Word of events in France quickly spread to Italy where Tirreno-Adriatico was in progress, and riders here organised their own protest against the UCI ruling. It was on stage five from Montegranaro to the ancient town of Osimo that the drama started. The peloton started the stage one hour late without helmets. Then at the five-kilometre and thirty-one kilometre marks they stopped in protest – on both occasions being warned that defiance of the UCI ruling would result in elimination from the race.

Riders sat in the road, chatting during the second confrontation pondering the situation, for 40 minutes. Finally, a compromise was reached: if the riders would continue racing with helmets, the officials would promise to find a solution.

Apart from this controversy, this year's edition of 'the Race of the Two Seas' was fairly unremarkable after a breakaway on stage one from Pompeii to Ottaviano largely determined the overall placings. In the eight-man break, which began 140km into the stage, were: Switzerland's Thomas Wegmüller (Weinmann), Spain's Herminio Diaz-Zabala (ONCE), Italy's Andrea Tafi (Selle Italia) and Federico Ghiotto (Ariostea), Dutchman Martin Ducrot (TVM), France's Philippe Casado (Z), Mexico's Raúl Alcalá (PDM), and Dutchman Maarten Den Bakker (PDM). It was Ghiotto who took the stage, and he retained the overall lead until the final stage.

But again, Ghiotto's place in the limelight owed less to his sporting prowess than the hot debate as to whether he should have been racing at all: in the 1990 Sicilian Week he had tested positive for the drug testosterone, and under Italian Cycling Federation rules the penalty was a two-year suspension. However, after intervention by the FICP the ban was cut to twelve months.

However, he had little trouble holding onto his lead as stage wins went successively to Switzerland's Pascal Richard (Helvetia-La Suisse), the Soviet Union's Dmitri Konyshev (TVM), Italy's Silvio Martinello (Gis-Ballan), France's Gérard Rué (Helvetia-La Suisse), Belgium's Dirk De Wolf (Tonton Tapis) and, on the penultimate leg, Denmark's TVM rider Jesper Skibby. But come the

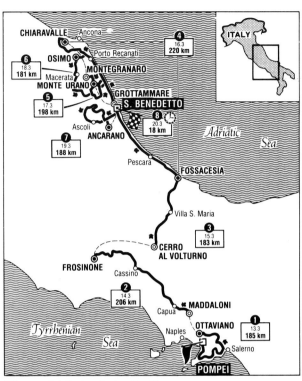

Tirreno-Adriatico, Italy: 1379km

eighth and final stage Ghiotto's aspirations crumbled: the flat 18.3km individual time trial at San Benedetto del Tronto was taken, in a repeat of his inspired performance in last year's race, by Dutchman Eric Breukink (PDM) in 22:10.

Ghiotto finished seventh at 0:31, while Diaz-Zabala came through with a second place on the stage at 0:05 to surpass his overnight 0:22 on Ghiotto and take overall victory. This win marked the 26-year-old Spaniard's first international success as a professional since he took a stage in the 1989 Tour of Spain; it also gave the ONCE team their third stage-race win of the season. Ghiotto took second place overall at 0:04, his disappointment at losing perhaps mitigated by the knowledge that he could easily not have been in the race at all.

RACE DETAILS

WEATHER *Mainly fine.*

FIELD *22 8-man teams. 175 starters.*

STAGE 1 – Pompeii-Ottaviano, 185km *...75km At top of Valico di Chiunzi, Rué attacks with De Wolf, Konyshev, and Martinez. They get 1:00 lead before Fondriest leads peloton back...140km Eight-man attack finishes 3:05 ahead of peloton. Ghiotto wins stage by 0:05 on Wegmüller to take race lead.*

STAGE 2 – Maddaloni-Frosinone, 206km *...189km On climb to Morola, Delion accelerates but is blocked by press motorbike. Leblanc attacks with Richard who wins stage. Peloton at 0:08; Ghiotto leads overall.*

STAGE 3 – Cerro al Volturno-Fossacesia, 183km *Konyshev wins in sprint from Sciandri and Vanderaerden. Ghiotto retains lead.*

STAGE 4 – Fossacesia-Chiaravalle, 220km *Martinello wins stage in bunch sprint from Leoni and Citterio. Ghiotto retains lead.*

STAGE 5 – Montegranaro-Osimo, 198km *...5km and 31km Peloton stops in protest at UCI helmet rule...185km Rué attacks with Maassen, Sunderland and Indurain...197km Rué attacks on cobbled uphill finish to win stage by 0:06 on Indurain and 0:27 on peloton. Ghiotto retains lead.*

STAGE 6 – Osimo-Monte Urano, 181km *...78km Pascal Simon attacks; De Wolf and Roscioli follow. They get 6:00 lead...145km*

Break has 1:00 lead now, and De Wolf and Simon drop Roscioli on the steep climb to Mont Urano...181km De Wolf wins stage alone by 1:46 on Skibby and 1:53 on Fondriest. Ghiotto retains lead.

STAGE 7 – Grottammare-Ancarno, 188km *...187.5km Skibby leads out sprint to win stage from Sciandri and Rué on uphill finish from a lead group of 20 riders. Ghiotto retains lead.*

STAGE 8 – San Benedetto-Del Tronto, 18.3km individual time trial *Diaz-Zabala finishes second at 0:05 to stage winner Breukink and takes overall victory. Ghiotto, 0:22 ahead of Diaz-Zabala overnight, drops to second overall at 0:02 after finishing seventh on stage at 0:31.*

The other *story of Tirreno-Adriatico 1991: Herminio Diaz-Zabala streaks across the finish line of the 18km time trial in San Benedetto del Tronto to snatch overall victory from Federico Ghiotto. Such was the force of the Basque rider's finishing kick that it lifted his back wheel clean off the ground!*

Milan-San Remo: 23 March

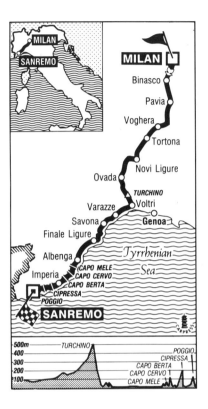

Milan-San Remo,
Italy: 294km

Grey clouds and sheets of rain accompanied the start of the 1991 Milan-San Remo: it was obvious that the winner would be a rider with the courage and aggression to shed the inhibitions so often engendered by wet weather racing. And in the person of Claudio Chiappucci (Carrera), the Italian former domestique whose hard-fought duel with Greg LeMond in the 1990 Tour de France made him an overnight star, and who maintained his form to finish the year ranked number two in the world, these two criteria were admirably met.

Chiappucci's 0:45 win, over Denmark's Rolf Sörensen (Ariostea) and 0:57 margin on the peloton led by Belgian sprinter Eric Vanderaerden (Buckler), kicked off the 1991 spring classics to a great start. And while 28-year-old Chiappucci still has plenty of critics, his fine attacking form in the *Primavera* inevitably earned him comparison with the great Eddy Merckx in his heyday, and put a hallmark on Chiappucci's seven-year professional career. It marked his first major one-day classic win, and only his sixth-ever professional victory. It also, incidentally, made him the first World Cup leader of the season. 'I knew that I was in form, but just the same I knew that that alone was not enough to win. People say that I am just a rider who makes a lot of noise but never wins. Today, I have taken my revenge, not only on my second place in the Tour, but on all the series of

Chiappucci and Bontempi safely installed behind Charly Mottet in the breakaway group as it battles through atrocious conditions along the Mediterranean coast after descending the Turchino pass

Sörensen resisted Chiappucci's strength longer than anyone. The Dane is seen here parrying the Italian's efforts on the sea-road leading to the Poggio, where Chiappucci finally dispenses with his companion's services in the style expected of all great winners of the Primavera

placings I have had in my career,' said Chiappucci who, despite his low tally of victories, is arguably the most consistent attacker in the peloton.

It was also a win that finally managed to subdue interest in the great helmet controversy which, at this point in the saga, was on ice as the UCI, FICP and riders' representatives had begun the previous day to negotiate towards a solution. These negotiations continued the following week, after riders agreed to wear helmets in this season-opening race, and were finally resolved when the UCI acceded to the peloton's demands and waived the rule for professionals until a helmet that met everybody's requirements was manufactured.

Looking back, it would have been hard to find a stronger rider in the line-up of 214 that departed Milan's regal Piazza del Duomo under a steady downpour of chilling rain that did not abate until the last hour of racing along the Mediterranean coast. Fit from winter cyclo-cross and full of confidence after his revelatory 1990 road season, Chiappucci wanted to start 1991 with

a winning ride. He had spent twelve days in January training on the Italian Riviera; in particular, the five critical climbs that pepper the final 60km of Milan-San Remo and usually determine the outcome of the race. Certainly, Chiappucci was entitled to the hysterical applause of the *tifosi* and the winner's laurels at San Remo's Corsa Cavallotti, but the muddied and grinning Carrera rider also owed a lot to his Italian team-mate, Guido Bontempi. For it was the veteran 1990 Tour de France stage winner who led out the decisive move near the top of the Turchino Pass at 140km, in pursuit of the two early attackers, Italians Stefano Zanini and William Dazzani (Italbonifica). Chiappucci, tucked into the slip-stream of the huge Italian, was one of five riders who joined the chase, the others being Sörensen, Frenchman Charly Mottet (RMO), Spain's Marino Lejarreta (ONCE) and Dutchman Adri Van der Poel (Tulip). The leaders' 3:30 lead by the start of the Turchino was 1:45 at the summit and, after a dangerous, twisting 12km descent through low cloud, rain and cold, they were reeled in by the Carrera-led chase group. Soon after, three more riders joined the leading eight – Frenchman Thierry Marie (Castorama) and Holland's Jelle Nijdam (Buckler) and Peter Stevenhagen (PDM).

With eleven riders in front, the winning cards seemed to have been dealt: by the first feed station at Savona their lead was 4:00 on the peloton, and had increased to 4:15 by the 201km mark. The race was now almost into Chiappucci's training ground, the final climbs, and as he said later, 'the race pattern was ideal for me'.

Back at the San Remo finish line, Chiappucci's critics began to fidget nervously. Radio and television broadcasts – albeit excitable Italian ones – relayed news on every pedal stroke he turned, and with every stroke, Chiappucci's stature grew in the eyes of his fans. Not only did he manage to stave off the chasing peloton, who got as close as 0:40 by 236km and the second feed station at Alassio, but he also shed his breakaway companions, with three lightning attacks that eventually left him alone in front. The first of these came on the Capo Mele climb, after 243km, and only Mottet, Nijdam and Sörensen could match it; the second, and more decisive, move was on the third of five climbs, the Capo Berta at 255km: only Sörensen was able to go with him. The final manoeuvre came, fittingly in view of the decisive role it has so often played in this race, on the Poggio climb: with 1:40 on the peloton, Chiappucci smoothly dropped the tiring Dane and scurried over the summit. He had

0:27 on Sörensen, and the odds on winning overwhelmingly in his favour. Admittedly, three mass crashes in the peloton hadn't damaged his prospects, particularly the last two, which involved riders of the calibre of Tony Rominger (Toshiba) of Switzerland and Italian Maurizio Fondriest (Panasonic). But Chiappucci had planned his race, and every move he made was part of his winning tactic. 'After we held back the peloton's chase, I put my plan into action,' he said afterwards. 'On the Capo Berta I saw the fatigue of Mottet and Nijdam. I accelerated, leaving only me and Sörensen. He suffered on the Cipressa climb [270km], but I didn't want to ride the last 20km alone, so I was happy to give everything on the Poggio, to respect my plan to the letter. Doing that makes me especially proud.'

The 4km descent into San Remo must have given Chiappucci some of his most nervous moments of the day: an almost unassailable position, vulnerable only to a crash on the slippery roads, and sheer elation at the prospect of his finest win to date, are a pretty volatile combination. But he arrived unscathed at the foot of the Poggio and spun his way to the finish line, urged on by a deafening chorus of cheers from the almost uncontrollable Italian crowds, bringing to a close a performance that was a welcome reminder of the rides that made cycling the institution it is in Italy today. Even Eddy Merckx would agree to that.

An apocalyptic image of Milan-San Remo: the peloton nears the fog-shrouded summit of the Turchino pass with Eric Vanderaerden, Marco Lietti and Marino Lejarreta literally leading the way

Home, and almost dry. Chiappucci's finest win to date certainly muzzled his critics

RACE DETAILS

WEATHER *Temperature in lower 50s, northerly wind, rain from start until last hour of race.*

COURSE *294km point-to-point, from Milan to San Remo, in north-west Italy.*

FIELD *214 starters, including the world's top 20 ranked teams. Maximum of eight riders per team.*

Peloton intact for first 50 km across flat Lombardy plain . . . 73km Two Italian domestiques, Dazzani and Zanini, launch the first real attack . . . 115km A crash splits the pack in two, and Kappes and LeMond are caught in the back half . . . 143km Just before the summit of the Turchino a counterattack is instigated by Bontempi and Chiappucci, followed by Mottet, Lejarreta, Sörensen and Van der Poel. Starting the wet, twisting, 12km descent to the coast, the two leaders are 1:45 ahead of the six chasers, and 2:15 ahead of the peloton . . . 150km Marie, Nijdam and Stevenhagen take up the chase . . . 185km At the Savona feed zone, the attacking riders have formed a lead group of eleven, 4:00 ahead of the peloton . . . 201km The break has a maximum lead of 4:15, and the pack starts a spirited pursuit . . . 236km The gap has reduced to only 40 seconds . . . 243km Approaching the Capo Mele climb, Chiappucci accelerates and only Mottet, Nijdam and Sörensen are able to follow . . . 254km A crash involving about 50 riders slows the peloton again . . . 255km Chiappucci drops Mottet and Nijdam on the Capo Berta . . . 270km Chiappucci and Sörensen hold the lead on the Cipressa, followed at 1:25 by Gilles Delion (Helvetia) and Johnny Weltz (ONCE), with the first part of the peloton at 1:40 . . . 277km A third crash disrupts the chase group, with Delion among the victims . . . 287km Midway up the Poggio, Australian Phil Anderson (Motorola) counterattacks, and is within 50 seconds of the two leaders when Chiappucci attacks and drops Sörensen . . . 200km At the Poggio summit, Chiappucci is 27 seconds ahead of Sörensen, and more than a minute ahead of a chase group of 52 riders that has absorbed Anderson . . . 294km On the finish line, Chiappucci wins by 45 seconds from Sörensen. 12 seconds later, Eric Vanderaerden (Buckler) wins the sprint for third place, from Djamolidin Abdujaparov (Carrera), Eddy Planckaert (Panasonic), Gérard Rué (Helvetia) and Anderson.

Criterium International: 30-31 March

In many quarters, scepticism greeted the suggestion that 1991 was going to be the comeback year for Stephen Roche. After his knee injury in 1988, the '89 and '90 seasons were supposed to witness glorious returns to form, but in the event were barren of the brilliance that had marked his *annus mirabilis* in 1987, when he won the Tours of Italy and France and took the World Road Championship.

But as the 1991 season settled into its spring programme it really began to look as though this year, finally, would see it all come good for the 31-year-old Dubliner. The strongest evidence for this prognosis was his victory in the Critérium International stage race in the rugged and picturesque Vaucluse region of southern France; his win over Frenchmen Gérard Rué (Helvetia-La Suisse) and Charly Mottet (RMO) in the two-day, three-stage event consolidated a run of several winning performances − clear indications that the much-heralded return to form was actually taking place. Victory in the Spanish Catalan Week and fourth place in Paris-Nice had also amassed him an important personal tally of 205 FICP world ranking points: for his Tonton

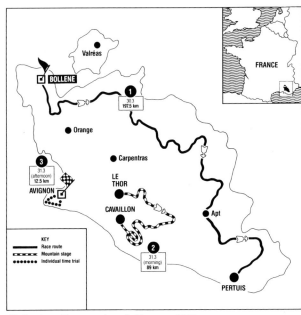

Criterium International, France: 298km

Tapis team − excluded from the opening World Cup race, Milan-San Remo, because they were ranked outside the top 22 teams − those points were very valuable, especially as Tonton Tapis had still to secure a place in the Tour de France.

'If it isn't a good year then I'll stop cycling for good' said Roche at the start of the season, after two years bedevilled by injury and sponsorship problems. 'It's my best performance since I started my comeback, and it was important not just because I beat someone like Charly Mottet, but because of the way I won it. I took the race into my own hands, making the key moves.'

Roche constructed his win on the second and third stages: the mountain race from Le Thor to Cavaillon, in which he came third, a member of the winning three-man break with Rué and Mottet that finished more than a minute clear of the peloton, followed by the 12.5km afternoon time trial at Avignon in which he came second, 0:02 behind the Soviet stage winner Viatcheslav Ekimov (Panasonic). It was in the time trial that Roche took the leader's lilac jersey; Mottet, the previous race leader after his victory in the second stage, two passages of the Côte de Vidauque, finished the time trial exhausted in 16th place.

Winning Critérium International takes a 'thinking' all-rounder. In fact, it is generally regarded as one yardstick of a potential champion and Tour de France winner, an opinion supported by the roll of past winners who include France's Laurent Fignon (1982 and 1990), Spain's Miguel Indurain (1989), Dutchman Eric Breukink (1988) and Irishman Sean Kelly (1983, 1984 and 1987). Roche himself had won the race in 1985. But after two disastrous seasons this latest triumph brought a wider smile to his face.

Criterium International, a two-day stage race through some of the most picturesque terrain of the Vaucluse region, is rated an accurate gauge of who will do what in the coming months

This winning breakaway of Mottet, Rué and Roche on Stage 2 set the battle lines for the final time trial that eventually took Roche to victory

RACE DETAILS

WEATHER *Sunny and warm throughout.*

FIELD *24 eight-man teams invited. 178 starters; 118 finished.*

STAGE 1 – Bollène-Pertuis, 197km *Undulating road stage* ...12.5km *After slow start, Frenchman Vincent Lavenu (Mosoca) attacks alone, staying away for 120km* ...135km *Lavenu is caught; a series of attacks begins* ...147km *12 men break away, but are caught after 30km. Roche prominent in attacks* ...173km *Attack by seven riders – Frenchmen Jean-Claude Leclercq (Helvetia-La Suisse), Robert Forest (Z) and Roland Le Clerc (Amaya), Belgian Johan Bruyneel (Lotto), Switzerland's Rolf Järmann (Weinmann), England's David Rayner (Buckler) and Denmark's Johnny Weltz (ONCE)* ...192km *Attackers get maximum of 0:40 on peloton; lead reduced to 0:17 at*

finish, where Le Clerc outsprints Weltz and Bruyneel to become overall leader.

STAGE 2 – Le Thor-Cavaillon, 89km *Americans Greg LeMond (Z) and Andy Hampsten (Motorola) are amongst those who abandon on this mountain stage* ...40km *Three riders attack on the first of two passages of 5% Côte de Vidauque: Ekimov and Frenchmen Eric Boyer (Z) and Laurent Madouas (Toshiba). Leaders are chased down by Mottet, Rué and Roche, and dropped on the second passage of the Vidauque* ...98.1km *Roche, Mottet and Rué enter Cavaillon's open velodrome 0:58 clear of peloton; Mottet wins stage from Rué and Roche to take overall lead.*

STAGE 3 – 12km individual time trial, Avignon *Ekimov wins convincingly on flat route, but Roche takes overall victory with second place at 0:02 as Mottet tires to finish 16th at 0:30, with Rué 11th at 0:20.*

The early season victory of the Criterium International looked like confirmation for Roche that 1991 would be his year

Tour of Flanders: 7 April

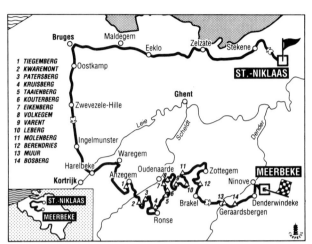

Tour of Flanders, Belgium: 261km

A pre-race favourite, Maurizio Fondriest failed to muster the tactical expertise necessary for the 'Ronde'. The Panasonic rider is seen here trying to bridge a gap to one of the front groups after the Patersberg climb had shredded the field

When Edwig Van Hooydonck astonished the cycling world in 1989 with his solo win in the Tour of Flanders, his tears of emotion as the young red-headed Belgian stood on the winner's podium made front pages throughout Europe. But this year, after a similarly convincing win, there were no tears. The Edwig Van Hooydonck cycling *aficionados* saw mounting the podium was a man, rather than the boy of three years ago. It was a transformation witnessed also by the media, impressed by his calm and mature demeanour and ability to orchestrate the barrage of press questioning, rather than stutter and stumble his way through as he used to. 'It's true that now I am more mature, less emotional than in 1989 when I cried with joy and suffering,' said Van Hooydonck (Buckler) after his victory over compatriot Johan Museeuw (Lotto) and the Ariostea riders Rolf Sörensen and Rolf Gölz.

The reasons behind Van Hooydonck's coming of age and victory in this, the second round of the 1991 World Cup, are several. Firstly, he has learnt to cope with the pressure of becoming a Tour of Flanders champion at the age of twenty-one, and the consequent expectation in Belgium that he would be the 'next Eddy Merckx'. Then last year, a near-fatal accident to his father, who fell from a ladder and subsequently went into a coma, further toughened Van Hooydonck's mental fibre. As he said after the race, 'Now my father has recovered and I have

also solved all my personal problems.' And thirdly, after such a disappointing 1990 season for himself and his Buckler team, his determination to do better this year was at its peak. 'It was absolutely vital for us to get a big win soon,' he said. 'Last year we lost in all the World Cup classics. Now, after a big win, the pressure will be less around our throats. Also this year, the team trained a lot harder. We got together earlier in the year than normal and then, recently, we had a training camp in the south of France.'

Van Hooydonck, nicknamed 'Eddy Bosberg' for his proven prowess on the Bosberg climb where he has trained – and now won – so often, won this year's edition with the panache characteristic of his performance in 1989. But he is still keen to avoid the inevitable parallels with Eddy Merckx. 'You only have to stick your nose out, and everyone starts comparing you to him. And him, I am not.' But what Van Hooydonck

The leading quartet consolidated their attack on the approach to the Mur of Geraardsbergen. Here Museeuw, Belgium's top sprinter, is forcing the pace ahead of Van Hooydonck, Gölz and Sörensen

Even without the Koppenberg the Tour of Flanders is no pushover. Sean Yates took an instant dislike to the Patersberg, the second cobbled hill of the day, and soon retired

Sörensen counterattacks on the Mur de Geraardsbergen. Museeuw is barely able to keep in touch with the Dane as he chases Van Hooydonck and Gölz

incontestably *is*, is the type of rider that the Tour of Flanders historically demands: a hard rider, a man of all-round ability, a man who can climb, sprint, and survive the rugged, windswept roads of Flanders. It's not surprising that people say the Tour of Flanders is the hardest classic to win. Another measure of Van Hooydonck's class is that his participation was in doubt before the race began at the ancient town square in St Niklaas. That doubt was due to a tendon injury in his right knee incurred during the Three Days of De Panne stage race in Belgium three days previously; Van Hooydonck, who had been optimistic about his chances after his victory in the Flèche Brabançonne, abandoned on the last day and took an enforced rest. 'In the morning [of Flanders] I was afraid. I spent one day resting after De Panne, then rode about 40km the next day. But I still had a throbbing pain in my knee. So, I wasn't very confident at the start. I thought that in the finale I wouldn't have the strength', he said.

But come the Old Kwaremont, the second of the fourteen monts, it was clear that Van Hooydonck's fears were groundless: he was always up near the front, in the company of Belgium's Michel Vermote (RMO), Italians Franco Ballerini (Del Tongo) and Maurizio Fondriest (Panasonic), Sörensen and Australians Phil Anderson (Motorola) and Allan Peiper (Tulip). Their performance

on the Kwaremont was no guarantee of success, but for others it was certainly the prelude to a day of frustration – just as the acceleration began for a front position in the peloton as it neared the Kwaremont, a crash brought down American Greg LeMond (Z), who would later abandon, Frenchmen Laurent Fignon (Castorama) and Charly Mottet (RMO), and Italians Moreno Argentin (Ariostea), defending his win last year, and World Cup leader Claudio Chiappucci (Carrera).

When Vermote attacked at the Kwaremont's summit, however, the selection of the first major break of 24 men began. As the race passed over the 12th difficulty of the day, Berendries after 229km, another and more select split occurred before the 'finalists' cast their lots five kilometres later, thanks to a desperate, but unsuccessful, surge by Frenchman Philippe Bouvatier (RMO). And, as the results showed, the winning split contained Van Hooydonck, Museeuw, Sörensen and Gölz.

With two Ariostea riders – Gölz and Sörensen – in the break, Italian interest in the race was still buoyant. Neither rider is Italian, but they belong to an Italian team – and the team of the defending champion Argentin at that. So the slight irregularity of their nationality could be regarded as inconsequential.

An attack by Van Hooydonck on the Mur de Grammont was foiled by Gölz, but on the descent the pair were caught by Sörensen and Museeuw. Gölz appeared to have mentally given up: as a smiling Van Hooydonck said later, 'One kilometre from the Bosberg, Rolf came up alongside me. He said –Hey, Eddy Bosberg, I am afraid of you here...!' And certainly, he could well have felt a bit betrayed that his break with Van Hooydonck was chased down by his team-mate Sörensen. But after the race, Sörensen – who had finished third and taken the World Cup leader's jersey

Van Hooydonck races over the top of the Bosberg. Now just twelve kilometres separate him from a stupendous victory in Meerbeke

Edwig Van Hooydonck, a convincing winner of the Tour of Flanders for the second time

from Chiappucci – defended himself. 'I said to Gölz before the Bosberg that we needed to stay together, because he would probably attack there. Our chances of winning were stronger if we all kept together – even though, in the end, Van Hooydonck proved stronger than anyone,' replied Sörensen to journalists' queries.

And Van Hooydonck was undoubtedly the strongest, as he bolted up the Bosberg without a shred of hesitation. He never faltered. He never turned his head to see if anyone was following. He never reduced his sprinting acceleration or cadence. It was the break of a man who knew he would win. And in that respect it is hard not to make the comparison Van Hooydonck so resents, with the legendary Eddy Merckx.

RACE DETAILS

WEATHER *Strong westerly wind, early drizzle but some sun in afternoon.*

FIELD *Maximum of 25 eight-man teams; 199 starters.*

No major breaks on flat plains of Flanders . . . 138km On first of 14 climbs, the Taigenberg, peloton still together but Fignon punctures . . . 150km Big crash delays many favourites as race approaches Old Kwaremont; amongst those delayed are LeMond and Argentin . . . 153km Vermote attacks alone at Old Kwaremont summit after Ballerini, Anderson and Van Hooydonck lead peloton to the top . . . 160km On Patersberg climb, Vermote is joined by Dutchman Frans Maassen (Buckler) and Sammie Moreels (Lotto) of

Belgium . . . 162km Three leaders are joined by four more: Denmark's Jesper Skibby (TVM), Peiper, Museeuw and Italian Guido Bontempi (Carrera) . . . 170km Seven leaders are caught by six more: Belgians Carlo Bomans (Weinmann), Marc Sergeant (Panasonic) and Eric Vanderaerden (Buckler), Ballerini and Frenchmen Marc Madiot (RMO) and Laurent Jalabert (Toshiba). Lead group now numbers 13 . . . 178km At Taaienberg summit, break has lead of 0:20 on ten-man chase group, 1:25 on a group including Fignon and World Champion Rudy Dhaenens (PDM) of Belgium and 2:15 on the peloton. In the first chase group are Van Hooydonck, Fondriest, Belgians Dirk De Wolf (Tonton Tapis), John Talen (PDM) and Rik Van Slijke (Lotto), Australian Stephen Hodge (ONCE), Bouvatier, Frenchman Martial Gayant (Toshiba),

Gölz and Sörensen . . . 185km Leaders and 10-strong chase group unite. On the Volkegemberg Anderson catches 23 leaders, who are now more than 3 minutes clear . . . 229km De Wolf accelerates on Berendries with Van Hooydonck, Ballerini and Museeuw. Riders dropped are Vanderaerden, Hodge, Anderson, Vermote, Moreels, Van Slycke and Gayant . . . 234km Bouvatier attacks and is caught by Van Hooydonck who attacks again, creating vital break which alo includes Sörensen, Gölz and Museeuw . . . 254km Van Hooydonck attacks on the 20% Mur de Grammont again. Gölz follows; they are rejoined by Sörensen and Museeuw . . . 240km On the final climb, the Bosberg, Van Hooydonck makes winning break and quickly secures a 0:17 lead . . . 261km Van Hooydonck wins by 0:45 over Museeuw, Sörensen and Gölz and 1:45 on the peloton.

Ghent-Wevelgem: 10 April

'**G**hent-Wevelgem without the Kemmelberg is like Paris-Roubaix without the cobbles'.

So said one of many roadside placard protests, as the midweek classic slogged to the close of what had been a sad day's racing for cycling purists. The reason for their downheartedness was simple: the race organisers had all but killed the race by taking out its heart − the notorious, cobbled Kemmelberg climb which the field normally covered three times and which nearly always provoked the winning split.

The omission of this much-loved landmark from the route sparked off a mighty protest from everyone with an interest in the race − the media, riders, team directors and thousands of Flemish fans who annually flock to this steep and narrow road to witness the winning move. And, when the protests went unheard, the end result was hardly a surprise.

That result was the staging of a virtual non-event. It only deserves a place in the annals of cycling because the Carrera rider Djamolidin Abdujaparov made history by becoming the first Soviet to win a professional classic. But his win in the inevitable bunch sprint, from Mario Cipollini (Del Tongo) of Italy, Olaf Ludwig (Panasonic-Sportlife) of Germany and Eric Vanderaerden (Buckler) of Belgium, barely shifted the focus of attention from why the Kemmelberg was omitted and, should it not be reinstated, what will be the future of Ghent-Wevelgem,

Diverting onto a cycle-path as the race approached its second feed at Poperinge proved the highlight of the day for many riders...

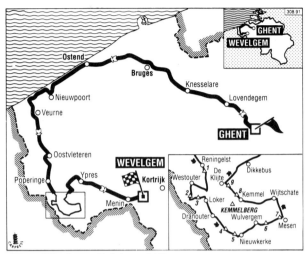

Ghent-Wevelgem, Belgium: 210km

already damaged by its failure to qualify as a World Cup race. And the sight of the Ghent-Wevelgem peloton ambling out towards Brugge and then Oostende on the coast, down to De Panne and then inland to Wevelgem without encountering a single difficult gradient will not have impressed those who have the destiny of the race in their hands.

The decision to omit the Kemmelberg from the race route stemmed from an original request by team directors to have the race pass it only once or twice. Recent years had seen team cars lose contact with their riders as the Kemmelberg split the field into numerous groups, and

...the pleasant undulations of the Heuvelland countryside failing to compensate for the lack of the Kemmelberg

passing them to join the leaders became impossible. The race organisation's response was redolent of notorious Flemish hard-headedness: they said there would be three passages or none at all. The rest we know, and as for the future, the banners held up by protesters at the town of Kemmel 169km into the race said it all. Ghent-Wevelgem without the Kemmelberg is like Paris-Roubaix without cobbles, Flèche Wallonne without the Mur de Huy, or the Tour de France without l'Alpe d'Huez: unimaginable.

Since it was first raced in 1934, Ghent-Wevelgem has survived on its strong historical interest; not only its impressive list of winners but also its connection with the First World War, whose front line ran only 10km north of Ghent-Wevelgem's final eastward stretch from the North Sea at De Panne to the finish line. And the Kemmelberg is an important element in this connection − its strategic importance in the race is directly paralleled by its wartime role. Standing out like a pimple from the flat lands of Flanders it was a valuable vantage point, and changed hands three times after heavy and costly battles to contest it. In recent years, the fighting has taken place between cyclists hoping to launch themselves to victory from its slopes; without it, such battles will not be seen again. Worse still, we may not even have the race.

RACE DETAILS

WEATHER *Fine, sunny, slight wind.*

FIELD *193 starters, 173 finished*

Field remains intact for the greater part of the race, from Ghent to the North Sea coast at Oostende and down to De Panne before turning east and towards Wevelgem ...141km *Peloton splits at Westouter* ...151km *The margin between the two*

groups is 0:35, with as many as 70 riders leading. Most favourites are in first group, except for Greg LeMond (Z) of the United States, Belgians Edwig Van Hooydonck (Buckler) and Eddy Planckaert (Panasonic) and Italy's Maurizio Fondriest (Ariostea) ...145-208km *Many attempted breaks follow the first real attempt, by Dutchman John Talen (PDM) and Belgian riders Roger Van den Bossche (La William) and Wilfried Peeters (Histor), which gets*

a 0:25 lead before being caught ...209km *15 riders crash, including Australian Phil Anderson (Motorola) who is badly grazed on hands, knees and hips, as peloton winds up for bunch sprint. There are several crashes during the day, most caused by changing wind direction, tram tracks and wheel touching in the bunch* ...210km *Abdujaparov outsprints Cipollini, Ludwig Vanderaerden to win.*

Paris-Roubaix: 14 April

Just when the habit of a professional lifetime – that of winning – seems to be a thing of the past you land a big one, and at thirty-two years of age Marc Madiot (RMO) was once again the toast of France. He had not won a race since July 1989, and although his racing is so aggressive that few people realised that the famine had endured so long, last winter he was starting to ponder on thoughts of retirement. But the wily and humorous Christian Rumeau, assistant director of RMO, is also a man of vision: four days before Paris-Roubaix he predicted that Marc would win. Lacking his inside information, but equally prescient as it turned out, was Motorola's *directeur sportif* Jim Ochowicz, who handed me a piece of paper on the eve of the race with his thoughts on the first five finishers: Madiot was listed as the winner. Why Madiot? Well, he had won Paris-Roubaix in 1985, the last Frenchman to do so, and he had shown a high degree of early-season form in the previous week's Tour of Flanders. And that was enough, in some quarters, to tip the comeback of this 11-year professional.

In Compiègne on the morning of the race the riders, as usual, were reluctant to appear. No matter how many races you have ridden, the feeling that this is the first time seems to apply especially to Paris-Roubaix. This 'Queen of Classics' is held in the utmost awe by her courtiers, who try desperately to be worthy of the greatest single-day race of them all. Less than half the field will reach Roubaix, and as they line up for a visit to Hell, the question uppermost in the riders' minds is who will drop out, and will it be from injury, exhaustion or just sheer frustration ... World Cup leader Rolf Sörensen (Ariostea), said: 'I have ridden well in Milan-San Remo [he was second] and the Tour of Flanders [third], but I have never finished this race in three tries. Today I want to see Roubaix.' This likeable Dane, whose father was recovering in a British hospital from a serious car crash whilst on holiday, would reach Roubaix this time: but not before three flat tyres had put him into 51st place – well outside the World Cup points.

It is the cobbles, potholes, ditches, dirt and dust of the race route that have earned *La Pascale* her eminence in the racing calendar; without them, excitement would barely enliven the long stretches of boringly flat countryside that remain largely undisturbed by cyclist and tourist for most of the year. It is the *pavé* that has made Paris-Roubaix the most coveted classic of all – an extreme test of a rider's skill and endurance – and the race organisers are doing all they can to make sure the threatened surfaces are preserved. No fewer than fifteen local mayors were invited to this year's edition of the race, in the hope that the experience would convince them of the value of their unique asset and dissuade them from pouring asphalt all over it.

The future of the race still hangs in the balance, but whatever happens, Marc Madiot will always be able to claim that he won it twice. The only other Frenchmen to have done this are Maurice Garin, the first winner of the Tour de France, who won *La Pascale* in 1897 and 1898, Luc Lesna (1901/2), Hippolyte Aucouturier (1903/4), Octave Lapize (1909/10/11), Charles Crupelandt

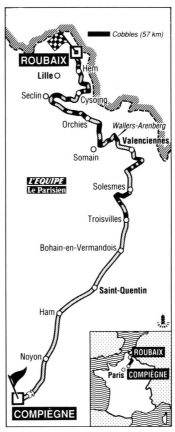

Paris-Roubaix, France: 267km

(1912/14) and Henri Pelissier (1919/21). The outstanding winner, and he still looks as fit as many of the current riders, is the Belgian Roger De Vlaeminck, now *directeur sportif* of the new Tonton Tapis team. 'The Gypsy', so-called because of his Romany features, rode Paris-Roubaix thirteen times, winning a record four times and finishing second another four! In Liège this year he said: 'I never had any mechanical problems in my first ten Paris-Roubaix, but when I punctured the next time I lost my will to succeed in it again.'

There were plenty of contenders for the title which last year Eddy Planckaert wrested from Steve Bauer by a millimetre, and this year as always it was the problems experienced on the *pavé* that deprived most of them of their chance. The race made a fast start, with the first serious attack coming after 50km when eleven riders broke clear. This group, comprising Dutchmen Gert Jakobs (PDM), Gerrit Solleveld (Buckler), Dane Hans Kindberg (Toshiba), Ludo De Koning (Panasonic), Erwin Nijboer (Telekom) and Adri Kools (Tulip), Belgians Johan Capiot (TVM), Bruno Geuens (SEFB) and Etienne De Wilde (Histor), Swiss Thomas Wegmüller (Weinmann) and Soviet Yuri Manuilov (Lotus), held a maximum lead of 5:15 over the main field, but by the first stretch of *pavé* after Troisvilles the

Madiot's triumphant solo lap of the Roubaix velodrome, an almost exact repeat of his 1985 performance, brought the ecstatic crowd to its feet

Johan Capiot, riding too strongly for his breakaway companions, leads the race onto an unsurfaced section before Valenciennes

As usual, the Wallers-Arenberg forest provided the first serious difficulties of the day. Unusually, this year there were very few crashes along the three kilometres of cobbles

chase was on. Punctures and crashes took their toll, and the peloton had been reduced from 185 to about 50 riders by the time the break was caught at 160km. A new escape of six riders, Englishman Sean Yates (Motorola), Frenchman Charly Mottet (RMO), Italian Mario Cipollini (Del Tongo), Belgians Hendrik Redant (Lotto) and Rudy Rogiers (Tulip) and Dutchman Nico Verhoeven (PDM), gained 65 seconds by Orchies (190km), but after 205km to go they were brought back by a chase instigated by Belgian Edwig Van Hooydonck (Buckler).

This new seven-man attack altered the race shape and developed the winning move; it comprised Van Hooydonck, his compatriots Eddy Planckaert and Marc Sergeant (both Panasonic), Italian Franco Ballerini (Del Tongo), Australian Allan Peiper (Tulip), Frenchman Jean-Claude Colotti (Tonton Tapis) and former Belgian champion Carlo Bomans (Weinmann). At Templeuve the front group swelled to 25 riders and soon after a group of six went ahead, from which Redant, chased by Madiot, Belgians Peter De Clercq (Lotto) and Wilfried Peeters (Histor), Ballerini and Dutchman John Talen (PDM), attacked with 23km to go. Redant built up a lead of 30 seconds, but punctured, and it was Madiot who entered the Roubaix velodrome with enough time in hand to lap the stadium before the rest arrived – an almost exact repeat of his performance in 1985. Marc Madiot had triumphed in his country's classic and he had done it in the style of a champion, alone. At 1:07 came his compatriot Colotti, beating Bomans and Canadian Steve Bauer (Motorola) in the sprint, and giving France their first one-two since the Pelissier brothers in 1921.

Planckaert defended his title with honour, and was still mixing with the front runners in the closing stages when a puncture robbed him of another crack at the finishing sprint. Steve Bauer, quietly confident all week, was hoping that his near-miss of a year ago would inspire his fast-improving form. He rode an outstanding race, latching onto the group chasing Madiot only as they entered the stadium. Bomans was forced to fight hard to hold him off, but Bauer is still waiting for the day he claims the cobblestone trophy that, along with a cheque for 150,000 French francs, goes to the winner.

Spare a thought for Hendrik Redant, who punctured when leading by 30 seconds at a crucial point. Afterwards I saw him covered in dirt, looking bewildered: 'Bad luck, Hendrik', I said. His reply was a painful shrug. Luck is an important asset in any cycle race; in Paris-Roubaix it is disproportionately so.

Ballerini's attack on a slightly uphill section of pavé *near Merignies, just before Seclin, provoked the final selection of seven riders*

RACE DETAILS

WEATHER *Dry weather prior to race made the route very dusty. Sun all day after an early threat of rain. Temperatures below normal; slight headwind.*

COURSE *267km from Compiègne, 800km north of Paris, to the velodrome in Roubaix. 57km of pavé split into 22 zones. No hills.*

FIELD *196 started and 105 finished, including ten riders who were not officially recorded: under the new FICP rule, the last 5% of the finishers are eliminated.*

38km After a fast start, 10 riders break clear, but are caught at Ham (43km) . . . 50km A more serious attack by 11 riders; after leading for 45km they hold a lead of 5:15 on the main field, but a chase is organised and at Valenciennes (148km) the lead settles to 3:15 . . . 160km Lead

down to a minute as Capiot leads the escape out of the Forest of Arenberg; the escape is caught 6km further on . . . 166km 6-man escape instigated by Yates gains a maximum 65 seconds . . . 192km On zone 11 pavé Van Hooydonck attacks and the reaction causes the recapture of the six leaders . . . 205km The winning move is developed by a 7-man attack comprising Van Hooydonck, Planckaert, Sergeant, Ballerini, Peiper, Colotti and Bomans. The front group swells to 25 riders by 232km and soon after a group of six riders goes ahead, from which Redant attacks alone . . . 244km Redant punctures; he rejoins the front but is unable to regain his lead. The six hold a 40-second lead and on the penultimate zone of pavé Madiot attacks. Ballerini chases, but Madiot increases his lead to win by 1:07; Colotti takes the sprint from Bomans and Bauer.

Allan Peiper recovered from this puncture with 30km to go and rejoined the leaders before the crucial section around Ennevlin, between Seclin and Cysoing

Would he have won? Hendrik Redant stormed to a 25-second lead in the closing stages, but a puncture 23km from home put paid to his bid for victory

The exact moment of Madiot's acceleration: Talen and Ballerini watch impotently as the flying Frenchman pulls inexorably away with 16km to go

Flèche Wallonne: 17 April

Moreno Argentin is one of those rare Italians who loves racing in Belgium. Three times winner of Liège-Bastogne-Liège, and last year winner of both the Tour of Flanders and the Flèche Wallonne, this season, after spending part of his winter training in South Africa, it was in his own words 'a matter of time before I win a classic.' Rumours about the Ariostea rider's strength had been rife among the riders for weeks, and they felt that sooner or later they would be on the receiving end of it. The good-looking Italian chose Flèche Wallonne to flex his muscles on, and by the end of the day he had proved one of the finest winners in recent editions of this underrated classic.

It was a field as good as any World Cup race (which this is not) that headed away from a sleepy Spa. Snow flurries sprinkled down on the riders as they climbed the 1.4km Mont Theux. Soon after, the rather damp

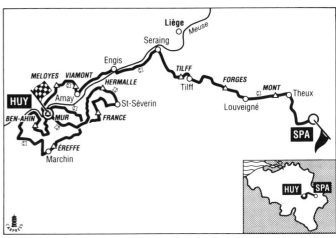

Flèche Wallonne, Belgium: 208km

Criquielion tried desperately to catch Argentin, but the Belgian hero's speed over the hills around the Meuse valley was never a threat to the Italian

moustache sported by Belgian Danny Neskens (La William) disappeared ahead for 50 kilometres. Like the Liège classic which followed four days later, the Flèche climbs and plunges around a most beautiful area of Belgium, but unlike Liège, this race climbs the Côte des Forges very early, so its significance is far less.

In Huy for the first time a large crowd had already moved onto the Mur, where they were hoping to see their home-grown hero Claude Criquielion (Lotto) land a killer strike on one of the four times up. 'Criq' was riding his last Ardennes weekend, and he had promised his fans a great farewell. To help his preparation he had missed the previous Sunday's Paris-Roubaix, instead training for 130 kilometres before watching the race on television, and then going out for a further 60km! The 34-year-old Belgian champion was desperately unlucky to come up against a rider on super-form, otherwise his farewell to Belgian classic racing would have been perfect. After the capture of Neskens, the 11 riders who escaped at St Severin looked good enough to fool both Criquielion and Argentin, especially as on-form Belgians Dirk De Wolf (Tonton Tapis) and Johan Bruyneel (Lotto), Dutchman Frans Maassen (Buckler) and Soviet Dmitri Konyshev (TVM) were driving hard. But, after working hard to gain 1:25, they were clawed back by the peloton. The dreary conditions dampened many a spirit, and no-one was expecting what happened next: with 73km to go, Argentin sprinted away after a sharp right-hand turn. Hail, lightning, the snow on the side of the road, could all have been signs from heaven of the danger posed by Argentin, but the stunned race found only individuals to attempt a resistance: Aussie Phil Anderson (Motorola), France's Charly Mottet (RMO) and Italian Maurizio Fondriest (Panasonic) all tried unsuccessfully to reel him in. He even fell on a descent when holding 20 seconds, but they never saw him remount and carry on. Heading up the Mur de Huy for the third time, Argentin was being pursued by an increasingly desperate Criquielion, in company with France's Jean-François Bernard (Banesto), at 0:25 and Italian Claudio Chiappucci (Carrera) and Soviet Dmitri Konyshev (TVM) at 0:40. The four regrouped, but could still make no impression on the flying Italian.

Chiappucci leads Bernard and Konyshev in pursuit of Criquielion and Argentin

Criquielion's hopes of a triumphal farewell were fading, dashed by the seemingly invincible form of an intruder from another country. On the Côte d'Eriffe at 174km his frustration overflowed, and he set off alone in pursuit. But it made no difference: Argentin's lead grew to 2:20, and he had won the race for sure when Criquielion surrendered to the other three, giving himself enough time to recover and leave them again on the final climb of the Mur. Argentin, world champion in Colorado Springs in 1986 and Italian champion in 1983 and 1989, could now boast two wins in Flèche Wallonne, as well as two second places in 1985 and 1988. Undoubtedly a man of pure class, who thanks the warm winter sun of South Africa for putting magic in his legs on a day when everyone was rooting for Criquielion.

Argentin's cool expression belies the physical cost of his 73km breakaway and the resulting achievement − the greatest performance in a one-day classic since Bernard Hinault won Liège-Bastogne-Liège in 1980

RACE DETAILS

WEATHER *Snow before the start in the hills. Cold with rain and sleet at times; occasional sun.*

COURSE *208km in the heart of the hilly Belgian Ardennes. Starts from Spa, skirts Liège and finishes at Huy on top of the steep Mur de Huy, having climbed it four times, at 70.7km, 118.6km, 160.9km and 208km.*

FIELD *192 starters and 85 finishers.*

21km Neskens attacks at Beaufays but is caught by Argentin on the first ascent of the Mur ...71km Field regroups ...96km 11 riders break clear at St Severin; field struggles back at Marchin ...130km Argentin attacks alone; crashes; but remounts and continues before he is seen by the field. Although he is chased hard by Criquielion, Chiappucci, Bernard and Konyshev he is never caught and finishes over 2 minutes ahead of Criquielion to repeat his 1990 win.

Liège-Bastogne-Liège: 21 April

Not since Eddy Merckx has one man been so feared in the Belgian Ardennes classics. For the second time in less than a week, the Italian Ariostea rider Moreno Argentin annihilated the retirement dreams of Belgian champion Claude Criquielion (Lotto) – the rider everybody, not just the Belgians, hoped would win. After 13 seasons as a professional, 'Criq' was doing his round of farewells on home soil, and had worked extraordinarily hard in training to be ready to take on the best. He was leaving the sport with two regrets (well, three, if you include the controversy surrounding the finish of the 1988 world championship road race with Steve Bauer): he had never won a stage of the Tour de France, and he had never won *la Doyenne*. Second in 1985 and third in 1987 – both times behind Argentin – are his best memories. He threw away his best chance in 1987: he and Irishman Stephen Roche had the race won between them when they started arguing, which gave Argentin his chance – he caught them and beat them both! Roche (Tonton Tapis) was also back to form for this year's race, saying 'I'm not sure if I will win, but I'll certainly be in when the final decision is made.' And he was.

Since the end of Flèche Wallonne, the riders had stayed in the Ardennes to ride the route of Liège-Bastogne-Liège, especially the two new hills, or *côtes*, one of which, the Côte de Haussire, according to the knowledgeable Belgian encyclopaedia Cotacol, is the most difficult in Belgium. It was certainly tough, included as it is in September each year in the

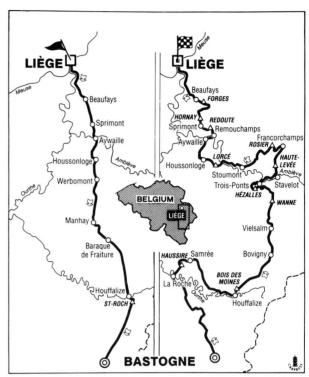

Liège-Bastogne-Liège, Belgium: 267km

At the head of affairs as ever, Criquielion, with Argentin to his left, heads for the Côte de Rosier. Behind and to his right are Sörensen, Roche, Van Lancker and Indurain

Roche and Lejarreta can only watch resignedly as Argentin's counterattack with Criquielion leaves them behind on la Redoute

Randonnée Claude Criquielion; now the big boys had their chance to show what they could do up the steep, wooded climb with a downhill in the middle and then a narrow climb to the top. But it came at 115km, too early in the race to break up the field that had settled into fast tempo riding to catch the first attack, by French Toshiba rider Thierry Bourguignon.

Much more decisive were the two *côtes* nestled near Trois Ponts, deep in the Ardennes woods. The first was the Côte de Wanne, soon followed by the Côte de Hézalles, a vicious ascent that started to show the cracks

among those who had had four hours to build up their confidence in this fearsome route. On the Côte de Wanne, with Bourguignon still stoically plodding on ahead, Belgian Dirk De Wolf (Tonton Tapis) attacked. De Wolf, a professional since 1983, but only last year showing the talent he had promised as a young amateur, was joined by Criquielion, but they were both quickly chased down by Argentin, who appeared to be using the hill for some interval training. For a while 10 riders merged, including the men who would shape the final kilometres of the race: Argentin, Criquielion, Roche,

Criquielion heads the front group of ten men as they approach the Côte de Lorcé

With just 200 metres separating them from their pursuers, the fabulous four descend from the Côte des Forges towards Liège

Fearful of being left on the climb, Sörensen attacked before la Redoute, thus ensuring his place in the final four

Denmark's Rolf Sörensen (Ariostea), Belgians Eric Van Lancker of Panasonic (last year's winner) and Edwig Van Hooydonck (Buckler), winner of the Tour of Flanders, and Italian Maurizio Fondriest (Panasonic). But the field were not yet willing to surrender, and on the 23% climb of the Côte de Hézalles Bourguignon felt his bronzed legs creak for the last time in attack. He was passed without a second glance by De Wolf, Argentin, Fondriest, Soviet Dmitri Konyshev (TVM) and Van Lancker, but not by Criquielion. Argentin and De Wolf kept the lead on the descent, but now the Belgian champion was again heading the chase.

All this fierce rivalry was taking its toll, and by Stavelot (185km) the leading group comprised about 40 riders, with the Haute-Levée next. Criquielion, with his characteristic designer stubble, looked magnificent as he attacked halfway up the Côte de Haute-Levée, dancing away on the climb. Clearly he was not going to give away his retirement present to an Italian without a fight, but again, with sickening ease, Argentin pedalled up to him. With the climb over, ten riders gathered to wave farewell to the field. Roche, Van Lancker, Sörensen, Mexican Raúl Alcalá (PDM), Spaniards Miguel Indurain (Banesto), Iñaki Gaston (Clas) and Marino Lejarreta (ONCE) and Belgian Johan Bruyneel (Lotto) were the others who used their climbing talents to join the front, and their lead was almost a minute by Remouchamps, the last town before the notorious climb of la Redoute.

Sörensen did not wait for the 20% climb that starts alongside the autoroute from the Ardennes into Liège; instead, he attacked along a cobbled street as they left Remouchamps, quickly building up a lead of 0:21. The counter-attack should normally have come from

Argentin's obvious delight at winning the 'Ardennes double' contrasts poignantly with Criquielion's disappointment ...

... while Roche's face expresses satisfaction at his strengthening form

Criquielion, but instead Argentin himself launched a vicious attack in pursuit of his team-mate. This split the ten riders into a 4-4-2 formation as Argentin, Criquielion, Sörensen and Indurain grouped at the front. Roche, Lejarreta, Alcalá and Van Lancker chased behind. Sörensen was putting in what he later said was the best performance of his career and began to look a dominant leader of the World Cup. Behind, with 24km and two climbs left, Roche was trying to organise the chase, and for a long time the gap hovered at 0:15. 'If only the other three had believed in themselves,' said Roche at the finish, 'then we would have caught them again.'

But they never did, as Criquielion continued to play to the thousands he knew were watching live on television. On the main road climb of Hornay, he attacked again, but once more Argentin left him in no doubt as to his strength. The chase was now 0:13 behind, and the slog

up the last, long Côte des Forges was next. At the top of this climb is a magnificent monument to Stan Okkers, the outstanding Belgian rider of the 50s who did the 'Ardennais double' – the Flèche Wallonne and Liège-Bastogne-Liège in the same year – in 1955. Argentin was now about to be the first Italian to join the august company of Okkers, Ferdi Kubler (who did it twice) and the legendary Eddy Merckx in their élite club.

There were no more attacks from Criquielion: the lion had been tamed. But he had ridden an admirable race, and could retire happy with his performance here. On the approach to the quai Mativa, Sörensen launched an attack to draw the sting of the rest and Argentin made light work of the sprint, although Criquielion appeared to push him close on the line. But afterwards, Criquielion was gracious in acknowledging the Italian's unbeatable form: 'I would never have beaten him unless he had punctured.'

RACE DETAILS

WEATHER *Generally clear skies with threat of snow showers; headwind for first hour. Cold, but an improvement on the poor weather of previous week's races.*

COURSE *267km, starting from the rue du Parc in Liège, crossing eleven climbs and returning to the quai Mativa, near the start point. The race passes through Bastogne at 75km. The climbs (côtes) are St-Roch (63.5km), Haussire (115.5km), Bois des Moines (140km), Wanne (169.5km),*

Hézalles (181.5km), Haute-Levée (193.5km), Rosier (206km), Lorcé (225km), la Redoute (240km), Hornay (246.5km), and Forges (253km).

FIELD *196 riders; 116 finished.*

The wind and general fear of the route causes a slow start; only 30km covered in first hour ... 62km Bourguignon attacks at Houffalize and passes through Bastogne with a lead of 4:0. On the Côte du Bois des Moines (240km) he leads by 7:30; the race is preoccupied by snow flurries and hail.

Bourguignon is caught on the Côte de Hézalles after leading for 120km. Criquielion attacks on the Côte de la Haute Levée (193.5km), forcing a break of ten riders: Sörensen, Argentin, Van Lancker, Alcalá, Lejarreta, Criquielion, Bruyneel, Gaston, Roche and Indurain. On the Côte de la Redoute the leaders split and Argentin, Criquielion, Sörensen and Indurain escape to fight out the finish along the quai Mativa. Argentin wins his fourth Liège-Bastogne-Liège; Criquielion is second.

Amstel Gold Race: 27 April

The duel between Dutchman Frans Maassen (Buckler) and Italian Maurizio Fondriest (Panasonic) as they lunged towards the finish line of the Amstel Gold Race signified more than a sprint for first place in this World Cup event, the fifth of the series and the last of the spring. It also mirrored the long-standing feud between two men − not Maassen and Fondriest themselves, but their respective *directeurs-sportifs* − Jan Raas (Buckler) and Peter Post (Panasonic).

The rivalry between Raas and Post is well-documented. But with the approach each year of the Amstel Gold Race, the only major one-day classic hosted by the Netherlands, it is always a popular subject for speculation, which of course enhances interest in the event.

This year, there was a lot at stake for both teams. At this point in the season, thanks to Edwig Van Hooydonck's successes in the Flèche Brabançonne and the Tour of Flanders, Buckler had the edge on Panasonic, but they needed to secure their domination with a victory in their home classic. Panasonic, Fondriest's new team, was desperate for a win: so far this season they had barely troubled the printer.

Maassen's eventual win over Fondriest and Belgian Dirk De Wolf (Tonton Tapis), who were all 0:16 clear of the peloton, certainly helped to stoke up the rivalry between Raas and Post. It also secured Buckler's place at the top of the World Cup ladder − ironically by one point over second-placed Panasonic − until after the Tour de France, when the World Cup competition resumed with England's Wincanton Classic. Denmark's

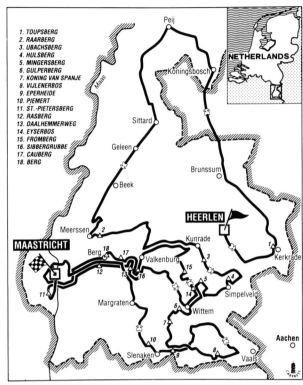

1. TOUPSBERG
2. RAARBERG
3. UBACHSBERG
4. HULSBERG
5. MINGERSBERG
6. GULPERBERG
7. KONING VAN SPANJE
8. VIJLENERBOS
9. EPERHEIDE
10. PIEMERT
11. ST.-PIETERSBERG
12. RASBERG
13. DAALHEMMERWEG
14. EYSERBOS
15. FROMBERG
16. SIBBERGRUBBE
17. CAUBERG
18. BERG

Amstel Gold Race, Holland: 244km

With just 14km to go, the Cauberg climb failed to split the leading trio. Fondriest leads Maassen and De Wolf ahead of an impressive phalanx of TV and photographers' motorbikes

The smile on the face of the tiger. Frans Maassen relaxes after the race

The Buckler domination of the race culminated in the sprint for fourth place. With 20 metres to go Vanderaerden, already well ahead, has team-mates Nijdam and Van Hooydonck hard on his heels

Rolf Sörensen (Ariostea) still led the World Cup individual standings with 68 points, but Buckler now had three riders in the top ten − Van Hooydonck (2nd, with 56 points), Maassen (4th, with 44 points) and Eric Vanderaerden (10th, with 38 points) compared with Panasonic's one, that being Fondriest, who was lying 9th with 38 points.

From Panasonic's point of view, Maassen's win not only shut the door on Fondriest's hopes of marking his first season away from Italy and in a Dutch team with victory in a Dutch classic, but also Post's desire to salvage something from the spring before the all-important national tours began.

For any Dutchman, to win the Amstel Gold Race is a high point in his career, and this year Maassen was particularly hungry for success. Fondriest was the more fancied rider, and Maassen was still smarting from the scathing remarks Raas had made about him at a pre-race team meeting, during which he indirectly criticised Maassen for not doing better in Liège-Bastogne-Liège. But whatever his motivation, it gave him the ability to outsprint the classy Italian in this year's finale.

RACE DETAILS

WEATHER *Sunny and warm; slight wind.*

COURSE *Total distance is 244km and 16 climbs. First 175km are mainly flat South, arriving at Maastricht for a hilly 69km circuit finish.*

FIELD *25 teams. 196 starters; 123 finished. Race stays calm for first two hours ...85km Bernd Gröne (Telekom) of Germany attacks and gets up to 3:45 lead after 130km ...133km At Vijlenerbos, Gröne's lead drops as Italian Argentin (Ariostea) attacks from peloton, followed by Frenchman Charly Mottet (RMO), Mexican Raúl Alcalá (PDM), Belgian Eric Van Lancker (Panasonic), Maassen, Australian Stephen Hodge (ONCE) and Italian Giorgio Furlan (Ariostea). They* catch and pass Gröne, and get a lead of 1:30 ...168km *Seven leaders caught as race makes first passage of Maastricht* ...178km *A series of breakaway attempts are made, starting with Maassen and Italian Claudio Chiappucci (Carrera) on the Saint-Pietersberg climb* ...190km *Nearing Valkenburg, Dirk De Wolf creates the first major split, taking with him Denmark's Brian Hölm (Histor), Dutchman Luc Suykerbuyk (Lotus), Belgian Michel Vermote (RMO) and Italian Andrea Tafi (Selle Italia)* ...204km *At the town of Eys, when leaders have 0:20 advantage, Hölm punctures on road under repair. So do 20 other riders in the peloton, including Moreno Argentin, Sörensen and Dutchman Adri Van der Poel (Tulip)* ...205km *On Eyserbos, Fondriest takes advantage of punctures to attack from peloton in pursuit of De Wolf who has* dropped Tafi, Vermote and Suykerbuyk. *Suykerbuyk and Maassen follow Fondriest who soon catches De Wolf* ...214km *Leaders have 0:30 on a peloton numbering about 100. Finally Frenchman Marc Madiot (RMO) succeeds in forming a chase group with Dutchman Nico Verhoeven (PDM), Belgian Marc Sergeant (Panasonic), Frenchman Martial Gayant (Toshiba) and Soviet Dmitri Konyshev (TVM)* ...226km *Chase group gets as close as 0:20 to the leaders* ...231km *Maassen sets fast tempo on the Cauberg and Suykerbuyk is dropped as the Madiot-led chase still fails to make progress* ...237km *Chasers caught by peloton, led by Del Tongo and Ariostea riders* ...241km *Frenchman Thierry Laurent (RMO) attacks from peloton, not knowing the three leaders are still away* ...244km *Maassen outspfints Fondriest and De Wolf.*

Four Days of Dunkirk: 7-12 May

The RMO team had an impressive spring season. They were consistently aggressive performers in the one-day classics, and Frenchman Marc Madiot had scored a great victory in Paris-Roubaix. But when they lined up for the Four Days of Dunkirk, in the north-west corner of France, one very important ingredient was still missing from the team's accomplishments. They needed a morale-boosting, inspiring win by their leader, Frenchman Charly Mottet.

Mottet's results had been disappointing. He had begun his 1991 season by announcing that he now accepted that he had to have ambitions in cycling other than the Tour de France, and that he was going to concentrate on the one-day classics. But the classics had come and gone, and thus far had not produced a win for Mottet.

But the memory of his poor early season was wiped out when Mottet and his team-mates battled through the eight stages of the Four Days of Dunkirk to a victory that was as important to him in 1991 as Stephen Roche's was to the Irishman in 1990; it restored his confidence and boosted his team's morale. After the race Mottet, who won the same race in 1989, told journalists: 'This victory puts me right back on top again. I'm ready for the Dauphiné Libéré now.'

Tactically, Mottet made two significant moves. The first was in the stage 6 uphill time trial at Mont Cassel,

Four Days of Dunkirk, France: 969km

Mottet's time trialling prowess brought him closer to the overall lead, but it was a winning break on the penultimate circuit at Cassel that secured it

where his 2nd place, three seconds behind Dutchman Frans Maassen (Buckler), reduced his deficit on overall leader, Frenchman Laurent Jalabert (Toshiba) from 57 to 51 seconds. The second came later the same day, in the stage 7 123-km circuit race at Mont Cassel, where Mottet won with a comfortable 1-minute lead on Jalabert, who was 9th, and picked up a 6 second bonus as well. So he ended an exciting day wearing the race leader's pink jersey and 15 seconds clear of Jalabert.

As nearly always with the Four Days of Dunkirk, it was the racing at Cassel which was crucial in deciding the winner. Thousands of spectators were packed into the small town, their gastronomic requirements being catered for by dozens of *frites* and beer stands, the latter also fuelling the intense speculation as to the outcome of the day's racing. The focus of attention was the town's cobbled main street, which was the finish of the Saturday morning time trial and was included in every lap of the afternoon's circuit race. In the event it was

Mottet who charged across the line first, 40 seconds clear of Belgian Peter Declercq (Lotto) and a minute ahead of Jalabert, in the peloton.

Saturday afternoon's racing was a triumph for the whole RMO team. They worked together very effectively, determined to collect a stage win. Putting Mottet into the race lead was a tremendous bonus. 'I thought above anything else, of the stage win – the most prestigious in the race' said Mottet later. 'It was not until I found myself alone on the last ascent up Mont Cassel that I started thinking of the overall win.' And Mottet kept the lead through the following day's uneventful final stage, which was taken by Belgian's Johan Capiot.

The result was a disappointment for Jalabert, who has been one of the up and coming French riders since he turned professional at the beginning of 1991. But Jalabert's turn may not be long in coming; his experience of wearing the leader's jersey may prove as invaluable to him as claiming it and keeping it has been for Mottet.

Jalabert came close to making the pink leader's jersey his for keeps, but had finally to surrender it to the more experienced Mottet

RACE DETAILS

WEATHER *Warm and sunny*

COURSE *8 stages over 4 days including 2 time trials – one uphill. Set in north-west corner of France.*

FIELD *14 teams (inc. one French amateur team) 108 starters, 88 finished.*

STAGE 1 – Dunkirk-Dunkirk, 170km ... 40km *Belgian Stefan Leeuwe (Tulip) attacks and gets an 8:00 lead* ... 150km *Leeuwe is caught* ... 170km *German Remig Stumpf (Histor) wins mass sprint.*

STAGE 2 – Dunkirk-Boulogne-sur-Mer, 112km *Jalabert wins stage to take overall lead from Belgian Kappes (Histor) who had 0:06 on the Frenchman.*

STAGE 3 – 8.2km time trial, Boulogne-sur-Mer *Maassen wins stage, but Jalabert holds on to overall lead.*

STAGE 4 – Béthune-Laon, 186.5km *Early kilometres, Toshiba controls race for Jalabert* ... 181km *Belgian Paul Haghedooren (SEFB) attacks* ... 186.5km *Haghedooren wins by 0:06 on Museeuw who leads peloton to get 0:06 bonus. Jalabert*

still leads by 0:03 on Museeuw.

STAGE 5 – Laon-Tourcoing, 185.7km ... 35km *Frenchman Jacky Durand (Castorama) and Belgian Patrick Dewael (Histor) attack and get 13:45 lead at 120km* ... 178km *Attackers caught by peloton* ... 185.7km *Museeuw takes stage and overall lead with 0:10 bonus. Jalabert is now second overall at 0:03.*

STAGE 6 – 6.8km uphill time trial, Cassel. *Jalabert takes back overall lead with fourth place at 0:06 to stage winner Maassen who clocks 9:29.90. Second is Mottet at 0:03.*

STAGE 7 – Cassel-Cassel, 123km ... 27km *Attacker Frenchman Richard Virenque (RMO) is caught by five chasers* ... 54km *Nine more join leading six riders, and peloton with all favourites is at 2:00* ... 68km *Peloton at 5:00* ... 100km *Breakaways are caught, but RMO continues to force the pace* ... 115km *Mottet attacks on last climb with De Clercq and wins stage alone.*

STAGE 8 – Gravelines-Dunkirk, 176.9km *No alteration to overall standings. Stage ends in bunch finish with Johan Capiot (TVM) winning.*

Tour de Romandie: 7-12 May

Tony Rominger of Switzerland won this year's Tour of Romandie with an almost surgical precision, clinching his success − like Charly Mottet in the Four Days of Dunkirk − at two strategic points. He won the important mountain stage on the second day, and he was fastest in the time trial over 19.4km which he took by 0:18 from Canadian Brian Walton (Motorola). True, most of the other favourites in the 119-strong line-up regarded the Tour de Romandie as training for the impending Giro, so they failed to pose a serious threat to the Toshiba leader's ambitions. This was reflected in the final results, with top riders like Italy's Gianni Bugno (Gatorade) and Spain's Pedro Delgado (Banesto) finishing ninth at 5:12 and 10th at 5:38 respectively. But so faultless was Rominger's performance in this five-stage race that those who also saw him win at Paris-Nice in March were inclined to think that he had redefined 'impressive'.

For Rominger, and his strongest rival Robert Millar (Z) of Scotland who was second overall at 1:31, the Tour de Romandie was a great opportunity to gain valuable FICP points. Rominger's efforts paid off − he moved

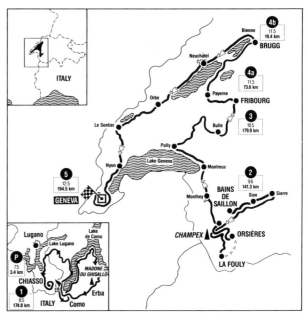

Tour de Romandie, Switzerland: 786.9km

Rominger was the outstanding rider of the Tour of Romandie. By Stage 3 from La Fouly to Fribourg, the last of the serious climbs, any real chance of a challenge from his rivals was gone

For Helvetia team-mates, Demierre and Leclercq, a stage win each was reason enough to smile

up five places in the world rankings, climbing from 12th to 7th.

The 1991 edition began in Chiasso, a town nestled on the Italian-Swiss border, with the 3.4km prologue followed by a circuit race which started and finished in the town. It was not the first time the race had ventured out of the Swiss region of Romandie over the border into Italy – on two previous occasions, in 1971 and 1986, when Jean-François Bernard won the prologue, part of the race had taken place on foreign soil – but it was certainly the first time that as much as 178km of the 787km route had been ridden on Italian roads.

At first, it appeared that the Swiss Helvetia team might succeed in making up for the mistakes they had made in 1990 and dominate the race in 1991. Last year, a disagreement between Frenchman Jean-Claude Leclercq and Australian team-mate, Michael Wilson, had resulted in Wilson's failure to defend the race leader's green jersey. This year, the team started extremely well. Pascal Richard of Switzerland took the short prologue time trial, and Leclercq added to the team's success by winning the first stage and with it the race leader's green jersey.

But Rominger began to turn on the pressure when the race returned to Switzerland. The Tour de Romandie always includes one important mountain stage, and this year's second stage gave Rominger the chance to make a quick killing. After three major climbs, with the finish at the summit of the third, Rominger took the first of his two stage wins and also the overall lead from Leclercq. As quickly as that, the race came down to a battle between Rominger and Millar. And just as in 1990, when he lost two minutes to winner Charly Mottet, it was Millar's poor performance in the time trial, held on the afternoon of the fourth day, which would once more cost him victory.

Already ahead on general classification, Rominger resisted any temptation to rest on his laurels and took more than a minute out of Millar, who could only manage 11th place. Such was the calibre of Rominger's ride that he beat the two time trial specialists – Walton, 2nd at 0:18, and Bernard (Banesto), 3rd at 0:34. And like Mottet after his win at Dunkirk, Rominger's win put him in a strong position as he faced the next challenge of the season – the ferocious slopes of the French Alps in the Dauphiné Libéré.

RACE DETAILS

FIELD *17 teams, 119 starters.*

COURSE *Race route takes riders around Switzerland and into Italy in five stages, including one time trial (stage 4a) and a hard climb on the col de Champex (stage 2).*

WEATHER *Mainly fine, some cloud. Rain on Stage 4.*

PROLOGUE – Chiasso, 3.4km *Richard wins in 4:13.51. Second is Swiss Daniel Steiger (Jolly-Club 88) in 4:13.88, third is Hodge in 4:14.00. Rominger is fifth in 4:17.00.*

STAGE 1 – Chiasso-Chiasso, 174.8km *Leclercq wins stage to take leadership from Richard.*

STAGE 2 – Bains de Saillon-La Fouly, 141km *Eight riders break away in the early kilometres: Frenchman Thierry Bourguignon (Toshiba), German Udo Bölts (Telekom), Swiss Weinmann team-mates Stefan Joho and Kurt Steinmann, Swiss Bruno Holenweger (Swiss Comp), Italians Stefano Giuliani (Jolly-Club 88) and Fabio Roscioli (Del Tongo) and Czech Jan Svorada (Colnago) ... 95km Bourguignon leads break over col des Planches (1411m) ... 120km On col de Champex (1466m) breakaways are caught. Hodge attacks with Rominger, Millar, American Michael Carter (Motorola) and Swiss Laurent Dufaux (Helvetia). Three kilometres from summit, Leclercq is dropped from peloton ... 135km On the col de La Fouly (1600m), Hodge and Dufaux are dropped and Rominger, Millar and Carter sprint for stage win. Rominger wins from Millar and Carter takes third at 0:06. Rominger also takes overall lead.*

STAGE 3 – La Fouly/Orsières-Fribourg, 179km ... 178.6km *Australian Stephen Hodge (ONCE) leads out bunch and wins stage from Joho and Italian Mario Cippolini (Del Tongo). Rominger leads overall.*

STAGE 4A – Fribourg-Brugg, 73km *Swiss Serge Demierre (Helvetia) wins from six other attackers. Peloton at 0:25. Rominger leads overall.*

STAGE 4B – 19.4 km time trial, Brugg *Rominger extends overall lead on Millar from 0:27 to 1:31 with stage win; 1:04 ahead of 11th placed Millar.*

STAGE 5 – Brugg-Geneva, 194.5km *Richard wins from Swiss Rolf Järmann (Weinmann). They finish 1:36 clear of four chasers and 1:46 clear of peloton. Rominger, in peloton, wins overall.*

Classique des Alpes: 18 May

Until this year, the climbers in the peloton had always lacked a showcase race. There were, of course, the two hilly Ardennes classics – Flèche Wallonne and Liège-Bastogne-Liège. But these failed to satisfy the appetites of the sport's champion ascenders, who were obliged to wait until the national tours served up some serious climbs – the Dolomites in the Giro d'Italia, or the Alps and Pyrenees in the Tour de France.

It was with these riders in mind that the Société du Tour de France created 'La Classique des Alpes'. Set in the French Alps, and boasting a menu of seven mountains, this new race provided the climbing specialists with ideal preparation for the looming Giro and Dauphiné Libéré stage races. It also provides cycling fans, whose attention was divided at this time between the Vuelta in Spain and the American Tour Dupont, with a great television spectacle: a factor which will certainly carry plenty of clout when the event comes to be considered for World Cup status.

The Société du Tour, already the organiser of four of the thirteen World Cup events, was careful not to seek World Cup status for their new race in its first year. But it will come as no surprise to anyone to see it added to the list of World Cup races in 1992, because it gives the season an even balance of races for every specialist.

There will be Paris-Tours for the sprinters, the Grand Prix des Nations for the time triallists, Paris-Roubaix for those who relish cobblestones, the Tour of Flanders for the 'strong men' who revel in its combination of short, sharp climbs and speed, Milan-San Remo for the calculating opportunists, Liège-Bastogne-Liège for the average climbers, the Tour of Lombardy for the hardy 'end of seasoners', and the Grand Prix de la Liberation team time trial for – obviously – the strong teams.

The inaugural Classique des Alpes, starting at Chambéry, where Greg LeMond won the 1989 world road championship, lived up to every expectation. There were attacks and chases; gripping, back-breaking slogs up mountains; breath-taking, neck-breaking flights down mountains. On the highest peaks, there was even some snow.

Classique des Alpes, France: 208.5km

It was anticipated that the real action would not begin until the final climb, the 1440m Col du Revard 23km from the finish, but in fact battle was joined much earlier. Frenchman Eric Boyer (Z) led the field over the penultimate climb, the 1130m Col du Granier, with a two-minute lead, but his lack of descending prowess meant that he was recaptured at the foot of the final climb. The central figure here was his compatriot Charly Mottet (RMO), clearly on form after his victory in the Four Days of Dunkirk, but with him also were such notable climbers as Scotland's Robert Millar (Z), Frenchman Luc Leblanc (Castorama), American Michael Carter (Motorola), Belgian champion Claude Criquielion (Lotto), and the Swiss trio of Alfred Achermann (Weinmann), Mauro Gianetti (Helvetia-La Suisse) and his team-mate, promising neo-pro Laurent Dufeaux.

But Mottet's confidence was as unshakeable as it had been in the Dunkirk Four Days, when he attacked on the second-last stage to take the lead. In the absence of Tour de Romandie winner Tony Rominger, he was easily able to shake off his rivals on the Revard, accelerating once to weed out the pretenders. And then, nine kilometres from the summit, he attacked. And as with Tony Rominger in the Tour de Romandie, the only man who could go with him was Robert Millar.

And, just as in the Tour de Romandie, Millar finished up second: the long 23km descent to the finish at Aix-les-Bains was hardly going to give him an opportunity to shed Mottet, and there was no chance that the Frenchman would let victory slip away from him in the finishing sprint. As Mottet said later, it was less a question of winning, than of not losing. 'It was one of my objectives for the season. And I am happy not to have lost it. I was in form and I knew the course,' he said.

Dufeaux and Abadie were two of the surprise riders in the decisive break

After they shed their breakaway companions on the col du Revard, the Classique des Alpes was a race between Mottet and Millar

Not for the first or last time this season, strong form wasn't enough for Millar to bridge the gap between a top placing and victory

RACE DETAILS

WEATHER *Fine and sunny. Snow on first-category mountain summits.*

FIELD *17 teams, plus eight individuals.*

COURSE *Principal difficulties: Col du Chat (2nd category at 12.5km), Côte de Berland (3rd category at 69.5km), Col du Cucheron (2nd category at 82km), Col du Coq (1st category at 98.5km), Col de Marcieu (3rd category at 115km), Col du Granier (1st category at 143km), Col du Revard (1st category at 185km).*

Early kilometres: Frenchmen Henri Abadie (Toshiba) and Yvon Ledanois (Castorama) attack ...137km Ledanois is alone and still leading at foot of Col du Granier but is soon caught ...143km At summit of Granier (1130m), Boyer leads by 2:00 on a small chase group including Mottet, Millar,

Carter and Leblanc. On descent, they reel in Boyer ...169km Boyer is caught ...173km Mottet accelerates to test rivals' strengths ...176km Mottet attacks but after 200 metres alone is joined by Millar. The two leaders are not troubled on descent to Aix-les-Bains. Behind them are Carter, Leblanc, Criquielion, Acherman, Gianetti and Dufeaux ...208.5km Mottet easily outsprints Millar, while in race for third place, nearly three minutes back, Leblanc does the same to Carter.

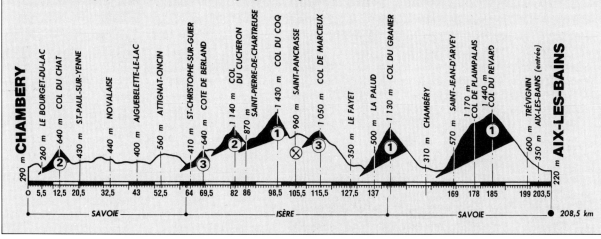

Tour Du Pont: 9-19 May

Sponsored by one of the world's largest corporations, and staged in one of the most beautiful regions of the eastern United States, the first Tour Du Pont should have been an out and out success. And compared with its predecessor, the Tour de Trump, this 11-day, pro-sanctioned race was more professionally organised and attracted a far greater representation of European teams. However the race itself was somewhat antiseptic, in that the outcome was always predictable – a victory for Eric Breukink of PDM. The 27-year-old Dutchman – a time trial specialist who was using the race as his lead-in to a Tour de France bid – won the difficult prologue time trial ... and then kept in close firing range of the opposition until the race ended with another, longer time trial, back in Wilmington, Delaware.

After the yellow jersey had been worn briefly by Belgian Patrick Roelandt (Tonton Tapis) and American Greg Oravetz, (Coors Light) it was Norwegian Atle Kvalsvoll who emerged on the vital Blue Ridge Mountain stage, as the race leader ... and Breukink's major opponent. A more than adequate climber, Kvalsvoll had the full backing of America's Greg

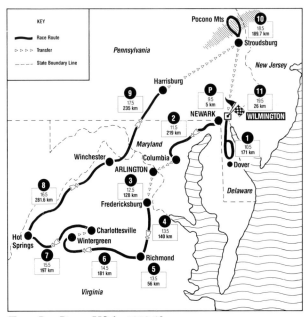

Tour Du Pont, USA: 1828.8km

After placing fifth in the prologue and second in the winning break at Arlington, former US champion Greg Oravetz was the race leader in Richmond

LeMond and his Z team. And it soon became apparent that they and Breukink's PDM riders were the race's dominant forces.

Less focused were the efforts of the top European-based squads, Motorola and Helvetia, who both made tactical errors, leaving them to play lesser rôles. Perhaps Motorola's biggest mistake was leaving its best two climbers – Andy Hampsten and Michael Carter – in Europe. In theory either of these two Americans would have been capable of matching Kvalsvoll in the key mountain stage, and would have thus given Motorola the opening that was not offered to its designated leaders for the Tour Du Pont – Australian Phil Anderson and Canadian Steve Bauer.

Bauer began the race well by coming in a close second to Breukink in the Wilmington prologue, featuring the steep, cobbled Monkey Hill and a further, challenging climb to the finish line, outside the Hotel Du Pont. Anderson, too, started strongly. He was the fastest in the prologue, 12 seconds down on Breukink; and, on the first stage, he was just beaten into second place by American Davis Phinney of Coors Light.

A feature of the first stage – held over a flat, out-and-back course at Wilmington – was a long, solo break by Belgian neo-pro Kurt De Muynck (Tonton Tapis). His 95km-long effort was extinguished 20km from the finish. But the following day, De Muynck's team-mate, Roelandt, had much more luck with a similar move on the second stage. After an intense period of attacks Roelandt slipped away to a lone lead, 46km from the finish. Soon out of sight on the twisting route through the rolling Maryland countryside, the 28-year-old Flemish rider moved to an unchallenged lead of 4:30 – a fact which was explained by PDM *directeur sportif* Jan Gisbers: 'Roelandt is not a dangerous rider for the general classification'. There was a belated chase, but Roelandt was still more than two minutes ahead at the stage end ... where the yellow jersey added to his joy.

The last of the race's mountain passes, Shenandoah Mountain, saw Atle Kvalsvoll emerge from the Appalachians with the yellow jersey he won at Wintergreen Resort

With a substantial overall lead, Roelandt could have been expected to hold it for a few stages; but he and his Tonton Tapis team-mates proved unequal to the challenge of controlling the Stage 3 circuit race at Arlington, Virginia. With three-and-a-half laps of the 12km circuit remaining, an acceleration by Bauer to catch four earlier breakaways was followed by the vigilant Coors Light team (with Oravetz and its three best climbers Americans Alexi Grewal, Mike Engelman and Scott Moninger), as well as by Breukink, Kvalsvoll, Helvetia's Rolf Aldag, Seur's Ronan Pensec of France and American amateur Bobby Julich.

The break was 20 strong, and by the time Tonton Tapis started chasing, was already more than a minute clear. The leaders gained more than 2 minutes by the end – except for the unlucky Bauer who punctured on the last lap and lost half a minute. Aldag, the rapid blond-haired German, sprinted to a narrow win over Oravetz; but it was the American who donned the yellow jersey. Having missed most of the 1990 season because of an injured knee, Oravetz seemed to be back on track with his promising career, that brought him the US national road championship in 1989, at age 21. He was now starting to show his former strength, and he raced well on the next day's two stages: a rolling, 140km road race to Richmond, Virginia, the former capital of the American South; and a hilly 56km criterium that evening.

Anderson, who'd missed out on the Arlington break, won the road race – thanks to a powerful surge over the uphill stretch of cobblestone, which set him up for the last 200-metre sprint. This time, Stage 1 winner Phinney messed up a gear change and could finish only fifth. Coming in second was the US amateur champion Bob Mionske, whose success inspired his team-mates for the evening's spectacular criterium. Covering 37 laps of a 1.5km circuit that was half climbing and half descending, with six corners per lap, this was a gruelling

Riding strongly, Greg LeMond was a perfect ally for Z team-mate Kvalsvoll on the marathon stage to Winchester, Virginia

event at the end of a very hot (34° C) day. It became even tougher when Bauer, Kvalsvoll and Grewal jumped across to two earlier attackers – the outstanding young amateurs, Lance Armstrong of the US and Dmitri Nelubin of the Soviet national team. The result was a violent chase by the PDM riders, with even Breukink and Ireland's Sean Kelly leading a 50 mph chase down Richmond's Ninth Street hill.

Shortly after the 11-man break was brought to heel, Z's François Lemarchand of France jumped away, and was joined by the senior member of the US amateur team, Nate Sheafor. They were later joined by Britain's Sean Yates (Motorola) and Frenchman Robert Forest (Z), and then by the effervescent Armstrong. American cyclists are reared on criteriums, and when Sheafor attacked at the top of the main climb, just over 2km from the line, he caught the pros by surprise. And he went on to win by three seconds from Yates and Armstrong, with Phinney taking the bunch sprint, 38 seconds down.

So Oravetz had retained the lead, and he held a three-second advantage over Breukink going to Stage 6 – which would finish atop the fiendishly steep climb to the Wintergreen Resort, 3800 feet (1160 metres) up in the Blue Ridge Mountains. The Belgian veteran Gino De

On the penultimate stage, in the Pocono Mountains of Pennsylvania, Kvalsvoll – seen here with Helvetia's Dominik Krieger – extended his overall lead to 50 seconds

The Poconos stage ended in a close sprint won by Motorola's Steve Bauer (centre), over former team-mate Davis Phinney (right) and the promising German Rolf Aldag of Helvetia

Backer (Tonton Tapis) and the Canadian amateur David Spears established a 7:30 lead halfway through the 181km stage; but a concerted chase led by Frenchman Gilbert Duclos-Lassalle, (Z) brought the race back together just before the final climb started.

Thunder rumbling over the adjacent mountains seemed to signal that decision time was approaching ... and it was the Z team that again took the initiative. LeMond orchestrated some short, probing attacks that softened up the opposition, and allowed Kvalsvoll to burst off the front, 4.5km from the finish. Rearing at an average gradient of 1-in-8 (13 per cent), this Wintergreen climb would have been at least category two in the Tour de France – probably category one in its context as the stage finish. It proved a perfect springboard for the in-form Kvalsvoll, who moved steadily away from the field, chased at first by Breukink (who blew, slightly, and lost 67 seconds); and then by the startling Swiss, Helvetia rider, Fabian Jeker (who showed great climbing form for a neo-pro, and came in second, at 30 seconds). Third place went to Grewal, at 59 seconds, while Pensec overhauled Breukink for fourth place. Jeker's better placed team-mate, Aldag, finished 1:45 down; Julich and Bauer came in at 1:52; LeMond was 20th, at 2:23; while overnight leader Oravetz lost 4:22 ... and the yellow jersey.

Kvalsvoll was in command, with a 48-second lead on Breukink and Coors Light's Grewal in third. And these positions would remain unchanged over the next three days, on a splendidly fast stage through the Appalachian Mountains to the Homestead resort, at Hot Springs, Virginia; a monotonously long trek, back through the mountains to Winchester; and a more aggressive, but equally inconsequential stage to Harrisburg, Pennsylvania. Bauer, Aldag and Spanish neo-pro Eladio Ambite (Amaya) were the three winners: the first two in field sprints – Bauer on a downhill, Aldag on an uphill effort – while the courageous Ambite won after a solo flight of 180km. Since the Wintergreen confrontation, Kvalsoll's Z team-mates had controlled the race perfectly. With LeMond riding stronger every day, they had pulled back a dangerous break led by Motorola's Andy Bishop, over the hills to the Homestead; and had neutralised an impressive move by the complete Soviet national team on Stage 9. But they were expected to have greater problems on the hilly Stage 10 circuit race at Stroudsburg, Pennsylvania.

However, after PDM's Jos Van Aert of Holland had stepped up a lethargic pace on the second of three loops in the Pocono Mountains, the only dangerous attack came from Jeker, who was joined by world pursuit champion Eugeni Berzin – but they were caught by the front half of the peloton 10km from the line, where Bauer took his second stage win in a sprint from his old rival Phinney.

The only change to the overall picture on that penultimate stage was a two-second time bonus gain by Kvalsvoll, whose lead over Breukink was thus 50 seconds going into the final, 26km time trial at Wilmington. Breukink had explained his lack of aggression by saying that he was confident that he could beat Kvalsvoll by a full minute in this final stage. It was

a slightly arrogant attitude, but one that appeared fully justified when, at the halfway mark, he was timed 40 seconds faster than the race leader.

At this point LeMond had already finished with the best-to-date time of 35:25 for the twisting, up-and-down loop through the more scenic parts of Wilmington's green and wooded parks. It was entering one of these woods, where thick shade masked his view, that Breukink rode into a pot hole and punctured his front tyre. 'I thought I'd lost everything,' exclaimed Breukink who rode as fast, and as dangerously, as he possibly could to eclipse LeMond's time by 35 seconds.

Now – like LeMond at the end of the 1989 Tour de France – Breukink had to wait until the man in the yellow jersey appeared at the end of the finishing straight. And, just as the American leapt with joy when Laurent Fignon finished eight seconds short of success, so Breukink could celebrate when Kvalsvoll crossed the line 12 seconds short of his target. And, finally, the Tour Du Pont had ended on an exciting note – albeit because of a puncture.

RACE DETAILS

WEATHER *hot and humid.*

COURSE *Prologue in Wilmington, Delaware, followed by 11 stages, including circuit races at Arlington (Stage 3) and East Stroudsburg (Stage 10); a criterium at Richmond (Stage 5); a mountain-top finish at Wintergreen Resort (Stage 6); and an individual time trial to finish, in Wilmington. Total distance: 1828.8km.*

FIELD *15 teams (11 pro, 4 amateur) of 8 riders. 105 starters, 91 finishers.*

PROLOGUE – *5km time trial, Wilmington Breukink scores 2-second win over Bauer, with Kvalsvoll 33rd, at 0:019.*

STAGE I – Wilmington-Wilmington, 171km ... 55km *Pace slow; De Muynck's solo break gains 7:00, but is caught after 151km. Uphill, bunch sprint won by Phinney from Anderson. Breukink retains lead.*

STAGE 2 – Newark-Columbia, 219km ... 150km *The PDM team thwarts dangerous, 30-second attacks by LeMond and Bishop ... 165km Kvalsvoll and 15 others join in with the attacks ... 173km Counter-attack from Roelandt, who gains 4:30, and is still 2:13 clear at finish. Roelandt takes lead.*

STAGE 3 – Arlington-Arlington, 128km ... 20km *LeMond attacks, and gains 1:00, when joined by McCarthy. After they are caught, a key attack is made by Bauer on 8th of 11 laps. He's joined by 19 others, who start last lap 2:00 ahead. Bauer punctures, loses 0:26. Aldag wins sprint from Oravetz, who takes overall lead.*

STAGE 4 – Fredericksburg-Richmond, 140km ... 85km *Mierzejewski attacks, gains 1:00, and is caught at 125km. Final, uphill bunch sprint goes to Anderson, from Mionske. Oravetz retains lead.*

STAGE 5 – Richmond criterium, 56km. *Midway through the hilly, 37-lap race, attack by Lemarchand is joined by Sheafor. They are joined with 12 laps to go by Yates and Forest, then by Armstrong. Sheafor attacks with 2.5km to go, wins by 0:03 on Yates, with pack at 0:38. Oravetz still leader.*

STAGE 6 – Richmond-Wintergreen Resort, 181km ... 111km *A 7:30 lead established by De Backer and Spears – to be wiped out by a long chase from the Z team at 161km. The pack is together approaching the 6km climb to the finish, until successive attacks by Forest, LeMond and Simon allow Kvalsvoll to launch the winning move 4.5km from the summit. At the line, he is 0:30 ahead of Jeker, 0:59 on Grewal, more than a minute on Pensec and Breukink and 4:22 on Oravetz. Kvalsvoll takes overall lead.*

STAGE 7 – Charlottesville-Hot Springs, 197km *From the start, Spain's Guerricagoitia breaks clear with Amaya team-mate Quevedo and Lammerts (Z) ... 55km The trio is 3:30 ahead. Quevedo drops other two on Reeds Gap climb, and is joined by Bishop after the descent. Bishop pushes lead from 2:00 to 7:17. Z team chases ... 183km Bishop drops Quevedo on last climb, but is caught at final kilometre. Bauer wins downhill sprint from American amateur Steve Larsen. Kvalsvoll retains lead.*

STAGE 8 – Hot Springs-Winchester, 281.6km *A truce creates a slow pace on this marathon stage, and the early hills fail to split the field ... 257km In the first break of the stage Spanish rider Eleuterio Anguita (Seur), Poland's Mierzejewski and Kaczmarcyk go clear. After gaining 0:50 lead, the break is caught with 1km to go. Short, uphill sprint goes to Aldag from Oravetz. Kvalsvoll retains lead.*

STAGE 9 – Winchester-Harrisburg, 235km *After initial attacks by Metorda's Yates, Anderson and Norwegian Dag-Otto Lauritzen a solo attack comes from Ambite. With his lead at 10:00, Bishop gives chase ... 166km By Gettysburg, he has reduced the gap to 6:40. An acceleration by the Soviet team causes Bishop to await the bunch, but Ambite stays clear to win by 6:00.*

STAGE 10 – Stroudsburg-Mt. Pocono, 189.7km *The first of three hilly laps of this circuit race produces no breaks ... 73km Van Aert attacks and gains 3:30 by the end of lap 2, where Kvalsvoll wins a time bonus to take his overall lead over Breukink to 0:50. Van Aert is caught on the second climb, where Jeker attacks, gaining 0:20. He's joined by Berzin after last hill, but the pair is caught 10km from the finish. Bauer wins long sprint from Phinney. Kvalsvoll retains lead.*

STAGE II – 26km time trial, Wilmington *At the halfway point of a twisting, hilly circuit, Breukink is 0:40 ahead, when he punctures, recovers to win the time trial by 0:35 over LeMond, and 1:02 over Kvalsvoll – so Breukink wins overall by 12 seconds.*

Stung by Breukink's confidence that he could wait until the final time trial to annihilate Kvalsvoll's 50-second lead, the Norwegian threw everything into his effort...

...but Breukink, despite a puncture, came through to win the Wilmington time trial and take the Tour Du Pont title by 12 seconds

Breukink succeeded PDM team-mate Raúl Alcalá, last year's Tour de Trump victor, as winner of America's most prestigious stage race

Vuelta a España: 29 April-19 May

Vuelta a España: 3393km

A nyone who knows Spain knows to expect the unexpected, and the unpredictable nature of Spain and the Spanish was confirmed in May 1991 when a little-known 25-year-old ONCE rider called Melchor Mauri caused a sensation by winning the Vuelta a España. Mauri, although his season had started well with two stage wins in the Ruta del Sol and overall victory in the Tour of Valencia, was a totally unexpected winner of Spain's national tour.

His victory also admitted Mauri to the select, but growing, band of 'rags to riches' riders. Like Belgian Rudy Dhaenens, when he won last year's World Championship road race; like Mauro Giovanetti when he won the Vuelta and finished third in the Tour de France; like Claudio Chiappucci, who last year took the Tour de France yellow jersey on Stage 12 and kept it, against all the odds, until the Stage 20 time trial, finally taking second place to Greg LeMond: like all these riders, Melchor Mauri seemed to arrive, as it were, from nowhere.

Other elements which contributed to the individual

Rivals Mauri and Indurain pose smilingly at Benasque the morning after Indurain had gained significant time over Mauri on the climb to Estacion Cerler, thus becoming the Catalan race-leader's main threat

After Mauri, Van Poppel was the man of the Vuelta – his devastating return to sprinting form brought him four stage wins. Here the Dutchman celebrates his third win at Zaragoza (Stage 13) which was really a team victory, the result of John Talen's unselfish lead-out and Uwe Raab's decoy tactics in the sprint

character of this year's race were the heated, and at times acrimonious, debate about rider safety in the Vuelta, and the dramatic fluctuations in the weather. The dwindling field, already decimated by crashes, found themselves pitted first of all against an enervating heat wave, followed by nearly a fortnight of rain, wind and heavy snowfalls, at the end of which a sticky, humid heat returned as the riders approached the finish in Madrid. The weather failed to deter Spain's growing number of cycling fans, however, and they lined the roads in their thousands as the Vuelta wound its way through some of Spain's most beautiful and inaccessible countryside. Picnickers drinking wine, off-duty workers, tourists and amateur cyclists sporting the jerseys of their favourite teams cheered on the riders every day, rain or shine.

The crashes which also characterised the race were far too common in the first week of racing. Belgian Patrick Robeet (Buckler) broke his arm in an accident on the fourth stage, and Soviet rider Dmitri Konyshev (TVM) broke his collar-bone during the fifth stage. The same day Mexican Raúl Alcalá of PDM took the first of three spills, bruising his right calf muscle and receiving a nasty tyre burn that never had a chance, in the changeable weather conditions, to properly heal. The crashes were caused partly by the poor surfaces of the narrow roads in southern Spain, which made the riders very jumpy, and partly by the incredibly fast speeds. The dangerous conditions did nothing to improve the relationship between riders and race officials, and when officials failed to respond adequately to the riders' expressions of concern there was a good deal of animosity between the two groups, which on two occasions led to protests by the peloton and the threat of strikes. There was also a barrage of protests about the poor hotels, about commercialization at the expense of rider safety, and about bad organization at the start and finish areas.

Then, as if the race officials did not already have enough on their hands, they faced a new calamity. The eighteenth stage of the Vuelta started from León, and the residents of León, angry about the region's economic recession, decided to block the race route as a protest. The response of the Spanish riot police was to charge at the demonstrators, firing on them with rubber bullets! Most demonstrators managed to hide in the fields and in deserted farm buildings, but sadly one person was reported to have been shot.

However, this was all in the future when the race embarked on its huge, 21-stage, anti-clockwise sweep around Spain, from the south-western town of Merida. The journalists whose job it is to speculate about the outcome of races had not even put forward Melchor Mauri's name as a rank outsider. How fast things change – during the last few stages, his name was being bandied about as a contender for the Tour de France! But Mauri's *directeur sportif*, the portly Manuel 'Manolo' Saiz, lost no time in quashing what he saw as damaging speculation. 'I just hope that the public and the press do not expect him to win the Tour de France,' he said. And Mauri himself agreed: 'The Tour de France is

a very tough race,' he said afterwards. 'I prepared especially for the Vuelta, and it's impossible for me to peak a second time for the Tour. In that respect, my win in the Vuelta doesn't change anything. I'll still be working for someone else in the Tour, whether it's Marino Lejarreta or Anselmo Fuerte,' he added, modestly.

Nevertheless, despite his modesty, Mauri achieved his victory in impressive style, and when after three weeks' hectic racing they packed their bags for home the big favourites – his ONCE team-mates Lejarreta and Fuerte, Alcalá, Banesto's Miguel Indurain, Federico Echave (Clas), and Colombian Fabio Parra (Amaya) – must have been pondering deeply on the comparisons that were being drawn between Mauri and Spain's most popular cyclist, Pedro Delgado. Delgado, twice winner of the Vuelta, was absent from this year's race; he had chosen instead to compete in the Tour de Romandie and the Giro d'Italia as preparation for his attempt to win the Tour de France for a second time. On the second to last day of the race, when it was almost inevitable that Mauri would win, Delgado made a guest appearance at the finish of the stage to his home town of Segovia, and congratulated Mauri on his performance.

Like Mauri, Delgado was 25 years old when he won the Tour of Spain for the first time in 1985, and to Spanish cycling fans, hungry for a new idol, the comparisons were irresistible. Because Mauri was not just a 'lucky' winner: he had demonstrated tactical ability in maximising his time-trialling strength, winning the opening three-man time trial with Anselmo Fuerte and Herminio Diaz-Zabala, and two more time trials, at Cala d'Or on Majorca and at Valladolid, for the latter using an amazing 55 x 12 gearing! He showed also that he can be a daring and courageous rider: he had constantly to watch out for and chase down attacks directed against him, yet he still had the intelligence and confidence to ride the race as he wanted to ride it. It was a fine display of maturity from a comparatively inexperienced rider – Mauri, who turned professional in 1987, had only one professional win behind him when he joined the ONCE team for the 1990 season.

His relationship with Manolo Saiz, his *directeur sportif*, has been a key factor in Mauri's rise to

Time stood still at this bridge over the Rio Esera while the peloton sped down from the mountains on its journey to Zaragoza on Stage 13

Mauri's superb performances in both long time trials put paid to any doubts that he was the strongest man in the race

The atrocious conditions at Valdezcaray failed to stop Fabio Parra from securing his first ever time trial victory in a major race. The Amaya rider is seen here in thick, freezing fog, two kilometres from the summit of the snow-covered mountain

The Vuelta a España was a celebration of Mauri's — and ONCE's — superiority. At the finish in Madrid, his success is saluted by his team-mate Eduardo Chozas

Only Laudelino Cubino could resist Herrera's strong attack at Lagos de Covadonga. Undeterred, Herrera began a second surge that secured the Colombian's first stage win in a major race since 1987

The Puerto de Navacerrada (Stage 20) was the last chance for Indurain to launch an attack against Mauri, but the tall challenger seemed tired by his efforts during the previous day's time trial and Mauri kept his lead

prominence. The two first met at the 1983 junior World Championships in New Zealand, where Saiz was the Spanish national coach. So when Saiz took the young Mauri under his wing in 1990 they already knew each other pretty well. That understanding, says Saiz, was of vital importance to Mauri's victory. 'Melchor's win was very much a psychological achievement,' asserted Saiz. 'It was very easy working with him because I've known him since 1983. It's always like that when you're working with a young person, because he has an open mind and is willing to learn. With older riders – Lejarreta for instance – they are already set in their ways and are less likely to change even though they aren't always right!'

Mauri's tactical intelligence and maturity were most clearly shown in the mountain stages – this year's route took the Vuelta over 34 major climbs. And when Mauri pulled on the leader's *amarillo* jersey for the second time he was still saying that he didn't think he would be very strong in the mountains. He was advised by Saiz to refrain from chasing down all the attacks and to find his own pace and rhythm. In the event, only the Colombians, in great shape after their national tour, and two of the Soviet riders, Ivan Ivanov and Piotr Ugrumov (Seur), were able seriously to attack Mauri's lead, and Mauri reacted with great tactical finesse, catching the escaping riders on the descents and keeping his time deficits to a minimum. And like all great champions, he owed something to luck: the mountainous Stage 10, from Andorra to Pla de Beret, on which he might have been toppled from the lead, was cancelled because of heavy overnight snow and avalanches.

One of the best indications of Mauri's physical strength came from the daily blood tests which are taken by every member of the ONCE team. While the results of his team-mates showed fluctuations, and more often than not plummeted, Mauri's were the same from the first stage to the last. Nor did his temperament falter. 'I never had one night's bad sleep, and I didn't dream about wearing the yellow jersey. I still understand and accept that I'm not the number one in Spain,' he said. 'I know there's still a long way for me to go and a lot of hard work to do.'

The value of Mauri's victory can be seen in his rapid ascent of the world FICP rankings, from 185th at the beginning of the season, to 105th before the Vuelta, to 8th place when it was over, thanks to the 660 points he earned by winning. The 18 days he spent wearing the yellow jersey (17 straight days and one individual), is the second longest leadership of any Spaniard in the Vuelta and the fourth longest on record; his performance has been bettered only by Spain's Julian Berrendero in 1942 (19 days) and two Belgians, Gustav Deloor in 1936 and Freddy Maertens in 1977, both of whom wore the leader's jersey for 20 days.

But whilst Mauri's was the outstanding performance of the race, there were opportunities for other stars to shine. The mountain stages gave the Colombians Fabio Parra (Amaya) and Luis Herrera (Ryalcao-Postobon) and Dutchman Steven Rooks (Buckler) the chance to demonstrate that their climbing brilliance was undimmed, and Holland's Jean-Paul Van Poppel (PDM) took four stages with his awesome sprint. His German team-mate Uwe Raab also took a stage with a sprint finish, as well as the blue points jersey for the second successive year. Other riders, however, went home disappointed with their performance. The hotly tipped Alcalá, whose chances of winning still seemed strong until the mountain time trial to the summit of the snow-covered Valdezcaray on Stage 14, faded as a result of a debilitating bout of sickness and the demoralizing effect of his three crashes – including one particularly unnecessary mishap at Valdezcaray, where he rode into a crowd of frantic race officials and reporters, crowding round the exhausted Mauri, who had overtaken Alcalá with 5km to go. His scathing comments about the race organisation earned him more headlines than his athletic prowess, and he left Spain declaring that he would never come back until the race organizers took steps to secure the safety of the competitors.

RACE DETAILS

WEATHER *Sunny, warm start and finish, but rain and severe snowfalls in middle fortnight.*

COURSE *21 stages (average distance 159.2km) over an anti-clockwise route including 34 mountain passes and five time trials (a three-man time trial, a team time trial and a mountain time trial, plus two flat individual time trials).*

FIELD *22 teams, 198 starters, 116 finishers.*

STAGE I – 9.3km three-man time trial, Merida *ONCE (Mauri, Fuerte and Herminio Diaz-Zabala) wins in 10:07. Mauri, first across the line, takes overall lead. Alcalá is at 0:08, Indurain at 0:12 and Lejarreta at 0:16.*

STAGE 2A – Merida-Cáceres, 138km *Dutchman Michel Zanoli (Tulip) wins in bunch sprint over Belgian Eddy Planckaert (Panasonic). Fuerte takes overall lead.*

STAGE 2B – 42km team time trial, Montijo-Badajoz *ONCE wins in 50:27. Second is Clas (Echave) in 51:08. Third is PDM (Alcalá) in 51:22. Banesto (Indurain) finishes poorly in eighth place and in 52:13. Mauri resumes overall lead.*

STAGE 3 – Badajoz-Seville, 229km *Peloton splits with 44km to go. Dane Jesper Skibby (TVM) wins in a bunch sprint from Raab. Diaz-Zabala leads overall.*

STAGE 4 – Seville-Jaen, 241km *Spaniard Jesus Cruz Martin (Wigarma) wins by 9:24 on the peloton after a 182km solo break. Mauri leads overall.*

STAGE 5 – Linares-Albacete, 232km *Raab wins over Holland's Adri Van der Poel (Tulip) in bunch sprint after peloton splits 30km from finish. Mauri leads overall.*

STAGE 6 – Albacete-Valencia, 250km *Main attack by Soviet Viktor Klimov (Seur) from 44km to 186km. Van Poppel wins sprint from German Olaf Ludwig (Panasonic). Mauri leads overall.*

STAGE 7 – Palma de Majorca-Palma de Majorca, 188km *Skibby wins in bunch sprint from Rooks. Mauri leads overall.*

STAGE 8 – 47km team time trial, Cala d'Or *Mauri wins by 0:11 from Alcalá. Others: Echave (4th at 0:46), Indurain (5th at 0:56), Lejarreta (18th at 2:43). Mauri leads overall.*

STAGE 9 – TVE San Cugat-Lloret de Mar, 140km *Van Poppel wins from Raab in bunch sprint. Mauri leads overall.*

STAGE 10 – Lloret de Mar-Andorra, 241km ... 23km *In freezing conditions Denmark's Per Pedersen (Amaya) attacks but is caught at 219km ...226km Italian Guido Bontempi (Carrera) and German Udo Bolts (Telekom) attack. Bontempi wins from Bolts. Peloton at 0:13. Mauri leads overall.*

STAGE II – Andorra-Pla de Beret, 135km *Stage cancelled because of heavy snowfalls and avalanches blocking second of three mountain passes.*

STAGE 12 – Bosost-Cerler, 115km *Very fast stage with three mountains, the last being the special category climb to Cerler ... 98km Peloton regrouped at foot of last ascent ... 99.5km Lejarreta attacks; Parra follows. Behind them are Indurain, Colombians Luis Herrera (Ryalcao-Postobon) and Oliveiro Rincon (Kelme), Spain's Federico Echave (Clas), Fuerte, Mauri ... 100km Parra attacks Lejarreta who is caught and passed by Ivanov. Ivanov catches Parra, and attacks again to win by 0:21. Mauri, at 1:48, leads overall.*

STAGE 13 – Benasque-Zaragoza, 224km *Van Poppel wins his third stage. His teammates, Raab and Dutchman John Talen, take second and third. Mauri leads overall.*

STAGE 14 – 24km mountain time trial, Ezcaray-Estacion Valdezcaray *Parra wins by 0:57 on Herrera. Alcalá, 21st at 3:48, drops to sixth overall at 3:27 after crash on finish line. Mauri, sixth at 1:35, leads overall.*

STAGE 15 – Santo Domingo-Santander, 218km ... 8km *Colombian Nestor Mora (Kelme) attacks with Spaniard Alberto Leanizbarrutia (Clas) ... 211km Mora, alone, is caught by nine riders, including Bontempi and Britain's Malcolm Elliott (Seur). Bontempi wins stage, with peloton at 0:32. Mauri leads overall.*

STAGE 16 – Santander-Lagos de Covadonga, 194km *Herrera attacks at foot of mountain finish. Behind, Lejarreta, Indurain, Echave and Rincon follow; then Rooks, Mauri, Parra and Spaniards Laudelino Cubino (Amaya) and Pello Ruiz Cabestany (Clas). Herrera wins stage by 0:58 from Soviet Piotr Ugrumov (Seur) and 1:00 on Lejarreta, Echave and Indurain. Mauri, at 1:28, leads overall.*

STAGE 17 – Cangas de Onis-Alto del Naranco, 152km *After attempts on first four climbs, Herrera attacks on the fifth to the finish. He is followed by Cubino who attacks again while Herrera is caught by Lejarreta, Ugrumov, Indurain and Echave. Lejarreta takes second place at 0:08 to Cubino. Mauri, at 0:32, leads overall.*

STAGE 18 – León-Valladolid, 147km ... 6km *Spaniard Antonio-Miguel Diaz (Kelme) and German Mario Kummer (Gatorade) attack. Diaz wins by 0:01, 0:08 clear of peloton. Mauri leads overall.*

STAGE 19 – 55km time trial, Valladolid *Mauri wins by 1:06 on Indurain and 1:36 on Belgian Eric Vanderaerden (Buckler). Lejarreta, seventh at 2:25, drops to third overall at 3:11. Mauri leads overall.*

STAGE 20 – Whisky DYC (Segovia)-Whisky DYC, 197km *Mauri defends lead despite being dropped twice on two of four early climbs ... 170km Six riders finally get away on last climb. Spaniard Jesus Montoya (Amaya) wins the stage by 0:06 on main group of 34 riders. Mauri leads overall.*

STAGE 21 – Collado-Villalba-Madrid, 175km *Procession to the first of five 4.7km finishing circuits. Van Poppel wins from Italian Giovanni Fidanza (Gatorade). Mauri wins overall.*

Milk Race: 26 May-8 June

Never since the days of the Independents (semi-professionals) and stages in excess of 160 miles – some would say, when men were men – have British riders enjoyed such a successful Milk Race. In 1953, Gordon Thomas led home six British riders, their finishing times spread over nine minutes, to become winner of the then Tour of Britain, which was sponsored by the Daily Express newspaper. The BSA rider succeeded in winning only one stage, at Bournemouth, but after riding 2624km he took overall victory and the lion's share of the £1013 prize money.

As 26-year-old Englishman Chris Walker (Banana-Falcon) sped to his most emphatic victory this year, he too headed six victorious British riders, but this time they all came within 62 seconds of each other at the end of 1878km. The winning margins have changed, and the prizes have changed too: £1000 for a stage win (Walker won three) and a total purse of £75,000. Times certainly change.

It was a race that was always going to be decided by a narrow margin. The course was fairly flat until the race reached Swansea, on Stage 8, and by then the peloton had all but surrendered to the restrictive grip of the well-drilled Banana-Falcon team, who led the race throughout in all the important classifications except the King of the Mountains and the Hot Spot sprint series. But it was never a boring race. Although most days ended in bunch sprints, the high speeds on the open road, and the attacks that stripped the field of its dignity on a number of occasions, made it interesting to watch.

Walker constructed his victory by taking the three most important stages of the race. His victories included the important stage to Hull, when he took the race leader's jersey from team-mate Jon Clay (riding his first Milk Race since 1987). It was a 30-man breakaway on this stage which had a decisive impact on the subsequent development of the race. Led by the King of the Mountains winner, Gary Baker (British Professionals), who was later dropped, this group included all the riders

The Banana-Falcon team of Shane Sutton, Keith Reynolds, Jonny Clay, Chris Walker, Chris Lillywhite and Rob Holden, with something to smile about

Milk Race, Britain: 1878km

who were to feature prominently over the next two weeks.

Good fortune in Stage 7 also helped Walker's cause. He got an unexpected bonus from the split-timed finish, the front half of the finishers being given a time four seconds faster than the back half. This placed him 0:22 ahead of his nearest rival Simeon Hempsall (England).

His second stage win came on Stage 8 from Gloucester to Swansea. From the Forest of Dean into Wales the peloton was a solid body of riders, led by the trio of Irish pro rider Ian Chivers, Australian Shane Sutton (Banana-Falcon) and Soviet professional Oleg Polovnikov. On Tumble Mountain Chivers dropped back, leaving Sutton and Polovnikov to cross the mountains together. They were finally caught on the descent to Cwm Parc near Port Talbot, and Walker outsprinted Belgian Bob Rasenburg (TVM-Sanyo) at the finish in Swansea.

Finally, still leader at Stage 10, Walker punctured just before the first category climb of Rowsley Bar in Derbyshire, and might have lost his yellow jersey, but he recovered so quickly that there was no rider capable of

Chris Walker might have been troubled by a talented Soviet team if they had possessed the tactical ability of the professional teams. But they were unable to outride him

taking advantage of the situation. Walker stormed up the steep climb, passing rider after rider. It took him about ten miles to regain contact with the leader Mark Walsham (British Professionals), and when he did the pace eased up. Surprisingly, Walker received no help from his team in this supreme effort. The field regrouped – more than 70 riders battled for the finish – but Walker had enough left to win the sprint for the stage in his home town of Sheffield.

Stages 11 and 12 were won by Belgian Jerry Cooman (SEFB-Saxon), but he was later disqualified for giving a positive dope test, leaving the way clear for Walker. Also on Stage 12 a crash marred the proceedings when a dog ran into the path of the peloton. Belgian Daniel Beelen (SEFB-Saxon) paid most heavily for this – he was taken to hospital needing treatment for facial injuries and a broken collar-bone, and lost his ninth place overall.

Chris Walker won the the Peter Buckley Trophy for top junior in '82 and '83 and turned professional in 1987 for the now defunct Watertech-Dawes team. From that moment on he was being touted as the up-and-coming star of British cycle racing. But it has taken him until 1991 to show his star qualities, and with his resounding success in the Milk Race, this must be counted as his best season to date. His next step must be to join a European team and get his foot firmly on the bottom rung of the difficult climb to international success.

The future for the Milk Race seems less rosy. Although 1992 will be its 35th year, unless another sponsor is found to back the Milk Marketing Board, it will also be its last. In addition, the governing body of professional cycling, the FICP, is currently discussing the possibility of imposing a maximum length of five days on open amateur races. If they did so an all-amateur event would be the only alternative, which would be a big blow to British professional racing – home

Two miles of main city centre roads to Liverpool were closed to welcome the finalists. It was an anxious two miles for the Banana-Falcon team, concerned primarily to make sure Chris Walker reached the finish safely, with his bike free from mechanical trouble on the last leg

Jonny Clay gave the Banana-Falcon team a winning start to the Milk Race by taking the Prologue time trial at Bridlington. After the first stage he handed the yellow jersey to team-mate and eventual winner, Chris Walker

professionals would lose their biggest pay day, and second category professionals, of whom there are a growing number in Europe, would be without a chance of proving themselves – important because their ranking is not officially recognised. They, more than anyone, need to demonstrate their talents to future sponsors.

Perhaps it was the intention of the competitors from the Eastern European countries to use the Milk Race as such a platform on this occasion. Renowned for sending very talented, much-feared competitors to international events, expectations were high of the Polish and Romanian teams who turned up for this year's race. The Romanians were appearing in the race for the first time since 1973, when two of their team members defected in Plymouth; the two riders who did finish took home a total of £10 in prize money! This year the team fared little better. Before the race began, one rider quit, others were badly prepared: one had no shoes, none had helmets. Hull Council and local business people helped out – the spirit of *glasnost* is alive and well in northern England!

One Romanian, at least, managed to distinguish himself. Costel Cracium showed a toughness which earned him admiration. By Stage 8 he was the sole surviving Romanian and in a nice gesture of support, a race mechanic, Tony Asplin, overhauled and updated his bike on the rest day. Cracium showed his appreciation by launching an attack on this most difficult stage from

The Milk Race is the biggest earner for Britain's home-based professionals. Here John Walshaw heads for his share of the £75,000 prize list, as leader of the sprints competition. He is flanked by Shane Sutton (left), overall winner in 1990 and Mark Walsham (right), the stage winner at Norwich

Gloucester to Swansea. After leading out for just 22 seconds he was dropped by the attacking bunch of Sutton, Chivers and Polovnikov – but for a fleeting moment, the glory was his.

The 34th edition of the Milk Race proved to be the challenge expected. It provided valuable experience to many riders, from the Romanians to the successful home team Banana-Falcon, and if it manages to survive the threats to its future, the race will continue to be one of the most important events on the British cycling calendar.

You may not win a multi-day stage race in the opening prologue time trial, but you can lose it! With this in mind, Chris Walker conserved his strength in the time trial so he could use it to greater effect in the next two stages – and take the overall lead

RACE DETAILS

WEATHER *Unseasonably cold, especially during the first week on the east coast of England. A typically British mixture of sunny, windy, cold days with rain on Stage 7.*

COURSE *12 stages, extending as far north as Bridlington and as far south as Cardiff. This includes the first category climb of Rowsley Bar, Stage 10, two circuit races and the prologue time trial.*

FIELD *101 starters from 17 teams, 5 professional and 12 amateur riders.*

PROLOGUE – *2.4km time trial, Bridlington. Clay dons the yellow jersey after beating Soviet newcomers Vladimir Abramov and Andre Dolgnikh by almost three seconds.*

STAGE IA – *Bridlington-Hull, 143km ... 14km Baker leads the attack and breakaway group of 30 forms. Baker is dropped. Group finishes with huge margin of 12:40 over the field, Walker wins stage and takes lead overall.*

STAGE IB – *Hull-Hull, 43km Belgian Jan Bogaert (Collstrop-Isoglass), sprints to victory after a crash thwarts earlier breakaway attempt. Walker retains lead.*

STAGE 2 – *Cleethorpes-Lincoln, 178km Hempsall romps up the cobbled hill to*

Lincoln to win from Walker and take second place overall, 0:18 behind Walker.

STAGE 3 – *Skegness-Norwich, 186km Jon Walshaw, (British Professionals) leads break from the gun in search of hot spot points at Boston. Race goes off course and is stopped, but break stays away and Walshaw wins prime. Peloton regroups ... 74km Walsham, John Hughes (Great Britain), and American John Loehner break clear. Walsham wins sprint; Walker retains lead.*

STAGE 4 – *Great Yarmouth-Bury St Edmunds, 127km Rasenberg and British rider Keith Reynolds (Banana-Falcon) have 0:22 lead on race leader Walker. They arrive in a group of five riders at the beginning of the finishing circuit and are caught by the field with 6 of 10 laps to go. Belgian Johan Van Den Dries (TVM-Sanyo) escapes, with 4 laps remaining, to win stage. Walker retains lead.*

STAGE 5 – *Ipswich-Milton Keynes, 200km Jacob Duwerkirk (Netherlands) leads attack from Ipswich ...21km He is joined by Darren Lawson (Australia), Paul Leitch (New Zealand), Casper van der Meer, (Netherlands) and Chivers. Low in overall standings, the five are allowed to gain 18:55. Lawson wins first stage for Australia. Adrian Timmis (British*

Professionals), third overall, crashes and retires with broken collar-bone. Walker retains lead.

STAGE 6 – *Kettering-Leicester, 103km Stage ends in confusion, a number of riders fall on tight finishing 8-lap circuit. A leading group of nine break away and enter circuit almost a minute ahead of the field. Two riders escape – Mark Gornall (Great Britain), who wins from Steve Douce (British Professionals).*

STAGE 7 – *Birmingham-Birmingham, 106km The peloton is split-timed at finish, Walker's lead goes up to 0:22 ... 104km Australian Patrick Jonker breaks away and wins by 3 seconds.*

STAGE 8 – *Gloucester-Swansea, 188km ... 50km Chivers, Sutton and Polovnikov break clear. Chivers is dropped others lead by almost 4 minutes. The pair are caught on the descent of Cwm Parc; Walker outsprints Rasenburg to take stage and retains overall lead.*

STAGE 9 – *Cardiff-Great Malvern, 159km Tom Bamford (New Zealand) takes lead in King of the Mountains breaking clear from the start and winning first three primes ... 48km He is caught by Tim Hall (Great Britain) who gains 6:46. Hall is caught by Douce, Kevin Kimmage (Ireland), Mathew Bazzano*

(Australia) and Duwerkirk at Eastnor, and dropped on the climb of Hollybush Hill approaching Malvern. Kimmage crashes on the second circuit of Malvern, remounts and catches leaders with 1km to go, winning stage by 300 metres from Douce. Walker retains lead.

STAGE 10 – *Telford-Sheffield, 140km Last mountain stage is full of attacks; a defensive Walker leads pursuit of Walsham. With 24km to go, the field regroups and Walker wins his third stage, to retain overall leadership.*

STAGE 11 – *Sheffield-Leeds, 171km ... 29km Rob Langley (Great Britain) attacks and is joined by Casper van der Meer (Netherlands), Jonas Carney (US professional), Belgians Peter Naessens (Collstrop-Isoglass) and Johan Devos (SEFB-Saxon) – they gain 10:00. Van der Meer is new leader on road – a chase begins ... 161km The field regroups; Cooman wins stage from Walker and Bogaert. Walker retains lead.*

STAGE 12 – *Manchester-Liverpool, 132km No attacks all day. Abramov and Dave Cook (England) both puncture on final circuit, losing high overall positions. Cooman wins stage from Walker and Bogaert, but is later disqualified. Walker holds on to lead to take overall victory.*

Dauphiné Libéré: 3-10 June

The Tour de France is inevitably the scene of many dramas, which are a reflection of the enormous prestige and importance of the race. Almost rivalling the Tour for drama, however, is the sight of the world's best climbers fighting tooth and nail in the Dauphiné Libéré, because they are not just fighting for victory in the Dauphiné: they are fighting either for a place in France's marathon three-week national tour, or to show that they already have the form to be serious contenders for honours in the Tour.

Sixteen teams had already been invited, on the basis of their FICP world rankings, to take part in the Tour. The line-up for the Dauphiné included the Castorama, Amaya, Ryalcao-Postobon, Panasonic, Tonton Tapis and Kelme teams, all competing for the six 'wild card' entries to the Tour. Other Tour contenders like TVM, Seur and another Castorama team led by Laurent Fignon (Castorama having sufficient riders to be able to field two teams), had been entered in the Giro d'Italia.

But by the time the race finished at the lakeside spa of Aix-les-Bains, the Dauphiné had produced a worthy winner in the 31-year-old Colombian Luis Herrera. His overall victory not only marked the resurrection of what many people had believed was a finished career, but ensured his new Ryalcao-Postobon team a place in the Tour; in 1990, overweight and disheartened by his mediocre form, Herrera had been able to manage only 25th place, and as a result had seen his team – the now-defunct Cafe de Colombia – excluded from the line-up for the Tour.

Herrera's opponents had mixed results. But Switzerland's Tony Rominger (Toshiba), Scotland's Robert Millar (Z) and American Andy Hampsten (Motorola) all gave Herrera a good run for his money. And although in the end he could not manage to wrest

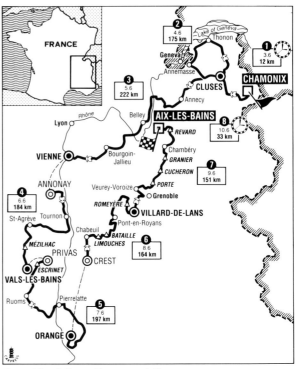

Dauphiné Libéré, France: 1138km

the race leadership from Herrera, Spanish champion Laudelino Cubino (Amaya) was his closest rival, only 0:46 behind him in the final standings. Cubino's performance also helped to add weight to the 'wild card' chances of his team, Amaya.

The early stages were inconsequential. Frenchman Thierry Marie (Castorama) won the first stage, and hung on to the lead for three days, thus compensating

The cruel ascent of the col de Revard was a natural ally for the climbing talent of Luis Herrera, whose acceleration drew Rincon, Cubino and Farfan away from him. Former race leader Rominger was left with a deficit that not even his time trialling prowess the following day could make up

somewhat for Laurent Fignon – in the other Castorama team – having to quit the Giro d'Italia because of injury. Then his compatriot Pascal Lino (RMO) took over the lead and kept it for another two days. But when the real climbing began after 20km on Stage 6, the race suddenly became a much more serious affair. Four major climbs, including a brutal final climb up to Villard, soon sorted out the sheep from the goats, pushing the potential winners to the fore.

At Villard-de-Lans, Rominger took over the yellow and blue race leader's jersey, but it was Herrera's bold show of strength in powering away from the other six riders in the breakaway group only 1000m from the finishing line that revealed him as the man to watch out for. Only 20 seconds down on Rominger after Stage 6, and not a strong contender for a winning ride in the final day's time trial, Herrera would have to pull a great ride out of the bag on the four major climbs of the next day's stage to Aix-les-Bains if he was to have a chance of overall victory. And he was fully aware of his responsibilities: 'To win the Dauphiné, I have to win the stage or gain about two minutes on Rominger, which won't be easy,' he said. 'Whatever ... I have to attack tomorrow.'

It was exactly this kind of competitive spirit in Herrera which helped to create cycling hysteria in Colombia in 1987, the year in which he won the Vuelta a España and took the King of the Mountains prize and fifth place overall in the Tour de France. And he attacked with a vengeance on Stage 7 of the 1991 Dauphiné. He and Cubino rode away from their rivals on the long,

Herrera's renewed form took him to a final third place in the concluding time trial at Aix-les-Bains

steep 22km climb of the col de Revard and stole the race from Rominger, who just could not find the speed in the final time trial the following day to regain the 2:08 he needed. And Herrera had one more surprise up his sleeve – a 3rd place in the time trial, which had been his only weakness in 1987.

So as July and the start of the Tour de France edged closer, it began to seem possible that this year Herrera, nicknamed 'the gardener of Fusagasuga' might rediscover the form that had made him the toast of Colombia and once again taste the thrill of success.

RACE DETAILS

WEATHER *Warm at start, with rain falling in middle days, followed by hot, humid weather in Alps.*

COURSE *Anti-clockwise route in South-eastern France. Two time trials and two major mountain legs (Stages 6 and 7) in French Alps.*

FIELD *Invited field of 16 eight-man teams. 128 starters; 102 finishers.*

STAGE 1 – 12km time trial, Chamonix. *Marie wins his fourth time trial of 1991 in 12:32.07, 0:18 faster than second-placed Rominger. Others: Herrera, at 0:45; Hampsten, at 0:48; Mottet, at 0:49; Roche, at 1:01; Millar at 1:12.*

STAGE 2 – Chamonix-Cluses, 175km ... 5km *Mottet attacks and has 6-minute lead at 40km ...*

45km *on 3rd category côte de Chatillon summit, his lead is 8:30 and chase starts ... 100km Mottet's lead reduced to 3:00 ... 125km Mottet caught when Frenchmen Patrice Esnault (Amaya) and Bruno Cornillet (Z), Soviet Viatcheslav Ekimov (Panasonic) and Dutchman John Talen (PDM) attack. They take 1:30 lead, just holding off the peloton. Talen wins sprint from Ekimov. Marie leads overall.*

STAGE 3 – Cluses-Vienne, 222km *Dutchman Jean-Paul Van Poppel (PDM) claims his ninth win of the season, from Frenchman Laurent Jalabert (Toshiba) and Belgian Johan Museeuw (Lotto) in bunch sprint. Marie leads overall.*

STAGE 4 – Annonay-Vals-les-Bains, 184km ... 134km *at foot of 2nd category Mezilhac climb, Frenchmen Henri Abadie and Thierry Bourguignon (both Toshiba),*

Yvon Ledanois (Castorama) and Lino attack ... 154km *On steep descent from Mezilhac, leaders are 2:30 ahead ... 180km Lead drops to 1:00. At finish, break is 0:34 ahead of Dane John Carlsen (Tonton Tapis) and 0:57 on peloton. Abadie wins photo finish from Ledanois while Lino, third, takes overall lead.*

STAGE 5 – Privas-Orange, 197km ... *Englishman Sean Yates (Motorola) wins after leading out bunch sprint with 300m to go. His winning margin of 0:02 secured when Museeuw and Jalabert, chasing him, crash on wet corner near finish. Lino leads overall.*

STAGE 6 – Crest-Villard de Lans, 163.5km ... *On four mountain passes, Colombians explode race ... 135km On second last climb, seven riders attack: Herrera, Rominger, Cubino, Colombian Henry Cardenas (Postobon), Rincon,*

Farfan and Millar. With 1km to go, Herrera attacks to win stage by 0:04 from Rominger who takes overall lead.

STAGE 7 – Villard-de-Lans-Aix-les-Bains, 151km ... 110km *Leading group of 30 reaches foot of fourth major climb, col de Revard, and Herrera attacks immediately. With Cubino, his lead grows to 1.00 ... 115km Seven riders chase: Frenchman Luc Leblanc (Castorama), Dutchman Eddy Bouwmans (Panasonic), Hampsten, Millar, Rincon, Rominger, Farfan ... 130km On Revard summit, lead is 2:25. At finish Cubino wins stage from Herrera with chase group at 2:22. Herrera takes overall lead of 0:45 on Cubino and 2:08 on Rominger.*

STAGE 8 – 33km time trial, Aix-les-Bains ... *Rominger wins undulating stage by 0:34 on Ekimov, 0:50 on Herrera and 0:51 on Cubino. Herrera wins overall.*

CoreStates Championship: 9 June

Easily the biggest one-day race in the United States, the CoreStates Championship in Philadelphia deserves to be part of the Perrier World Cup series. And yet, because this international event also decides the destiny of the US national professional road race championship, it's not eligible for the Perrier series. This is a great shame, as the event is promoted to higher standards than many of the World Cup races – boasting exceptional prize money of $110,000, a demanding 24km circuit, and an enthusiastic crowd that in 1991 numbered more than 70,000.

The race itself was also outstanding, even though for the first time in its seven-year history the event ended in a 60-rider sprint. The winner was Dutch colossus Michel Zanoli (Tulip), who finished 5 metres clear of two past Tour de France stage winners, Davis Phinney (Coors Light) – who took the US title – and Australian Phil Anderson (Motorola).

The race is sponsored by the CoreStates Corp, a Philadelphia-based financial and banking group, which has a high profile in the populous Pennsylvania-New Jersey area. The sponsor uses the event as a giant public-relations operation, with the race commanding more than four hours of live television coverage.

Ever since the first edition – won by former Olympic speedskating champion Eric Heiden – the race has seen intense rivalry between home teams and European visitors. Going into this race, the winners' tally was America 4, Europe 2, the two overseas winners being the Italians Roberto Gaggioli in 1988 and Paolo Cimini in 1990. Gaggioli now lives in San Francisco and races for the powerful Coors Light team, numbering Phinney and 1989 winner Greg Oravetz among his team-mates. As well as Coors Light, other home teams were Motorola, Subaru-Montgomery and Spago; the European challenge was headed by Tulip (with Zanoli, Australian Allan Peiper and Dutchman Adri Van der Poel) and Gis-Ballan (with Italians Angelo Canzonieri and Ettore Pastorelli).

Comprising 10 laps of the main circuit, followed by three laps of a 5km version of the same loop, the CoreStates Championship has always produced an early breakaway. The 1991 race was no exception, with four riders going clear on the first lap: they were the Americans Scott McKinley (Motorola), Scott Moninger (Coors Light), Todd Gogulski (Subaru) and Peter Davis (Spago), who moved to a six-minute lead within two laps, forcing the Tulip and Gis teams to increase the tempo of the peloton. The break gained a maximum advantage of 7:34 halfway through lap six, but by now, almost four hours into the race, the leaders were showing signs of fatigue. On the 16 per cent slopes of the short, but significant, climb of the Manayunk Wall Gogulski showed he was the strongest of the front runners when he jumped away alone on the seventh ascent. By the end of the lap he was 4:50 ahead of his companions, now absorbed by the chasing pack.

With 87km remaining, the race entered its second phase. Gogulski, suffering badly from cramp, was caught and passed by 11 chasers, who had moved a minute clear of the bunch. In this group were three Coors Light men

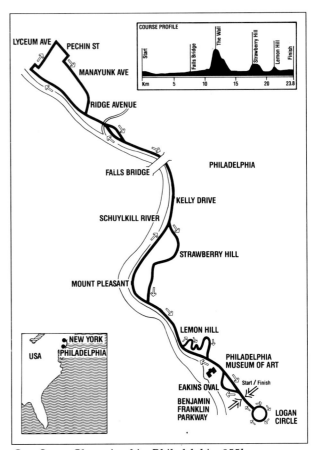

Core States Championship, Philadelphia: 255km

(including Gaggioli) as well as Anderson and Canzonieri. It seemed like a great opportunity for Coors Light, but *directeur sportif* Len Pettyjohn didn't feel comfortable helping Anderson towards a possible victory, so – with only Anderson working – the break lost its momentum, and nine others caught up by the end of lap nine, including Zanoli and Phinney.

Almost immediately, Zanoli punctured, while a new combination of 11 riders streaked away, as they headed into the final 24km loop with 39km remaining. Gaggioli and Phinney were there, along with other powerful sprinters Pastorelli, the German Marcel Wust (RMO) and British professional Dave Mann (IME-Bolla). On the last climb of the Manayunk Wall, Mann, Phinney and Wust were dropped; chased back; and just as they rejoined with 20km to go, what looked like the vital move was made by Gaggioli, Walton and the lone Z rider, neo-pro Paul Willerton. As these three riders began the three laps of the short finishing circuit, 54 seconds clear they looked certain to produce the winner. But Motorola was afraid of giving the race to Gaggioli, so Walton stopped working. Willerton, as the only American in the attack, was keen to win the US title, but he didn't want to go too hard and risk being dropped before the finish. With 5km to go, Walton made a solo bid for victory, but as he crested the last climb of Lemon Hill, the bunch swallowed him up. Inevitably, there was a tumultuous finishing sprint along the crowd-packed Benjamin Franklin Parkway – and nobody could beat Zanoli.

Colorado-based professional Todd Gogulski, seen here on his way to winning the King of the Wall award, was the strongest member of the early break

Well before the exciting spring finish, Anderson and Zanoli showed their strength on the Manayunk Wall and it stayed with them to the end

There was an international podium at Philadelphia, with Phil Anderson (3rd), Michel Zanoli (1st) and Davis Phinney (2nd and US champion)

RACE DETAILS

COURSE 10 laps of 24km circuit, including climb of Manayunk Wall, with 3 laps of 5km finishing circuit.

FIELD 113 starters; 63 finishers. Six US teams plus individuals. Four European teams.

WEATHER Hot, sunny, 28°C 50° humidity.

5km Break by Gogulski, McKinley, Moninger and Davis ... 140km Lead reaches maximum of 7:34 on lap six ... 164km Gogulski breaks clear of other three escapers ... 178km Gogulski 4:51 ahead of peloton ... 202km 11 riders catch Gogulski, who drops out. Lead is 1:00 ... 212km Another nine riders catch break, which has 0:54 lead going into last big loop ... 215km

11 riders split from break, gain 1:00 by hill ... 231km Walton, Willerton and Gaggioli break from front, reach lap end with 0:43 lead ... 241km Three leaders 0:54 ahead of regrouped peloton of 60 riders ... 246km Walton drops other two, leads pack by 0:13 ... 248km Walton caught by pack ... 251km Zanoli wins final sprint from Phinney and Anderson.

Chioccioli's outright domination of the Giro was never clearer than on the stage to Aprica, where the race leader delighted his tifosi *with a 70km solo breakaway* à la Coppi *over three major climbs*

Giro d'Italia: 26 May – 16 June

It is 38 years now since the Italian *tifosi* thrilled at the sight of their national hero, Fausto Coppi, a thin rider who was somewhat bird-like in appearance, wearing the bright pink jersey of leadership in the Giro d'Italia. Those who were old enough to remember him, however, were granted a rare reminder of the legendary Coppi when Italian Franco Chioccioli (Del Tongo) became a decisive winner of the Italian national tour. Chioccioli, 31, is nicknamed 'Coppino' because of his striking resemblance to Fausto Coppi, the five-time Giro winner who died in 1960 at the age of only 40, having triumphed in the Giro for the last time in 1953. In 1991, Chioccioli stood up on the winner's podium, engulfed by a throng of fans, photographers and journalists, having just brought off the biggest victory of his entire career.

Chioccioli's victory, by 3:48 over Claudio Chiappucci (Carrera), 6:56 over Massimiliano Lelli (Ariostea) and 7:49 over last year's winner, Gianni Bugno, was convincing evidence that the renaissance in Italian cycling which began in 1990 is set to continue strongly into the future. It was the first time since 1986 that the first three places had all been taken by Italian riders, and the first time since 1969, when Felice Gimondi won, that all of the first four places had been taken by Italians.

The 1991 Giro was one of the toughest ever, and the pressure on the riders was terrific. There were 35 mountains to climb and the competition to earn FICP points was at boiling point. Several teams were still in the running for 'wild card' places in the Tour de France, so they were at their most anxious to impress the selectors; the Alpine roads were dangerously narrow and twisting; the weather was capricious, varying from freezing sleet to buffeting winds and then to an intense and suffocating heat. Chioccioli came through this ordeal with flying colours. He won three stages and arrived in Milan having worn the pink jersey for a total of 19 days. What a ride! And what a reversal in fortunes for a rider who had previously won only 19 races in his whole ten-year professional career!

One result of this victory was that much began to be made of the physical similarities between Chioccioli and Coppi. More important to Chioccioli himself, however, were the 870 FICP points which took him from 106th to 9th place in the world rankings. In fact, Chioccioli will never be able to rival Fausto Coppi's achievements, because his career is already well advanced – he doesn't have enough years of competition left. The fans, however, saw no reason at all why that fact should put a brake on their enthusiasm; the people of his home town, Pia di Sco, cleared the shops of pink wrapping paper and cans of pink paint so that they could festoon their streets and give Chioccioli the hero's welcome they felt he deserved. The tall Tuscan was thus able to avenge himself for the six occasions when he has finished in the top ten in the Giro. As recently as 1988 he wore the pink jersey for two days, only to have Andy Hampsten take it from him after the notorious stage over the Gavia, raced in appalling blizzards.

What was the secret of his success in 1991? Essentially, he was strong in every department of the

Giro d'Italia, Italy: 3724km

The steep Mortirolo climb on Stage 15 spelt the end of Lejarreta's race-winning ambitions.

As early as Stage 6, Chioccioli looked every inch a winner. Here the 31-year-old leads his closest challengers over the snow-packed summit of the Terminillo

race. He climbed well, and he showed courage, flair and a willingness to take risks when it was crucial to do so. After the Gavia stage of the 1988 Giro, people had said he lacked the temperament to endure adversity, but this year he demonstrated that it is not so; he also, in the Stage 20 time trial, gave the lie to his reputation as a mediocre time triallist. He laid the foundation for victory with solo attacks in his first two stages in the Dolomites, and clinched it in the time trial. It was a performance that Coppi himself would have been proud of.

The much-publicized feud between Chiappucci and Bugno was also to Chioccioli's advantage because it kept the pressure off him. When the race began in Sardinia, Chiappucci and Bugno were the definite favourites for victory, and their mutual antagonism was made much of in the media: Bugno was reported as wanting the first ten days to be uneventful and was waiting for the time trial at Langhirano, whilst Chiappucci made no secret

of his intention 'to attack every day, if I have to'. But for the first three days of the race there was a media strike in Italy, so the war of words between Bugno and Chiappucci could be conducted only with difficulty. This was bad news for Chioccioli, too: his team sponsor, Del Tongo, was threatening to withdraw from bicycle racing in 1992, so Chioccioli and his team-mates were under a lot of pressure to do well. After Chioccioli's victory, however, Del Tongo decided to stay in the game, and will sponsor a team in 1992.

Chioccioli first took the pink jersey on Stage 2, and thenceforth had to endure continual media speculation as to whether, being a relatively unknown rider, he could go the distance. He lost the jersey when Frenchman Eric Boyer (Z) put in a storming performance on Stage 4 to Sorrento, and regained it after his late Stage 5 break with Spaniard Marino Lejarreta; but he was still not seriously considered as a winner.

The volatile Chiappucci became the focus for media attention on Stage 6 from Scanno to Rieti when, on the Terminillo climb, he broke a riders' resolution to 'go slow' as a protest against the badly-lit tunnels through which they were expected to race. An insignificant Colombian, Demetrio Cuspoca (Pony Malta), escaped, and Chiappucci ordered his team-mates to chase him down. This behaviour made him extremely unpopular with the other riders; as Greg LeMond said, 'It's not so much a feud between Bugno and Chiappucci as between the whole peloton and Chiappucci. OK, it was a Colombian who attacked first, but as a big-name rider, Chiappucci had a responsibility to stick by the pact.

Gianni Bugno unselfishly lent his strength and experience to the 'ganging up' on Lejarreta on the unscheduled ascent of the Marmolada Pass on Stage 17. Though he paid dearly for his efforts later that day, Bugno saw to it that only Italians would mount the podium in Milan four days later. The 1990 Giro winner has Chioccioli to his right, while his arch-rival Chiappucci follows, ahead of Massimiliano Lelli and Roberto Conti

He didn't. He'll pay for it one day.'

As the Giro headed north, and Chioccioli won his two mountain stages, people began to say that maybe he *would* hold off his august challengers. But it was always very close. After the wet and windy Stage 10 time trial, brilliantly won by Bugno, Chioccioli held on to his lead by the slimmest of margins – one second! There was also some surprise that Bugno did not move into the lead. His supporters said he was just biding his time, that he would wait until the Dolomites and would then annihilate Chioccioli. He did put in a very strong challenge, winning three stages and placing fourth overall, but with hindsight, it's obvious that Bugno – like the other favourites – simply did not have the strength to wrest the *maglia rosa* away from its unexpected occupant.

The top foreign contenders had a poor race. LeMond, the Z team leader, pulled out of the race exhausted at the end of Stage 14, just before the serious climbing began in the Dolomites. In 51st place overall, 52:14 down, he once again found himself in the position of heading towards the Tour de France plagued by doubts about his fitness and strength. Frenchman Laurent Fignon (Castorama), still suffering from the injured thigh muscle he sustained in the Tour of Flanders, was despondent about his resulting poor performance. 'It's hard to believe. I don't know what the answer is, but I just can't push the big gears – my leg is sore whenever I try,' he said after the Langhirano time trial. A week later, on Stage 17 to the Passo Pordoi, he gave up the struggle and retired from the race.

But even if some of his rivals had not been concentrating

Chioccioli's victory in the difficult time trial to Casteggio vividly recalled Melchor Mauri's efforts in the Vuelta a España a few weeks earlier – and was no less surprising

RACE DETAILS

COURSE *21 stages, taking the race roughly from south to north, including 35 mountains and three time trials. Stages 1-3 held on the island of Sardinia; then the race transferred to the mainland at Sorrento.*

FIELD *20 nine-man teams. 180 starters, 133 finishers.*

WEATHER *Mainly hot and sunny, but some rain and fog during middle stages in Appennines and especially humid in last days.*

STAGE I – Olbia-Olbia, 193km ... 32km *Spaniard Alberto Leanizbarrutia (Clas) attacks and stays away for 145km ... 178km Peloton catches Leanizbarrutia but is split in two, with several sprinters in second group: Italians Mario Cipollini (Del Tongo) and Adriano Baffi (Ariostea), Denmark's Rolf Sörensen (Ariostea) and Soviet Djamolidin Abdujaparov (Carrera).*

Frenchmen Philippe Casado (Z) and Didier Theux (Castorama) attack 300m out; Casado wins, becoming overall leader.

STAGE 2A – Olbia-Sassari, 127km ... 125km *Chiappucci, Lelli and Australian Stephen Hodge (ONCE) attack, and with 700m to go Bugno chases and wins stage. Chioccioli, 2nd on stage, becomes race leader.*

STAGE 2B – 7.7km individual time trial, Sassari ... *Chioccioli extends overall lead to 0:05 with third place, 0:05 behind stage winner Italian Gianluca Pierobon (ZG-Mobili). Lejarreta second at 0:05, Frenchman Jean-François Bernard (Banesto) fourth at same time, Chiappucci fifth at 0:08, Bugno sixth at 0:10 and LeMond eighth at 0:13. Fignon penalised 0:20 for allegedly taking draft from team car and placed 55th at 0:43, but later wins appeal against penalty.*

STAGE 3 – Sassari-Cagliari, 231km ... 231km *Cipollini wins stage in bunch sprint. Baffi, 4th, Belgian Johan Capiot (TVM) and Frenchman Francis Capelle (Z) crash on finish line. Baffi breaks collar-bone and withdraws. Chioccioli leads overall.*

STAGE 4 – Sorrento-Sorrento, 170km ... 155km *On last of five 34km circuits, Boyer attacks alone on the climb. After descent he wins stage by 0:23 on Portuguese rider Acacio Da Silva (Lotus) and Chiappucci to take overall lead by 0:08 on Chioccioli.*

STAGE 5 – Sorrento-Scanno, 246km ... 225km *Chioccioli attacks, taking Lejarreta, with 5km to go on the third of three climbs, first category Passo Monte Godi ... 230km Two attackers have 0:26 on other favourites, led by Boyer. LeMond and Fignon, with a thigh muscle injury, are meanwhile dropped. ... 224km Lejarreta wins stage, but Chioccioli retains overall lead with 0:08 on Lejarreta and 0:50 on Boyer.*

Amidst the rocky spires of the Dolomites, two ascents of the formidable Passo Pordoi await the peloton of the Giro d'Italia

Once Bugno had done his work and got rid of Lejarreta, Chioccioli and Chiappucci took off themselves on the Marmolada Pass, a move that laid the groundwork for Chioccioli's brilliant stage victory on the summit of the Pordoi

Bugno's victory at Brescia hinted at some real form at last, but his defeat by Chioccioli in the time trial next day only reflected his unpredictable early season performances

'Friend or foe?' Chiappucci got a surprise shower during the final time trial, while would-be rival Delgado produced his best performance of the race after reputedly wolfing down five of these gelati on the stage to Brescia

on 'preparation' for the Tour de France, by this time Chioccioli would have been hard to beat. In the Dolomites he took the initiative with an aggressive attack on Stage 15 to Aprica, where last year Leonardo Sierra became the first Venezuelan to win a stage of the Giro. This year the victory went to Chioccioli, with an inspired solo ride covering 52km and three mountains. And then, two days later, on the most difficult Stage 17 to Passo Pordoi, Chioccioli did it again; leaving behind Boyer and Chiappucci 4km into the climb, and finishing

with a lead of 0:33 on his nearest rival, Chiappucci. The thousands of cycling fans who rode up the mountain to picnic and drink wine on the side of the road, hoping to see a sensational race, got a show that will stay in their memories for many years. 'To win the Pordoi stage like that, wearing the pink jersey, that's something you daren't even dream about,' said Chioccioli later. The mountain stages, which were wearing out the legs and lungs of his rivals, seemed only to inspire Chioccioli to further confidence. The times on this 17th stage showed

STAGE 6 – Scanno-Rieti, 205km ... 136km *Because of badly lit tunnel, peloton makes 'go-slow' pact for climb to Terminillo (summit at 174km) ... 171km Cuspoca attacks and Chiappucci orders team-mates to chase, breaking the pact. At summit, Cuspoca is caught, but behind Delgado, Fignon and LeMond are dropped, by 0:30, 1:15 and 2:30 respectively ... 175km On descent, 14 riders get away, including Soviet Vladimir Pulnikov (Carrera), Spaniard Iñaki Gaston (Clas), Italian Mauro Giovanetti (Gatorade), Bugno, Chiappucci, Lejarreta and Sierra ... 203km Gaston attacks, with Pulnikov and Giovanetti. Pulnikov wins. Chioccioli retains lead.*

STAGE 7 – Rieti-Città di Castello, 179km. *Cipollini wins in bunch sprint from Abdujaparov; Chioccioli retains overall lead.*

STAGE 8 – Città di Castello-Prato, 163km. *Italian Davide Cassani (Ariostea) wins from compatriots Mario Mantovan (ZG-Mobili) and Fabiano Fontanelli (Italbonifica). Peloton is split in two, first*

group at 0:02 to stage leaders. LeMond is in second group because of puncture and bike change in last 7km. Chioccioli retains lead.*

STAGE 9 – Prato-Felino, 229km ... 159km *Italian Massimo Ghirotto (Carrera) attacks alone on descent from Passo di Lagastrello. Despite tail wind, Ghirotto's lead never exceeds 1:00. Chase from Italian Italbonifica team-mates Michele Moro, Franco Vona and Bernard and Echave, but Ghirotto still wins with 0:31 spare and 1:28 on peloton. Chioccioli retains lead.*

STAGE 10 – Collechio-Langhirano, 43km time trial ... *In wet conditions, Bugno wins by 0:08 on Bernard, 0:45 on Italian Luca Gelfi (Del Tongo) and 0:53 on Hodge. Chioccioli, 8th at 1:02, hangs on to overall lead by 0:01 on Bugno. Others: Chiappucci, 7th at 1:01; Lejarreta, 10th at 1:20; LeMond, 13th at 1:36.*

STAGE 11 – Sala Baganza-Savona, 223km ... 153km *Exiting tunnel at Bogliasco, LeMond and Italians*

Maximilian Sciandri (Carrera) and Michele Coppolillo (Italbonifica) attack from 80-strong front group. They get up to 2:00 lead, but with 500 metres to go this is down to 100 metres. At finish, Coppolillo is caught by peloton as Sciandri wins from LeMond, 0:05 ahead of peloton. Chioccioli leads overall.*

STAGE 12 – Savona-Monviso, 182km. *Bugno loses 1:57 after being dropped on ascent to Monviso (2020m) where Lelli wins by 0:03 from Bernard, Chioccioli and Lejarreta. Chiappucci is fourth at 0:38. LeMond loses 12:13. Chioccioli leads overall by 0:30 on Lejarreta and 1:07 on Lelli.*

STAGE 13 – Savigliano-Sestriere, 192km ... 180km *Spaniard Eduardo Chozas (ONCE) attacks with Mexican Miguel Arroyo (Z) at foot of last climb to Sestriere (2035m) ... 189km Arroyo is dropped 3km from summit, but Chiappucci chases and finishes 0:01 behind Chozas. Lejarreta is 3rd at 0:03 with Chioccioli. Bugno loses 0:43, LeMond loses 23:12 and falls to 51st overall at 52:14. Chioccioli leads overall.*

just how strong Chioccioli was. Bugno lost 3:33, and Lejarreta an incredible 6:36, which left the hordes of Spanish journalists, not usually present at the Giro in such great numbers, absolutely horrorstruck. This win gave Chioccioli an almost unassailable lead of 2:54 on Chiappucci and 3:38 on the Ariostea revelation, Italian Massimiliano Lelli, who was 9th last year on his Giro debut and had been wearing the white jersey of best young rider since the 5th stage. Chiappucci and Lelli regained some of their lost time on Stages 18 and 19, but Chioccioli put paid to their aspirations once and for all with a stunning victory in the penultimate day's time trial. On one of the hardest courses imaginable, in sweltering mid-summer heat that was like riding in a furnace after the cool air of the Dolomites, Chioccioli's time was 0:52 ahead of Bugno, with Chiappucci in third place at 1:02 and Lelli sixth at 3:18. After three weeks of punishing racing, this 66km race of truth on the narrow, twisting, hilly roads between Broni and Casteggio, under the eyes of thousands of fans, produced the finest performance of Chioccioli's career.

Bugno took his defeat with a good grace, happy to be moving up to 4th place overall. Chiappucci, disappointed not to have won a stage even though he had finished in the top ten 15 times in 21 stages, was compensated by his confirmation as a leading stage racer and by moving into first place in the FICP rankings. Chioccioli himself was thrilled that after ten years of virtual anonymity he had finally brought off a victory beyond his wildest dreams. And as he rode the final stage from Pavia to Milan, it was as though the whole of Italy had come to the roadside to express their gratitude to 'Coppino' for having brought Fausto Coppi's memory to life again.

But at the end only champagne was good enough for Franco Chioccioli

STAGE14 – Turin-Morbegno, 231km ... 8km *Attack by Italian Franco Ballerini (Del Tongo), Spaniard Juan Martinez Oliver (Banesto), Denmark's Brian Petersen (Amore & Vita) and Casado; lead reaches 8:00 before dropping to 1:55 at finish where Ballerini wins from Casado after the longest breakaway (223km) in the history of the Giro. LeMond withdraws after stage. Chioccioli leads overall.*

STAGE15 – Morbegno-Aprica, 132km ... 74km *Chioccioli attacks from nine-man breakaway on steep 12km climb to the Passo del Mortillo. At summit, he has 1:20 lead, increasing to 2:30 after descent. Chase begins but Chioccioli wins by 0:32 from Bernard and Boyer. Chioccioli retains lead.*

STAGE16 – Tirano-Selva di Valgardena, 208km ... *Stelvio Pass (2758m) is replaced by Passo del Tonnale (1882m) after avalanche threats* ... 187km *Eight riders attack: Lelli, Bugno, Sierra, Chiappucci, Chioccioli, Lejarreta, Bernard and Giovannetti. Lelli wins from Bugno in sprint with others at 0:02. Chioccioli leads overall.*

STAGE17 – Selva di Valgardena-Pordoi Val di Fassa, 195km ... 153km *Mud slide on Passo di San Pellegrino summit forces another deviation; route cut by 30km, but San Pellegrino is replaced by harder Passo di Fedaia. After first passage of Pordoi at 91km, Vona and Italian Giorgio Furlan (Ariostea) lead, followed by Ghirotto and Giovanetti. They regroup on descent. On climb to Fedaia, Giovanetti attacks as chase behind starts. At summit, Giovannetti is 0:37 ahead of Chioccioli, 0:47 ahead of Chiappucci, Lelli and Italian Roberto Conti (Ariostea), followed by Bugno, Sierra and Boyer. On last passage of Pordoi to finish, where Fignon abandons, Giovannetti is passed and Chioccioli and Chiappucci lead. Boyer joins, but is unable to respond to Chioccioli's winning solo attack 4km from summit. Chioccioli wins stage by 0:38 on Chiappucci, 0:41 on Boyer, to save overall lead. Major time losers: Bugno (3:33) and Lejarreta (6:36).*

STAGE18 – Pozza di Fassa-Castelfranco Veneto, 163km ... 113km *9 riders attack but are caught 500m from finish. Bunch sprint sees local Silvio Martinello (Gis-Ballan) win. Chioccioli retains lead.*

STAGE19 – Castelfranco Veneto-Brescia, 185km ... 160km *Slow early pace sees many attacks start. After 9km climb to summit of Castello di Serle, Da Silva and Italians Enrico Zaina (Carrera) and Valerio Tebaldi (Gatorade) are 0:10 ahead of group of 26 riders but are caught on descent. Bugno wins his third stage, in sprint from Chiappucci and Ghirotto.*

STAGE20 – Broni-Casteggio, 66km time trial. *On very hilly, technical route and in 33° C heat, Chioccioli wins stage by 0:52 on Bugno, 1:02 on Chiappucci, 2:08 on Giovannetti and 2:09 on Lejarreta. Chioccioli retains lead.*

STAGE21 – Pavia-Milan, 153km ... 138km *on 15 5km circuits, Spaniards Eleuterio Anguita and Jose Camacho (both Seur) and Italian Dario Nicoletti (Colnago) attack, but are caught after 10km. Chioccioli wins overall.*

Tour of Switzerland: 18-28 June

Over the past two years, Luc Roosen's name has often been put forward by Tour de France pundits as one to watch for in the contest for mountain stage wins, if not for overall classification. He first rode the event in 1989, finishing in 27th position, but since then, for one reason or another, the 26-year-old Belgian has always lacked the opportunity to test the prognosis. In 1990, when he was riding for Histor-Sigma, he let it be known that he would not ride for Stephen Roche, nominally his team leader, in the Tour: he would play his own card in a bid for victory. Roosen's stand developed into an ugly feud between himself and Roche, and when Roosen announced that he would ride for himself or not at all, nobody was very surprised when he was left out of the team's line-up for the Tour.

He joined the new Tulip team for the 1991 season, and lost his chance to ride the Tour again when Tulip failed to qualify for one of the six 'wild card' places in the Tour announced after the Giro d'Italia. But whilst there was nothing that Roosen could do to alter the fate of the Tulip team, he did succeed in making the judgement of the Tour de France selectors look questionable with a convincing win in the Tour of Switzerland. Many of the riders in the Tour of Switzerland were using it as final preparation for the

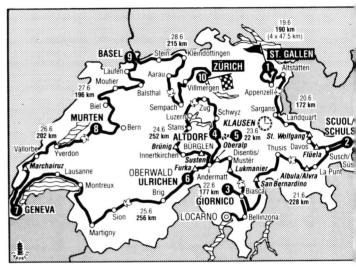

Tour of Switzerland: 1912km

imminent 'Grand Boucle', but even so it was a worthy victory: Roosen led from Stage 2, which he won, until Stage 10, his form clearly benefitting from a determination to prove that his omission from the Tour de France was a mistake.

For Greg LeMond, the mountainous Swiss route was to have been the key to finding winning Tour de France form. He fared well in all but one stage; yet unlike 1990 was unable to repeat his Tour performance a few weeks later

All past winners of the Tour of Switzerland who competed this year were awarded 'honorary' yellow jerseys. Andy Hampsten gets his for two previous wins, in 1986 and 1987

The Tour of Switzerland is always one of the most lucrative events of the season, with as many as thirty-odd sprint primes on every stage; this year, with its four Alpine stages, it was also one of the most mountainous. Roosen's main rivals for the mountain stages, American two-time winner Andy Hampsten (Motorola) and Scotland's Robert Millar (Z), dropped out of contention after missing the early break and losing 11 minutes on Stage 2 to Bad Scuol; thereafter, they never posed a real threat to Roosen's lead.

However, having lost their realistic chances of victory did not prevent Hampsten, Millar and other stars from putting in star performances. Millar led the way with his win in the Stage 5 uphill time trial, in which Hampsten was second and Dutchman Eddy Bouwmans (Panasonic), who had enjoyed such fine form in the Dauphiné Libéré, third. The calibre of their performances was amply demonstrated by the fact that Dutchman Eric Breukink (PDM), who won the mountain time trial in last year's Tour de France, came in fourth at 1:28. Also under close scrutiny was the progress of Greg LeMond, who had abandoned the Giro d'Italia a week previously. After losing more than 15 minutes of his eventual overall deficit on the first mountain stage, and then finishing the time trial in 36th place at 6:18, he had an overall deficit of 23:27, but by then had picked up his form to finish with all the other main contenders for victory in the Tour de France.

For Roosen there was to be no July, at least not in terms of professional cycling. But he had made the most of June, and could sit at home in Belgium nursing his trophy whilst the rest of the cycling world turned their attention to France.

Luc Roosen was unable to compete in the Tour de France but victory in the Tour of Switzerland was some consolation

---

RACE DETAILS

WEATHER *Snow in mountains; changeable weather with sun and showers.*

COURSE *Prologue plus ten stages taking the race clockwise around Switzerland. Four mountain stages with 16 major climbs.*

FIELD *Invited field of 20 eight-man teams. 160 starters; 125 finishers.*

PROLOGUE – St Gallen, 1.66km *Frenchman Jean-Claude LeClercq (Helvetia) wins by 0:02 from Dutchman Steven Rooks (Buckler) and Italian Maurizio Fondriest (Panasonic). Breukink is 4th at 0:05, Hampsten 10th at 0:09 and LeMond 13th at 0:11. Leclercq leads overall.*

STAGE 1 – St Gallen-St Gallen, 190km ... 187km *Fondriest, Italian Flavio Vanzella (ZG-Bottecchia), Germany's Rolf Gölz (Ariostea) and Swiss Heinz Imboden (Helvetia) break away; Imboden wins sprint with peloton at 0:03. Leclercq leads overall.*

STAGE 2 – St Gallen-Bad Scuol, 172km *Roosen takes lead with 40km solo attack on first major mountain. He wins stage from Gölz and Swiss Pascal Richard (Helvetia) by 0:56. Hampsten, Millar and Irishman Sean Kelly (PDM) finish more than 11 minutes behind.*

STAGE 3 – Bad Scuol-Giornico, 228km *Imboden wins; his team-mate Leclercq crashes and abandons. Roosen retains lead.*

STAGE 4 – Locarno-Altdorf, 177km ... 172km *Mexican Miguel Arroyo (Z) attacks 5km from summit finish, with Belgian Jan Nevens, Hampsten, Frenchman Jérôme Simon (Z) and Dutchman Jos Van Aert (PDM). Nevens wins from Arroyo. Roosen retains lead.*

STAGE 5 – Bürglen-Klausen, 22km uphill time trial *Millar wins in 54:33, Hampsten 2nd at 0:37, Bouwmans 3rd at 1:16, Breukink 4th at 1:28, LeMond 36th at 6:18. Roosen, 11th at 2:59, retains lead.*

STAGE 6 – Altdorf-Ulrichen, 252km *Italian Franco Vona (Jolly-Club 88) wins stage in solo break. Roosen retains lead.*

STAGE 7 – Oberwald-Geneva, 256km *Bunch sprint taken by German Olaf Ludwig (Panasonic) from Belgian Etienne De Wilde (Histor) and Britain's Sean Yates (Motorola). Roosen retains lead.*

STAGE 8 – Geneva-Murten, 202km *Australian Phil Anderson (Motorola) beats Dane Rolf Sörensen (Ariostea) to win stage, 1:08 clear of six other riders, with American Ron Kiefel (Motorola) 3rd and peloton at 3:45. Roosen retains lead.*

STAGE 9 – Murten-Basel, 196km ... 156km *After 70km solo attack, Japanese Masatoshi Ichikawa (Blieker) is caught and passed by Sörensen and Swiss Fabian Jeker (Helvetia). Sörensen drops Jeker on finishing circuit to win; peloton at 0:22. Roosen retains lead.*

STAGE 10 – Basel-Zürich, 215km ... 65km *Italian Stefano Colage (ZG-Bottecchia) attacks alone, winning by 2:20 on Belgian Jim Van de Laer (Tulip) and Italian Felice Puttini (Carrera) and 2:38 on peloton. Roosen wins overall with Richard 2nd and Hampsten 3rd.*

Ore-Ida Women's Challenge: 20-30 June

The American bike racing community was a little astounded in June when a rumour began that multi-world champion Jeannie Longo – who had retired from racing at the end of 1989 – was in the country, and was going to compete in the world's longest women's stage race, the 11-day Ore-Ida Women's Challenge, in the north-western state of Idaho. The story was that she wanted to keep a low profile and had entered the race under the name Jane Ciprelli – taking her husband's surname.

It seemed an unlikely tale until 'Ciprelli' turned up at the Telluride stage race in Colorado, saying that she was on vacation ... and entered the men's category one/two event. After the three stages – one of which included 1500 metres of climbing – she finished second overall, beaten only by the outstanding 18-year-old American, Jonathan Vaughters. The Ore-Ida began the following weekend ...

Longo was put in a hastily arranged team sponsored by the Ore-Ida potato company's sister firm, Weight Watchers. This team also included the outstanding Finnish rider Tea Vikstedt-Nyman. But they would have a tough task against the might of American women's teams, that included TGI Friday's (sponsored by a restaurant chain), Shaklee-Ritchey (a department store chain and bicycle manufacturer) and Kahlua (a brand of rum).

However the race started with a win for Longo in the prologue time trial: she left the best of the Americans – TGI Friday's Maureen Manley – 24 seconds in arrears on the 3km climb to Boise's Bogus Basin ski area. And more than a minute later came on-form Sally Zack of Shacklee-Ritchey, who was expecting to benefit from the generous time bonuses awarded to the top six finishers on every road stage. And benefit she did.

Zack used her snappy sprint to win all of the first three stages, which also enabled her to take over the race

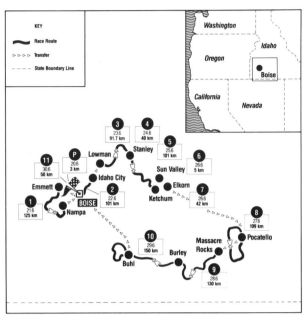

Ore-Ida Women's Challenge, USA: 947km

leadership from Longo. Her success showed that the Longo comeback wasn't going to be as easy as it seemed. This was particularly true on Stage 3, from Lowman to Stanley, which includes a gruelling climb over Banner Creek Summit. Longo attacked on the 30km-long ascent, and topped the pass with a lead of 2:30 over a small chase group. But she was thwarted by a stiff head wind, and after the chase group caught her, Zack sprinted hard for the stage, taking its 30 second win bonus and the overall lead.

By now Longo, who was riding this event for the first time, realised that earning bonuses was the only way she could win; and it was by taking the second place bonus in the next day's 40km team time trial – behind the well-knit Lithuanian national team – that the 32-year-old French rider was able to regain the lead ... albeit by only two seconds. Uncomfortable with such a tiny lead, Longo went on the attack on the Stage 5 climb over Galena Summit. Zack clung to the French rider for a long time, but when she dropped back, she exploded, and was overtaken by the nine other riders who would eventually catch Longo. Zack finished almost a minute down, while the stage win went to the former world junior champion, Dede Demet of TGI Friday's.

The seventh day of the Ore-Ida saw a vintage Longo extend her overall lead to more than two minutes. She didn't win the morning's short, flat time trial – losing by three seconds to Vikstedt-Nyman – but she romped away on the afternoon's hilly circuit race, winning alone by more than a minute.

The race appeared to be in the bag for Longo, but she had a shock on Stage 8, a tough 110km loop in eastern Idaho. Although Longo dropped everyone on an early climb, she was reeled in and a four-strong counter-attack took the dangerous Demet into a two-minute lead.

Mo Manley leads the bunch through the Stage 3 feed zone in pursuit of Longo's solo break

Jeannie Longo, also known as the low profile Jane Ciprelli, on her way to victory in the Elkhorn circuit race in Sun Valley

Tea Vikstedt-Nyman leading Demet, Bolland and Tchepliene on their Stage 8 break through eastern Idaho, with the bunch two minutes behind

Longo was angry that Vikstedt-Nyman worked in the break, even though the Finnish rider won the stage. And without a late charge, Longo would have had less than the 31-second overall advantage she retained over Demet.

Two days later, the former world champion was again unhappy, and she almost capitulated on Stage 10 – the longest ever in women's racing at 150km. It was cold, wet and windy, and Longo was dropped by the peloton at one point; but she struggled through and even increased her lead by taking a fifth place bonus at the

end. Demet had been hoping to win the stage, but she was brought down in a ten rider pile-up in the last kilometre, and dropped to a 44-second deficit on Longo.

Only a 50km criterium remained, in a sunny, crowded Boise, and Longo had no trouble in policing Demet, her only threat to overall victory. It was a remarkable result for the Frenchwoman, who declared her interest in renewing her quest, so far unsuccessful, for an Olympic gold medal. So watch out for Ciprelli at Barcelona in 1992 ...

RACE DETAILS

WEATHER *Unseasonably cool and wet, with strong winds, and temperatures some days around 5°C.*

COURSE *Prologue hill climb at Boise, Idaho, followed by 11 stages, including a team time trial (Stage 4); an individual time trial (Stage 6); a circuit race (Stage 7); and a criterium to finish, in Boise.*

FIELD *15 teams (10 American, 5 international) of 4 riders each. 60 starters; 50 finishers.*

PROLOGUE – *3km hill climb, Boise-Bogus Basin Longo sets fastest time of 6:40, beating Vikstedt-Nyman by 0:08, with Manley third at 0:24.*

STAGE 1 – Emmett-Nampa, 125.5km *Uneventful stage ends in sprint, taken by Zack from Jacqui Nelson (New Zealand) and Cindy Walters (Kahlua).*

STAGE 2 – Boise-Idaho City, 101.4km *After peloton is split at Shoshone Dame Hill,*

30 riders regroup and field sprint is won by Zack, from Lithuanian Daiva Tchepliene and US rider Jeanne Golay (South Bay). Longo retains lead.

STAGE 3 – Lowman-Stanley, 91.7km *On the opening part of the 30km climb to Banner Creek Summit, 16 riders break clear. Longo makes solo attack from this group and tops the pass ... 52km With a 2:30 lead she slows in strong headwind. Peloton regroups. Zack wins again from US rider Linda Brenneman (TGI Friday's) and Tchepliene. Zack takes overall lead.*

STAGE 4 – 40.2km team time trial, Sawtooth *The Lithuanian team wins with a time of 55:46, 0:49 ahead of Longo's Weight Watchers squad. Zack's Shacklee team comes in fifth, and Longo regains lead by two seconds over Zack.*

STAGE 5 – Stanley-Ketchum, 101.4km *Longo splits field on Galena Summit, and breaks clear. Zack follows,*

but soon drops back ... 42km *Longo tops climb 1:00 ahead of small chase group, with Zack further back. 10 riders regroup, with lead of 2:00 over 16 chasers. At finish, Demet wins from team-mate Eve Stephenson, with Longo in third. Zack group comes in at 0:54.*

STAGE 6 – 5.1km time trial, Sun Valley *Raced in head-to-head format, time trial is won by Vikstedt-Nyman 0:03 ahead of Longo, with Stephenson third at 0:08.*

STAGE 7 – Elkhorn circuit race, 41.5km *Longo attacks twice before getting clear on third lap of hilly, 16-lap race. She wins by 1:03 from small group, in which Nelson takes second place sprint from Zack. Longo now with 2:20 overall lead on Stephenson.*

STAGE 8 – Pocatello-Pocatello, 109.4km *After a lone break by Longo on an early climb, field regroups, and Jan Bolland (Shaklee-Ritchey) breaks clear at 40km. She is joined by Demet, Tchepliene and Vikstedt-Nyman, and the four riders move 2:15 clear.*

Bolland is dropped before end, where Vikstedt-Nyman wins from Tchepliene and Demet. Longo leads late chase that arrives 1:58 down. Demet moves into second overall, 0:31 down on Longo.

STAGE 9 – Massacre Rocks-Burley, 130.3km *No attacks are successful on this long stage, which ends in a downhill field sprint, won by Brenneman, from Zack and Nelson.*

STAGE 10 Burley-Buhl, 149.7km ... 80km *The longest break was made by Canada's Kelly-Anne Carter-Erdman who established a lead of 1:00. After she was caught, Donna Rae-Szalinski made a short break before her team-mate Jaqui Uttien went clear to win stage by 0:24. Field sprint went to Ruthie Matthes (Shaklee-Ritchey) over Zack and Nelson.*

STAGE 11 – Boise criterium, 49.6km *An eight-woman break is established at half distance, with Zack winning the final sprint from Brenneman and Nelson. Longo wins overall.*

Tour de France: 6-28 July

On the eve of the finish of the 1991 Tour de France, at Mâcon, Greg LeMond (Z) gave a press conference attended by several hundred journalists. To the barrage of questions about his erratic performances of the previous three weeks, the 30-year-old American answered with both candour and humour. As he spoke, a 27-year-old Spaniard, Miguel Indurain (Banesto) – who would be crowned Tour champion the next day – entered the interview room. A handful of Spanish journalists clustered round him in a corner, but the bulk of the press corps remained focused on LeMond.

The three-time Tour winner continued to field questions, until Indurain was finally ushered to the chair next to LeMond's. However neither the American nor his audience acknowledged the presence of the Spanish rider, who sat in silence for another five minutes. Eventually, after glancing to his left, LeMond saw who was sitting next to him. He shook hands with the tall, handsome Castilian, and complimented him on his victory ... and then continued with his press conference.

As fine an athletic achievement as it was, Indurain's 1991 Tour win will not go down in history as one of the finest. That was one message that emerged from the Mâcon press conference. Another was that Indurain –

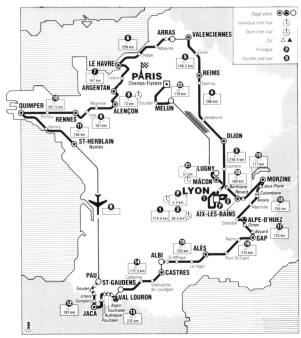

Tour de France: 3919km

Greg LeMond's hopes of a fourth Tour de France victory were dashed by the superior strength of Miguel Indurain

whom the Spanish journalists describe as 'boring', 'not forthcoming' and 'doesn't have an opinion on anything' – has yet to acquire the charisma of a champion. And that's why all the attention was on the American. Even in defeat he has something interesting to say. He makes a better story. And for many, the story of the 78th Tour de France was not so much 'how did Indurain win?' as 'why did LeMond lose?'

The answer to the latter question – which is also the key to understanding this Tour – is a complex one. For the first week of the race, LeMond had shown dominant form, matching the specialists in two time trials and stealing two minutes on all the favourites except for PDM's Eric Breukink (Holland) and Raúl Alcalá (Mexico) in the opening road stage. His team was riding well, the only problem being a crash that almost put one of its climbers, Norwegian Atle Kvalsvoll, out of the race.

Things started to go wrong when the then race leader, Denmark's Rolf Sörensen of Ariostea, crashed out of the Tour at Valenciennes. This put Z and LeMond back into the rôle of controlling the race. Then, another of Z's climbers, Scotland's Robert Millar, crashed heavily and injured his back, on the stage that Castorama's Thierry Marie (France) – already winner of the prologue in Lyon – briefly regained the lead. But LeMond was back in the yellow jersey following the Argentan to Alençon time trial, and the Z team riders were again called upon to ride hard in its defence.

The next three stages, through Brittany, were particularly difficult to control because of high speeds and constant attacks. And this put added pressure on LeMond's team – particularly the more lightly-built riders, such as Millar, Kvalsvoll and Frenchmen Bruno Cornillet and Jérôme Simon, who were having to ride at team time trial speeds to control the race, thus expending the strength they should have been conserving for the mountains. Matters worsened with the withdrawal of the powerful PDM team, which had been helping control the race on behalf of their own top men, Alcalá and Breukink.

Indurain, meanwhile, except for his efforts in the time trials, had taken a back seat for the first eleven days of the Tour, and he'd been lucky not to lose more than two minutes when he missed the Stage 1 break at Lyon. His Banesto team's negative tactics continued on the first mountain stage, when it was severely criticized for its inaction behind a break headed by Frenchmen Charly Mottet (RMO) and Luc Leblanc (Castorama), and American Andy Hampsten (Motorola) ... and this negative tactic is what destroyed LeMond's chances.

After the first big mountain climb, the col de Soudet, the race leader had only two team-mates, Cornillet and Frenchman Gilbert Duclos-Lassalle, at his side. These two rode so hard to contain the break and subsequent counter-attacks that they were dropped on the early slopes of the final climb, leaving LeMond to control a group of thirty riders containing all his main rivals. The temperature was in the 90s, and as LeMond had no team-mates to fetch water for him he became severely dehydrated.

This was the prelude to his seven-minute loss to Indurain and Italian Carrera rider Claudio Chiappucci on the next day's epic stage from Jaca to Val Louron. On this stage, LeMond had been riding strongly, exploding the peloton with his attack on the Tourmalet; but then he himself exploded near the summit, losing just 14 seconds, but giving Indurain an opening to attack on the descent. It was Indurain's only attack in 23 days of racing, but it earned him those seven minutes.

Less courageous competitors than LeMond would probably have dropped out of the race at this point, but the American battled through his physical difficulties and ended the race in an honourable seventh place overall. In contrast, Indurain remained the healthiest, strongest competitor, who took the maximum advantage of his assets. And it was his dominance in the time trials that eventually gained Indurain his overall victory by 3:36 over Italian Gianni Bugno (Gatorade) and almost six minutes over Chiappucci.

Before this 78th Tour de France had started, these three riders – along with Indurain's co-team leader Pedro Delgado, Breukink and Alcalá – were all among the pool of favourites expected to challenge defending champion LeMond in the 3919km race. There was some concern that LeMond's withdrawal from the Tour of Italy had upset his preparations, but he soon squashed such speculation by taking the yellow jersey in Lyon.

After a close-up third place, behind Marie and Breukink, in the prologue time trial (in which Indurain was only 7th), LeMond masterminded a spectacular attack on the opening road stage. It was a move similar to the one in the 1990 Tour that gained the American five minutes over Chiappucci, on the stage to St Etienne. And once again, LeMond was abetted in his enterprise by Breukink – who this time had team-mates Alcalá and Ireland's Sean Kelly along to help. These men, along with Carrera's Soviet Djamolidin Abdujaparov, had joined an initial attack by Sörensen, Cornillet and RMO's Belgian rider Michel Vermote, just before the halfway mark on the 114.5km stage.

Kelly never got closer to beating Abdujaparov than on Stage 1 into Lyon, but the Irishman gives his best despite the long lead out from the Soviet

Ariostea, the surprising winner of the team time trial around the suburbs of Lyon, survived a last 500-metre crash to put Sörensen into the race lead

Riding flat out, LeMond and Cornillet, Sörensen and the three PDM riders led the other five men in the break, and quickly mopped up earlier Swiss solo attacker Rolf Järmann (Weinmann). As the gap grew to a minute, on a twisting, hilly road, the leaders were aided by some confusion in the peloton caused by the crash which saw Kvalsvoll fall heavily. However, even when Indurain's Banesto riders and Chiappucci's Carrera team took up the chase, the break continued to gain time. The gap was two minutes on entering Lyon, and was still 1:44 at the line, where Abdujaparov galloped to a narrow stage win over Kelly, with LeMond third.

It was an impressive start by the defending champion, who several times on the 60km-long break had dropped the other ten riders. But LeMond's fortunes changed a few hours later, when he punctured right at the start of the 36.5km team time trial. By the time he'd got a replacement bike and the nine men had organised themselves into a fast moving line, the Z team had lost about half-a-minute ... and they passed the midway check in eleventh place, 41 seconds slower than the surprise leaders, Ariostea.

Shaking out the morning's efforts from his legs, LeMond did the work of two men on the return leg of the triangular-shaped course, to pull his Z team up to seventh, only 14 seconds down on third placed Panasonic. PDM also showed the effects of their leader's hard work in the Stage 1 breakaway, and placed only fourth, nine seconds ahead of Z. Meanwhile, a rejuvenated Laurent Fignon pulled himself into contention by leading the Castorama team into second

The ambitions of the big teams ensured a hot pace between Villeurbanne and Dijon, and at the end Ariostea had succeeded in keeping Rolf Sörensen in the yellow jersey

place, 27 seconds faster than Panasonic. But not even the French team could make an impression on Ariostea, that held onto its first place, by 8 seconds, despite crashing on the penultimate corner ...

Sörensen admitted causing the crash by going too fast into the turn; his team-mates Italian Moreno Argentin and German Rolf Gölz fell over him, with two others coming down. Sörensen picked himself up and sprinted to the line, losing 16 seconds to his colleagues, but retaining enough time to take the yellow jersey from LeMond by 10 seconds. If these unexpected developments weren't enough for one day, the most bizarre turn of fortunes was the elimination of former Tour winner Stephen Roche: the leader of the Tonton Tapis team had mistakenly arrived six minutes late for the start, rode the entire course alone, and finished 11 minutes behind his team-mates, well outside the time limit.

After the excitement of the opening two days, the Tour had settled down into its expected, first week pattern of fast stages, tight finishes and a profusion of crashes. Working its way north from Lyon, Stages 2, 3 and 4 were won by sprinters Etienne De Wilde (Histor) of Belgium, Abdujaparov and Holland's Jelle Nijdam (Buckler) respectively. Of more significance in the overall picture were the repeated attacks by Chiappucci and the long chases taken on by the Ariostea, Z and PDM teams to maintain the time gains they made in Lyon.

In Dijon, De Wilde won his stage by counter-attacking 2km from the line, just after Bugno had made a similar solo bid for victory. The Belgian gained no more than 50 metres, but that was enough for him to hold the desperately charging Dutchman Jean-Paul Van Poppel (PDM), and two other green jersey contenders, German Olaf Ludwig (Panasonic) and Abdujaparov. These sprinters – except for Van Poppel, who was dropped with 34 others on the third category climb just before the finish in Rheims – again played leading roles in the spectacular Stage 4 bunch sprint. Abdujaparov had a great lead-out from Carrera team-mates Swiss Erich Mächler and Italian Guido Bontempi, and then the thick-thighed Soviet used his own in-built speed (as well as some intimidating swerves that almost put Belgian Lotto rider Johan Museeuw into the barriers) to win his second stage ahead of Ludwig and the fast-finishing Kelly.

It was halfway through this long, 286km stage that Chiappucci made his presence felt when he put the hammer down on the descent of the fourth category Grand Mallet hill. With the aggressive Spaniard Eduardo Chozas (ONCE), Frenchmen Thierry Claveyrolat (RMO) and Simon, and Belgian Peter De Clerq (Lotto), he gained 45 seconds over a reluctantly chasing peloton. The Z team did most of the chasing, and the five-man break was caught after covering 41km in just 52 minutes.

Chiappucci justified his 'suicidal' tactic by saying he was there to race, and he would take any opportunity to attack. He'd been suggesting that LeMond's attack the first day had been a bluff; and he took great delight in overtaking the American and Bugno, after they'd

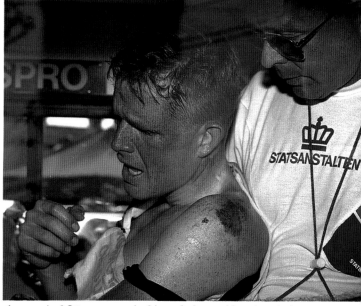

An agonised Sörensen awaits his ambulance ride to hospital after crashing in Valenciennes on Stage 5

accelerated at the start of the Champillon hill — between the champagne vineyards near Epernay. This uphill bout of sabre-rattling also involved Delgado, Italian Maurizio Fondriest (Panasonic), Argentin and Dutch champion Steven Rooks (Buckler), before Abdujaparov made a short solo attack on the descent towards Rheims ... where the Soviet would take the honours.

With the time bonuses he was collecting, Abdujaparov was edging ever closer to the yellow jersey of Sörensen. But it was again the Soviet's team-mate Chiappucci who exploded into the picture, 20km from the end of the 150km Stage 4, Rheims-Valenciennes. Following a string of small attacks — that contributed to the stage's 45km/h average speed — Chiappucci made a surge on the short climb out of Solesmes. With Fondriest and Colombian Reynel Montoya (Postobon) on his wheel, the Italian bridged to two earlier breakaways, Belgian Dirk De Wolf (Tonton Tapis) and Swiss Mauro Gianetti (Helvetia), and these five had gained 40 seconds by the 15km-to-go-banner.

The chase didn't come from Sörensen's Ariostea riders, but from an almost complete line-up of LeMond's Z squad. Working a 55km/h pace-line, the Z riders stretched out the peloton on the narrow roads, and slowly pegged back the leaders, until they were only 17 seconds clear at the 5km marker. Moments later, after negotiating a small roundabout, American Andy Bishop (Motorola) and Italian Giuseppe Calcaterra

(Gatorade) fell into each other, and yellow jersey Sörensen crashed over the top of them. The Dane soon received a spare bike from his Italian team-mate Bruno Cenghialta, and chased back to the bunch ... the pain in his left shoulder was confirmed as a broken collar-bone that would put the race leader out of the Tour.

While this drama was being enacted, the peloton had split, and 20 riders caught the Chiappucci break in the streets of Valenciennes. Fondriest counter-attacked, followed by Motorola's Canadian Steve Bauer; but a winning coup was being prepared by Nijdam's Buckler team. Approaching the red 1km kite, Nijdam was in front, as if leading out sprinter Eric Vanderaerden, but then Vanderaerden intentionally allowed a gap to open, and team-mate Nijdam dashed away to win.

RACE DETAILS

WEATHER *High temperatures throughout: humid at the start, dry in the south. Only one stage (Bourg d'Oisans-Morzine) affected by rain and thundery showers.*

COURSE *Prologue at Lyon, followed by 22 stages, including one team and two individual time trials. Mountain climbs included on two stages in the Pyrenees (Stages 12 and 13) and three in the Alps (Stages 17, 18 and 19). One transfer/rest day, from St Herblain to Pau (after Stage 11). Total distance: 3918.9km.*

FIELD *22 teams of 9 riders; 198 starters, 158 finished.*

PROLOGUE — *5.4km time trial, Lyon Marie scores two-second win over Breukink, with LeMond third. Indurain finishes 7th at 0:09.*

STAGE 1 — *Lyon-Lyon, 114.5km After fast start, Järmann escapes to two-minute lead. He is joined by 10 counter-attackers — LeMond,*

Cornillet; Breukink, Alcalá, Kelly, Sörensen, Frenchman Gilles Delion (Weinmann), Abdujaparov, Belgian Rudy Dhaenens (Panasonic) and Vermote. After 56km the break arrives 1:44 ahead of the pack, with sprint being won by Abdujaparov from Kelly. LeMond takes the yellow jersey.

STAGE 2 — *36km team time trial, Bron-Chassieu LeMond punctures at start and his team finishes seventh at 0:49, allowing Sörensen to take overall lead. Stephen Roche is late for start, rides course alone and is eliminated. Ariostea, despite crash near finish, wins by 8 seconds over Castorama, with Panasonic third.*

STAGE 3 — *Villeurbanne-Dijon, 210.5km Attacks are all short lived ... 174km Break by Belgian Sammie Moreels (Lotto), Spaniard Pello Ruiz-Cabestany (Clas) and Denmark's Jesper Skibby (TVM). They gain 0:53, but are caught; then De Wilde jumps away to win alone, just ahead of the sprinters.*

STAGE 4 — *Dijon-Rheims, 286km ... 116km No attacks until the Grand Mallet hill where Chozas, Belgian Peter De Clercq (Lotto), Claveyrolat, Chiappucci and Simon broke clear. They gain 0:45 but are caught at 157km after chase led by Z team ... 146km Belgians Benjamin Van Itterbeeck (Histor) and Guy Nulens (Panasonic) and Italian Valerio Tebaldi (Gatorade) gain 1:07 in a breakaway formed just outside Epernay. The gap is cut to 0:25 by summit of Champillon hill, where peloton splits. The break is caught in streets of Rheims. Abdujaparov winning bunch sprint from Ludwig and Kelly. Sörensen retains lead.*

STAGE 5 — *Rheims-Valenciennes, 149km 35 riders break clear at the start including Sörensen and Alcalá. They are caught after 18km ...40km Frenchman Marc Madiot (RMO) and Belgian Willy Willems (Collstrop-Isoglass) attack, and gain 1:00. They are joined at 55km by American*

Ron Kiefel (Motorola), De Clercq and Spaniard Melchor Mauri (ONCE); their lead is 3:50 at 70 km, making Kiefel leader on the road. A chase led by Ariostea and PDM closes gap by 90km. Another break by 10 riders — including Englishman Sean Yates (Motorola), De Wolf and Gianetti — moves 0:42 ahead. Just before they are caught, De Wolf and Gianetti counter-attack and they are joined, after Solesmes hill (130km) by Chiappucci, Fondriest and Montoya ...135km These five are 0:40 ahead when chase is led by Z team. The peloton splits before break is caught 3km from the finish. Nijdam (Buckler) jumps away in last kilometre to win from German Remig Stumpf (Histor) and Ludwig. Sörensen crashes in final kilometres, gets back to the bunch, and retains the yellow jersey. But his injury is later diagnosed as a broken collar-bone and he is unable to start Stage 6.

Just when it seemed either Greg LeMond or Sean Kelly would take Sörensen's place as race leader during the stage to Le Havre, Castorama's Thierry Marie produced the second longest solo breakaway in the Tour's history to put himself in the yellow jersey

With the unfortunate Sörensen out of the race, LeMond was entitled to wear the yellow jersey for Stage 5 from Arras to Le Havre. But he turned down the opportunity to acquire the leader's jersey in such a fashion; he was also prepared to concede the overall lead to Kelly – who began the stage only one second behind LeMond on overall time. Kelly did overtake LeMond during the day, thanks to winning the overall time bonus, but both men were left more than a minute in arrears by Marie.

The prologue winner made impudent use of a lull in the pace, just after Ludwig won the day's first sprint, 21km out of Arras. As the sprinters eased, Marie burst from the pack, and was on his own within a kilometre.

There were still 237km of the stage to go, a distance that only one other rider in Tour history had ever covered alone to win a stage. That was another Frenchman, Albert Bourlon, who in 1947, rode the whole of the 253km Carcassonne-Luchon stage on his own to win by 15 minutes. Forty-four years later, Marie rode to a 22-minute lead after 105km on his own; he slowed somewhat on the hilly road parallel to the Channel coast between Dieppe and St Valery-en-Caux, emerging with a 16-minute advantage; and over the final 80km, he maintained a steady pace, close to 40 km/h, to arrive beside the docks in Le Havre almost 2 minutes ahead of the pack. He would be riding through his native Normandy next day resplendent in yellow ...

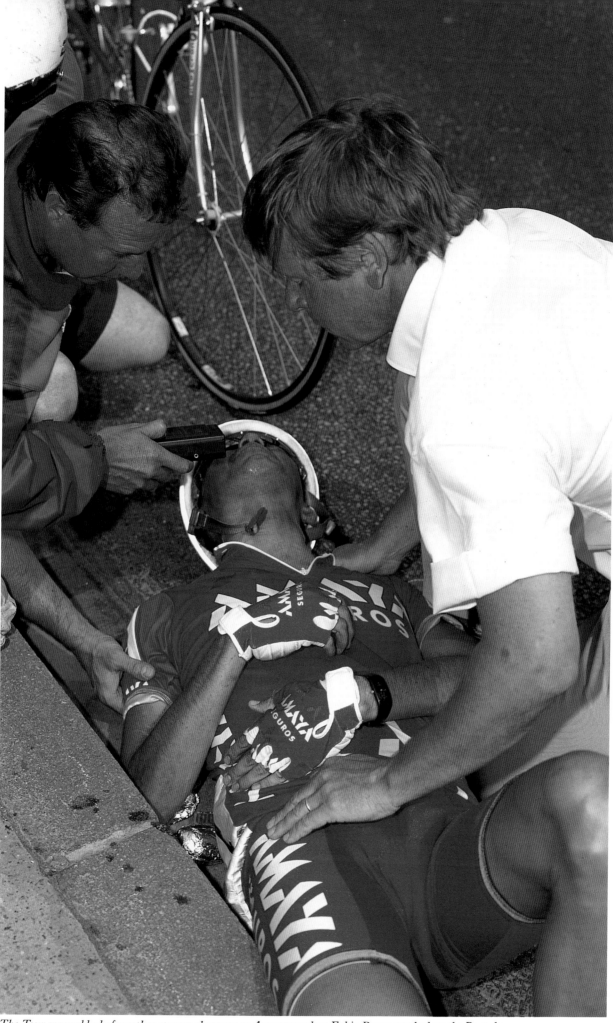

The Tour was robbed of another star on the stage to Argentan when Fabio Parra crashed on the Pont de Tancarville, Le Havre

The peloton ambled through the picturesque town of Honfleur en route *to Argentan*

During the final kilometres of Stage 6, there was yet another crash, this one putting Frenchman Martial Gayant (Toshiba) out of the race, while Robert Millar damaged vertebrae − and was forced to ride with a neck brace for the following four days. Despite his injuries, the Scot would contribute to every chase launched by the Z team on the stages through Normandy and Brittany.

Breukink's overall ambitions ran into problems on the long time trial to Alençon when he blew up within 15km of the finish while matching the pace of stage winner Indurain

This time sophisticated componentry couldn't help Thierry Marie as he fought to save his yellow jersey on the stage to Alençon

Jean-François Bernard's third place at Alençon was the Frenchman's best stage performance in the Tour since his Mont Ventoux victory in 1987. His rediscovered form became an important factor in helping Indurain to win the Tour, and vindicated his decision to move to Banesto for the 1991 season

The first of these stages was won by PDM's Van Poppel, whose team-mates gave him the perfect opening to sprint clear in the final 400 metres well ahead of Museeuw. With the first week over, only Marie, Abdujaparov and Kelly led LeMond, with Breukink still seven seconds behind him. That picture changed the following day when the rolling 73km time trial between Argentan and Alençon saw Breukink streaking out to an early lead. The Dutchman seemed headed for first place and the yellow jersey ... but he faded badly to finish fourth, 1:08 down on the stage winner, Indurain, whom Breukink had led by 33 seconds entering the final 20km.

Riding in his hall-mark calm style, Indurain showed the benefit of having made a detailed reconnaissance of the course when he was in the area to ride the Circuit de la Sarthe pro-am stage race, two months earlier. Rarely taking his hands from his clip-on aero' bars, the tall Spaniard took the tightest lines on the frequent curves, and timed his effort to perfection, going faster over the final 20km than any of his rivals.

LeMond meanwhile made a typical storming finish, failing to win the stage by just eight seconds, but retrieving the race lead, with an advantage of 1:13 over Breukink, and 2:17 over the emerging Indurain. Bugno came in fifth, to move up to seventh overall (at 3:51); Alcalá faded after a fast start and dropped to ninth overall (at 4:14); and Chiappucci lost more than four minutes (finishing only nineteenth in the time trial).

With the general classification more firmly established, the major teams were content to reserve their next major efforts for the first mountain stages, still five days off. But that did not mean that the stages through Brittany would be easy, and the six hundred journalists following the race would have no trouble in finding things to write about. In fact one of the biggest stories of the Tour emerged during the stages through Brittany: the sickness that sidelined the whole of the PDM team.

As the story broke the media gave second billing to the stage wins — by Mauro Ribeiro (RMO) at Rennes, the first-ever by a Brazilian; by Motorola's Australian Phil Anderson at Quimper; and Mottet's at St Herblain, at an amazing 47.229 kph, a record for a stage longer than 200km. It was during these three days that the PDM 'affair' evolved.

The story began when team rider Irishman Martin Earley felt sick after the stage to Rennes: he changed rooms at the team's hotel, so as not to pass the illness on to his room-mate, Kelly. However next morning, several other PDM riders were sick. German Uwe Raab and Dutchman Nico Verhoeven didn't start Stage 10; Van Poppel and Earley climbed into the sag wagon before the stage ended; and whilst German Falk Boden completed the full distance, he arrived well beyond the time limit. The remaining four PDM riders — Alcalá, Breukink, Kelly and Dutchman Jos Van Aert — developed a high fever at their hotel in Quimper, and none of them could start Stage 11.

It was revealed later that the team's sickness was a bacteriological infection caused by a bad injection of Intralipid — a natural lecithin-based product that contains concentrated carbohydrates and proteins that help an athlete recover more quickly from an intense effort (such as the Argentan-Alençon time trial). The injections were given by the team's doctor, Wim Sanders, who was alleged to have used a batch of Intralipid that was either infected or out-of-date.

The PDM team's withdrawal from the Tour — and the absence of key riders Breukink, Kelly and Alcalá — cast a dark cloud over the race on the eve of its most awaited stages. It also had an incalculable effect on the outcome of the race. If the Dutch-based team had remained at full strength, then it's certain that the racing in the mountains would have altered dramatically. But PDM was out ... and the race continued in Pau after the travel/rest day.

Phil Anderson continued his season's good form by winning the stage into Quimper on the Brittany coast. The Australian is seen here driving the successful breakaway clear of the peloton with 20km to go

After the most promising Tour de France start he had made in years there was no one sadder than Kelly as the PDM team prepared to quit the Tour at their Quimper hotel

At St Herblain an in-form Charly Mottet stole the sprinters' thunder on the last flat stage of the race before the Pyrenees

RACE DETAILS

STAGE 6 – Arras-Le Havre, 259km ... 21km *Following intermediate sprint Marie attacks and rides unchallenged to a lead of 21:25 ... 75km A strong sidewind slows down the solo leader, but he then recovers. His lead is 22:00 at 127km, and 16:00 at 177km. Carrera team eventually organise a chase, but Marie retains a 1:54 margin to win stage and take overall lead.*

STAGE 7 Le Havre-Argentan, 167km *There are constant attacks from the start ...68km The first clear break is made by Gölz. He gains 5:00, making him leader on the road ...137.6km Castorama-led chase reduces gap to 1:00. Chozas then chases and joins the leader, followed by Ribeiro and Dane Per Pedersen (Amaya) ...147km The four leaders are 0:11 ahead of 10 chasers, and 0:26 ahead of pack. The Panasonic team gives chase, and pack is together for final sprint, won by Van Poppel (PDM). Marie retains lead.*

STAGE 8 – 73km time trial, Argentan-Alençon *The rolling course through the Normandy countryside suited the classic time triallists like Breukink, leading at all check points until he suddenly slowed 20km from the end. The steadier Indurain came through to win by 0:08 from LeMond – who regained the yellow jersey. Frenchman Jean-François Bernard (Banesto) came in third followed by Breukink and Bugno. Chiappucci lost 4:04.*

STAGE 9 Alençon-Rennes, 261km *An early break of 30 riders gains 0:19 but is caught after 18km. A counter-attack with Hampsten takes 0:13 before being caught. Further attacks follow ... 63km Mottet heads an attack that within 9km contains 40 other riders, including Kelly and Alcalá ... 84km The 0:32 gap is closed by LeMond and Z team, and Frenchman Henri Abadie (RMO) breaks clear. He is chased and joined by Soviet Dmitri Konyshev (TVM), and then, at 118km, by 8 others : Ribeiro, Bontempi, Frenchmen Thierry Bourguignon and Laurent Jalabert (both Toshiba), Belgians Johan Bruyneel (Lotto) and Edwig Van Hooydonck (Buckler) and Italians Giuseppe Calcaterrra (Gatorade) and Massimiliano Lelli (Ariostea) ... 128km Break's lead is 4:00, which is reduced to 0:53 at finish, where Ribeiro attacks in last kilometre to win from Jalabert and Konyshev. LeMond retains lead by 1:13 over Breukink.*

STAGE 10 – Rennes-Quimper, 207.5km *A slow early pace allows Frenchman Thierry Laurent (RMO) to break clear at 83km. He gains 4:05 and is reeled in at 147km ... 177km A series of counter-attacks ends when four men escape: Belgians Michel Dernies (Weinmann) and Nico Emonds (Clas), Anderson and Denmark's Brian Holm (Histor) ... 188km The break is 0:32 ahead, and maintains just 0:06 at Quimper, where Anderson easily outsprints Emonds and the other two. Abdujaparov takes bunch sprint to move into second overall, 1:09 behind LeMond. Five riders from the PDM team quit the race, while the other four will not start next day, due to bacterial infection. Rearranged general classification sees Indurain* move into third, 1:17 down on LeMond.

STAGE 11 – Quimper-St Herblain, 246km ... 70km *Incessant attacks result in the first clean break by Frenchman Pascal Lino and Mottet (both RMO), Anderson, Belgian Carlo Bomans (Weinmann), Norwegian Olaf Lurvik (Toshiba) and Spaniard Fernando Quevedo (Amaya). They gain a minute, but are caught at 107km. Within 5km, another break moves clear: De Wolf, Quevedo, Kiefel, Argentin, Vermote, Belgian Marc Sergeant and Dutchman Marc Van Orsouw (both Panasonic), Frenchman Christophe Lavainne (Castorama), Belgians Patrick Jacobs (Tonton Tapis) and Rik Van Slycke (Lotto). The 10 men gain 2 minutes, which is reduced to 0:10 at 203km ... 228km The lead is 0:55 when – Järman attacks. The rest of the break is caught 2km from the finish. Mottet counter-attachs with 1km to go and just holds off the fast-finishing Museeuw, Abdujaparov and Jalabert. The stage is the fastest ever over 200km: 47.229km/h.*

Greg LeMond, surrounded by his rivals on the col de Soudet, never seemed motivated to defend his race lead into the Spanish town of Jaca ...

... unlike his fellow American Andy Hampsten, who found himself in good form on the climb of the col de Somport where he is seen leading Charly Mottet and Luc Leblanc

After eleven days of pounding their biggest gears, the riders experienced their usual difficulties in adjusting to their smallest gears as the race entered the Pyrenees. And, as in the first mountain stages of many past Tours, an early breakaway was allowed to develop. In this 22-man group − which arrived at the base of the first-category col du Soudet with a lead of 3:20 − were such potentially dangerous riders as Hampsten, Fondriest, Swiss Pascal Richard (Helvetia), Ruiz-Cabestany, Australian Stephen Hodge (ONCE) and Frenchman Luc Leblanc (Castorama). As the climb steepened, 12km from the top of the 1540-metre peak, and with the gap at 5:35, Hampsten, Fondriest, Richard, Leblanc and Belgian Jan Nevens (Lotto) moved clear.

At the same point, Mottet broke clear of the pack to begin a solo chase. Following his year-long statements that he was riding the Tour to win stages, not to contest the overall victory, Mottet was allowed his freedom; he reached the Soudet summit 2:13 behind the five leaders,

and 1:40 ahead of the yellow jersey group, that was just preceded by Bugno and Delgado. The long climb had completely shattered the field on this day of 30°C temperatures, and would be spread over 52 minutes by the finish, at Jaca, still more than 100km away.

On the fast, steep descent, Mottet linked up with Hodge to chase the leaders, while the Z riders Cornillet and Gilbert Duclos-Lassalle (who'd both been in the original 22-man break) dropped back to help race leader LeMond lead the chase. A crucial moment came halfway up the next climb, the second-category Col d'Ichère, where Mottet and Hodge caught the leaders, and were now only 1:20 ahead of the LeMond group − now joined by a separate chase group headed by Bugno, who had crashed on the Soudet descent. As these two groups merged, there was an inevitable slowing down by the peloton, and with 74km remaining, the chase virtually stopped.

In front, Hodge was soon dropped by the other six leaders; and after they'd sped down the Ichère descent to begin the much easier, but longer Col du Somport, the break's lead multiplied at an alarming rate. Well before reaching the 1640-metre summit, which marks the border between France and Spain, the gap was over five minutes. Leblanc then made an unexpected attack to reach the prime 16 seconds ahead of Richard and Mottet, 1:05 ahead of Mottet; 1:37 over Fondriest; and an enormous 7:15 over the LeMond group.

On the mainly descending roads into Spain, the three at the front linked up to gain two minutes on Hampsten and Fondriest, while in the chase group LeMond was without team support. This 28-strong group arrived in Jaca, in broiling temperatures, still seven minutes down. Mottet won the stage by outsprinting Richard and Leblanc, 24, was crowned the new yellow jersey, with a 2:35 advantage over LeMond, and 3:52 over third-placed Mottet.

LeMond finished the stage severely dehydrated, remaining in the medical control caravan for almost an hour, drinking cokes and mineral water, before he could supply enough urine for the drugs tests. In contrast, Indurain had finished with four other team-mates, and had even dashed away at the end, taking seventh place on the stage, 6 seconds ahead of the rest of the group. The Spaniard looked to be in top form for the next day's monster stage to Val Louron ...

The peloton took its time moving across the province of Hueva in Spain, nervous of the five mountain climbs awaiting them on the stage to Val Louron

Miguel Indurain was quick to join the attack of Greg LeMond and Claudio Chiappucci on the col du Tourmalet, in a move that set the Spaniard up for his own attack on the descent

Meanwhile the new race leader Leblanc was saying 'it will be much harder defending the jersey than winning it'. However, the young French rider rode admirably on Stage 13 – until he blew up on the fourth of the long day's five mountain passes. This seven-hour stage from Jaca to Val Louron would prove to be the most decisive of the 1992 Tour, seeing a series of rapidly changing fortunes between the race favourites.

The decisive moments of this stage – and of the whole race – took place on the mighty Col du Tourmalet, the third of the day's climbs. LeMond, fearing a repetition of the Jaca stage, launched a dramatic attack 10km from the 2115-metre summit. 'I attacked because I didn't have any team-mates with me, and I only wanted to be against the top guys'. His move had the desired effect: Chiappucci was the first to join him, followed by Indurain and Mottet, and then by Hampsten, Bugno, Leblanc and Frenchman Gérard Rué (Helvetia). These eight riders joined forces halfway up the giant pass, and soon overtook a few earlier breakaways.

However the Tourmalet held one more surprise – 500 metres from the summit, Chiappucci and Indurain were setting the pace when a gasping LeMond suddenly lost contact. He lost only 17 seconds by the top, but before he recaught the leaders, Indurain had bolted. By the foot of the descent the tall Spaniard was 53 seconds ahead of the chasers. On reaching the valley Chiappucci sped away to join Indurain, who said later, 'I was beginning to wonder what I should do. Then I heard that Chiappucci was coming up, and I knew we'd be able to work together'.

Then 3.5km from the summit of the Aspin climb, Bugno attacked. Leblanc was dropped, while Mottet and Frenchman Laurent Fignon of Castorama (who'd chased back from a two-minute deficit on the Tourmalet) rode away with the Italian, leaving LeMond to plough a lonely furrow, with Hampsten, Rué and Chozas on his wheel.

The beautiful col du Tourmalet, with its towering guardian the pic du Midi in the background, was the highest point of the 1991 Tour de France

Indurain and Chiappucci approach Val Louron at the end of their incredible breakaway

Out front, Chiappucci and Indurain were riding with strength and confidence, in the knowledge that all their rivals were having a hard time. Only Bugno showed true resistance: he dropped Mottet (4th) and Fignon (5th) on the final ascent, pulling back to within 1:28 of the two leaders − with Chiappucci taking the win from Indurain. Hampsten also finished strongly, taking sixth place 6:01 back, with LeMond in ninth place 7:18 behind. The baton had passed to a new Tour leader: Miguel Indurain.

The steady but fast cadence set by Gianni Bugno was enough to dislodge everyone but Indurain himself at Alpe d'Huez. The pair are seen here through the gloom; later, Luc Leblanc fought his way up to them before the finish

With the epic battle of the Pyrenees behind them, some easing of the pace was expected over the following three days, especially because the temperatures remained high. But there were some intense periods of racing on each of the three stages—which were, incredibly, all won by Italian riders from the Ariostea team: Bruno Cenghialta at Castres; Argentin at Castres; and Marco Lietti at Gap. Cenghialta won with a 30km solo effort after breaking clear from a small leading group. Argentin scored a masterful win by attacking from the entire pack on a short climb, and time trialling the 65km to the finish at more than 47km/h. And then Lietti, on the descent into Gap, caught solo attacker LeMond and outsprinted him to take the Stage 16 victory.

Argentin's remarkable Stage 15 break was rewarded by the second of three consecutive Ariostea stage wins

Despite a severed artery in his elbow and severe grazing on his leg, Sean Yates battled back to the peloton before the finish of Stage 15 to Alès, only to be forced to withdraw the following morning because of his injuries

LeMond suffered badly on Stage 18 to Morzine, having been dropped on the col des Aravis

Miguel Indurain was also below his best for the very wet stage to Morzine, and is seen here getting soaked on the valley road leading to the col de la Joux Plane

The prelude to LeMond's attack in the final 10km of this pre-Alpine stage – which gained him 26 seconds – was an almighty battle that almost cost Indurain the Tour. When the Spaniard missed an eight-man break on the St André hill, 65km before Gap, Indurain found himself in a hostile 54-rider group, a minute behind. The group in front were headed by his two most dangerous rivals, Bugno and Chiappucci, who also had the help of Fignon, and the revitalised Dutch climbers, Steven Rooks (Buckler) and Gert-Jan Theunisse (TVM). At first, the race leader tried to cross the gap on his own, but failed. Furthermore, he had only team-mates Delgado and Rondon to help him in the resultant chase – before the Banesto team manager José-Miguel Echevarri ordered French rider Fabrice Philipot back from the break, and then Mottet eventually asked his team to join in the pursuit. As a result the break sat up after racing 47km in the hour ... and Indurain was safe.

So the Banesto rider entered the Alps with overall margins of 3 minutes over Mottet, 3:10 over Bugno, 4:06 over Chiappucci and 4:42 over LeMond. If he faltered, Indurain could still lose this Tour; but he was favoured by the vital stage to l'Alpe d'Huez being only 125km long, and containing only minor climbs before the traditionally decisive, uphill confrontation at the Alpe. The result of the battle was a repeat stage win for Bugno – in a sprint against Indurain and a revived Leblanc – with Chiappucci conceding 43 seconds, while Mottet and LeMond both lost almost 2 minutes. This result provided the Tour's eventual finishing order of Indurain-Bugno-Chiappucci, and the remaining five stages became mere battles for stage honours.

There remained the final procession into Paris, where a revitalised LeMond shook up the peloton with a 30km solo break that only ended on the Champs Elysées. The inevitable bunch finish looked likely to go to green jersey Abdujaparov, but the squat rider from Uzbekistan rode head-down into the barriers, when leading less than 100 metres from the line, and Konyshev came through to win from Ludwig. Many minutes later, the concussed Abdujaparov, with a broken left collar-bone, was helped by the Tour doctors to walk across the line, so that he could finish the Tour and receive his award as its best sprinter.

Meanwhile, a few metres away, Indurain was receiving his final yellow jersey and posing for the photographers with his runners-up, Bugno and Chiappucci. But the man who'd come to France looking for his fourth Tour win was, for the first time in his career, not on the winners' podium. LeMond was dignified in defeat, and had generously said at the Mâcon press conference, 'Indurain was the strongest man in the race. He deserved to win.'

Even so, the race left many questions hanging in the air. Would the result have been different if Breukink and his PDM team hadn't been forced to quit? Was this the end of the LeMond era? And will Indurain dominate the next generation of the Tour de France champions? We will never know the answer to the first question; we would have to wait a year to find out the answer to the second; but we do have an insight into the third ...

At six feet two inches, and twelve-and-a-half stones, Indurain is probably the biggest man ever to win the Tour. He is also, despite his successes in the past two or three years, one of the least well-known of the riders. Indurain started bike racing at the age of eleven, when he was persuaded by three cousins to compete in a small event near their home in Pamplona, in the Spanish province of Navarra. He came in second, and then won his next race: the young Indurain had been persuaded that cycling was his sport, having already shown promise as a cross-country runner and soccer player.

Through the lower cycling categories, he would win six or seven races a year – 'I never trained in those days,' said Indurain, 'I did it just for fun.' At the time, he was in the Ciclo Club Villaves, until he was spotted racing by Eusebio Unzue, who was then in charge of the Reynolds team junior squad. By coincidence, Unzue's family owned a fertilizer business used by Indurain's parents, who are crop farmers in Villava.

The 17-year-old Indurain – already over six feet tall and weighing 14 stones – joined the Reynolds amateur team in the same year, 1983, that its pro squad entered the Tour de France for the first time. It was the Pamplona rider's first serious season of racing, and he showed his talent by winning the first Spanish national amateur title. 'That was the first time I knew that I could be a champion,' Indurain remembered.

A year later, after coming fourth at his national amateur road race championship, he was selected to race for Spain at the Los Angeles Olympics; but he did not finish the road race. However, his year ended on a strong note, when he won the time trial stage of the pro-am Tour de l'Avenir, beating such riders as Charly Mottet and Jean-François Bernard. Indurain's weight was a big problem in those days, as was shown when he turned pro at age 20, in 1985. He could finish only 84th in his first Tour of Spain, and then abandoned his first Tour de France. A year later, after losing about eight pounds, he won the first edition of the European Community Tour (the former Tour de l'Avenir). However, he'd again abandoned the Tour de France, and could only finish 97th in the following year's Tour ... almost three hours behind the winner Stephen Roche.

Indurain was a valued team rider for the Reynolds and its leader Delgado – who was narrowly beaten by Roche in 1987 – but the team manager Echevarri was concerned that his young protégé was not improving his climbing ability. As a result, the *directeur sportif* had a meeting with Francesco Moser's former trainer, Professor Francesco Conconi, and a new regime was mapped out for Indurain. By changing his diet and training more intensively, the Spanish rider's weight would drop a further 12 pounds, which gave him a much higher power-to-weight ratio.

However, there was no overnight miracle. Indurain abandoned the 1988 Tour of Spain, and finished 47th at the Tour de France. It wasn't until the spring of 1989 that the world saw the 'new' Indurain – when he won Paris-Nice and the two-day Critéruim International. He again quit the Tour of Spain, but went on to take 10th place at the Tour of Switzerland and a more promising

17th place (including a stage win in the Pyrenees) at the Tour de France.

In 1990, an even slimmer Indurain matured into a well rounded performer by scoring eight victories, which included a World Cup race, the Clasicá San Sebastian, and another stage win at the Tour de France, in which he finished tenth overall. That position could have been much higher had he not ridden the race as the main support rider for his Banesto team leader, Delgado. By unselfishly working for his friend 'Perico' on the Alpe d'Huez stage, Indurain conceded 10 minutes on the hellish climb; on the crucial St Etienne stage he even dropped off the winning break to help the ailing Delgado; but when his leader was sick in the Pyrenees, Indurain ably followed the attacks by LeMond on the Tourmalet and Luz-Ardiden, and went on to beat the American for the stage victory.

So when the 1991 Tour began in Lyon, everyone was asking, 'what if Indurain doesn't ride for Delgado this year?' As the world was to witness, Delgado would ride for Indurain, whose combination of time trial power, descending skills and 'undropability' in the mountains proved unbeatable, and the 27-year-old Spaniard from Villava became the toast of Spain.

Miguel Indurain savouring his triumph

The ferocity of Abdujaparov and Ludwig's sprinting at Mâcon was undiminished, despite the fact that they were only racing for second place behind Ekimov

Greg LeMond prepares for the time trial at Lugny, his privacy shared by old rival Laurent Fignon who started three minutes before him

RACE DETAILS

STAGE 14 – St Girons-Castres, 172.5km *De Clerq attacks from start and is caught after 11km ... 76km On Saintes hill, Chiappucci takes King of the Mountains sprint from Hampsten and Norwegian Dag-Otto Lauritzen (Motorola) ... 86 km Lauritzen continues effort and is 1:30 clear, chase taken up by 27 riders including Hampsten, Bernard and Konyshev. The peloton organises a chase, and the 27 are about to be caught at 100km, where Lauritzen is 0:15 ahead. He is caught by eight counter-attackers... 118km 13 others join the attack – including Leblanc and Abdujaparov – to make a lead group of 22 riders ... 120km The gap is 3:15. A 5-strong splinter group headed by Konyshev takes a 0:30 lead but is caught at 143km. An immediate solo attack takes Cenghialta 1:00 clear of the lead group, at 15km to go, with pack at 2:55. Cenghialta holds on to win by 0:20 over chase groups, with Frenchman Jean-Claude Colotti (Tonton Tapis) second. Indurain retains lead.*

STAGE 15 – Albi-Alès, 235km *There are no breaks before nine men – including Bauer and Ekimov – get clear on descent ... 162km On the steep third category Sumène hill, Weltz and Philipot attack from break, but are soon passed by counter-attacking Argentin, who crosses summit 0:14 clear ... 195km Argentin's lead climbs to 3:00 and he holds on to win stage by 1:07 over chase group headed by Swiss Thomas Wegmüller (Weinmann), with pack at 1:53. No changes to general classification.*

STAGE 16 – Alès-Gap, 215km *... 146km No action until the start of St André hill, where sprint for King of the Mountains points is followed by Bugno and Fignon, catching Indurain by surprise ... 149.5km Claveyrolat is 0:27 ahead of Chiappucci, Spaniard Alberto Leanizbarrutia (Clas), Tebaldi and Bruyneel; 0:20 ahead of Fignon, Bugno, Theunisse, Rooks and Philipot; and 0:30 ahead of first part of peloton.*

Tebaldi drops back, while other 9 leaders link up on descent ... 169km the lead is 0:43 over a 54-strong group, with the peloton well behind ... 180km The gap increases to 1:00 while Philipot drops back to help in chase. RMO team joins the chase and eight leaders sit up at 198km. Within 2km a counter-attack forms headed by Anderson, Fondriest and LeMond; LeMond attacks on descent, 10km from finish. He is joined by Lietti at foot of descent, and the Italian wins sprint for stage win, 0:19 ahead of Fondriest, with the Indurain group at 0:28.

STAGE 17 – Gap-l'Alpe d'Huez, 125km *... 5km After leading the peloton over the col de Bayard, Ruiz-Cabestany attacks on the descent and is joined by Bourgignon, Abdujaparov, Winterberg and Lavainne. The five riders gain 2:00 before Bourgignon and Ruiz-Cabestany move clear ... 61.5km At La Mure, the two leaders are 2:00 ahead of Abdujaparov and 4:05 ahead of the pack ... 96km At the summit of the col d'Ornon*

Bourgignon and Ruiz-Cabestany are 2:20 ahead of the peloton, which is headed by the Banesto riders. On descent, Frenchman Frédéric Vichot (Castorama) begins chase with Rooks, Claveyrolat and Pensec ... 112km These four reach the foot of the Alpe d'Huez climb 1:35 behind the two leaders, with the peloton at 2:05 ... 115km The leaders are caught; Bugno attacks causing Fignon, LeMond, Mottet and Delgado to drop back. Only Indurain and Chiappucci can follow Bugno, while Bernard, Leblanc and Claveyrolat catch back when the pace eases. Bernard now takes over the pace-making, and Chiappucci and Claveyrolat drop back ... 120km The four leaders are 0:25 ahead of Chiappucci with Fignon/Delgado at 0:55, and Mottet/LeMond at 1:25 ... 122km Bernard drops back, Leblanc falls, remounts and recatches Bugno and Indurain. At finish Bugno outsprints Indurain and Leblanc, with Chiappucci at 0:43, and Mottet/LeMond at 1:58. Indurain retains lead with Bugno in second place at 3:09.

Ludwig (left) and Konyshev found themselves with much more space than they'd expected at the Champs Elysées finish after Abdujaparov rode himself into the barriers within sight of another stage win. It was Konyshev's second win in three days

STAGE 18 – Bourg d'Oisans-Morzine, 255km ... 117km *No attacks until now, Wegmüller breaks clear with DeClerq and Frenchman Dominique Arnaud (Banesto). They gain 1:45 by Ugine ...* 135km *They are caught on slopes of first category col des Aravis – where LeMond is dropped. In front Claveyrolat attacks, taking with him Conti, Vichot, Spaniards Miguel Martinez-Torres (ONCE) and Francisco Espinosa (Clas) and Colombian Alberto Camargo (Postobon). At the summit these six men are 1:01 ahead of peloton, and 3:57 ahead of LeMond group. Camargo and Vichot break clear on descent, but are caught on next climb, the col de la Colombière ...* 185.5km *By the summit Claveyrolat and Conti are 0:10 ahead of Camargo, Espinosa and Martinez-Torres; 0:31 up on Vichot; and 2:20 ahead of the Indurain group. The wet, slippery descent sees Conti drop back, while Camargo and Vichot join Claveyrolat in lead ...* 205km *At Cluses these three are 1:45 ahead of chase group headed by Konyshev and Conti; and 2:40*

ahead of peloton ... 216km *Chasers are joined by Bourgignon, Montoya and Ruiz-Cabestany, they all catch the three leaders at Samoëns ...* 227km *Final climb begins to the col de la Joux Plane: Conti, then Bourgignon, then Claveyrolat attack on the climb and by the summit,* 273.5km, *Claveyrolat is 0:20 ahead of Bourgignon; 0:33 ahead of Conti and Montoya; and 1:00 ahead of the Indurain group. Bourgignon chases on descent and catches Claveyrolat in streets of Morzine. In uphill finish, Claveyrolat pulls away to win stage from Bourgignon, while at 0:30, Chiappucci leads in main group. LeMond finishes 59th, at 7:52.*

STAGE 19 – Morzine-Aix-les-Bains, 177km ... 6km *Mauri attacks on descent and moves to a lead of 7:15 by Thônes (73km) ...* 118km *He is caught on the ascent of the col des Leschaux, where Winterberg and Bruyneel break clear. They are recaught on descent, and Richard and Konyshev attack at the foot of the second category Mont Revard. A chase group forms,*

comprising LeMond, Rooks, Rué, Conti, Chozas, Espinosa and Pulnikov ... 153.5km *At summit the two leaders are 0:13 ahead of the seven chasers, with the peloton at 1:58. Konyshev sets fast pace on descent, and wins stage from Richard, with Chozas in third at 0:11. Peloton comes in at 1:50.*

STAGE 20 – Aix-les-Bains-Mâcon, 160km *Peloton remains clear until Bourg-en-Bresse ...* 115km *22 riders break clear, headed by Anderson, Fondriest and Bruyneel. As pack closes, Sergeant, Belgian Hendrik Redant (Lotto), Soviet Dmitri Zhdanov (Panasonic) and Holm leave lead group and establish lead of 1:00 by 132km ...* 152km *The peloton chases and catches four leaders. A series of counter-attacks follow until Ekimov breaks clear with 3km to go. The Soviet wins by 0:07 over Abdujaparov and Ludwig.*

STAGE 21 – 57km time trial, Lugny-Mâcon *Chiappucci makes fast start, and at 20km check is 0:22 ahead of Bugno and Indurain,*

and 0:31 faster than LeMond ... 36km *Indurain has the fastest time, 0:33 ahead of Chiappucci and 0:20 over Bugno. The yellow jersey adds to his advantage by winning the time trial by 0:27 over Bugno and 0:48 over LeMond. Chiappucci is fourth at 1:08, with Ekimov fifth.*

STAGE 22 – Melun-Paris, 178km ... 112km *No attacks until LeMond breaks clear in Chaville. He gains 0:58 by start of the Champs Elysées circuit ...* 142km *On the third of eight laps LeMond is joined by 25 riders, with 0:30 lead on bunch. Before they are caught, nine riders counter-attack, headed by Chozas, Ekimov and Van Hooydonck. They gain 0:24, but are caught on lap 7. Chiappucci breaks clear, and is joined by Sergeant, Pedersen, Indurain and Bauer. On final lap, Bugno catches break, and as peloton closes Bauer moves clear, but he is caught 2.5km from the line. Abdujaparov is winning when he crashes into barriers 100m from the line, Konyshev comes through to win stage from Ludwig and Jalabert; Indurain wins Tour.*

Wincanton Classic: 4 August

After the Tour de France and all the publicity that surrounds a race of such reputation and fame, it is difficult for the riders on the professional circuit to rekindle their thoughts and ambitions, and face up to the second half of the season which includes the World Championships and the last seven World Cup races.

Greg LeMond, no longer the Tour de France champion, had returned home to the States, while the new Tour champion, Miguel Indurain, was basking in glory in France and Spain. His attempt at the World Cup would begin again in San Sebastian — a race too close to home to miss.

Still the lure of FICP points from the third Wincanton Classic in Brighton was enough to put five of the top ten Tour finishers on England's south coast, and along with them was World Cup leader, Denmark's Rolf Sörensen (Ariostea), who left the Tour by ambulance after crashing near the finish at Valenciennes.

This year's testing course was unquestionably a sharp reminder to the peloton that the season was not over, although the sight of France's Laurent Fignon (Castorama) riding at the back for 80km and then peeling off for his hotel, could have made some think otherwise. Ditchling Beacon, a local beauty spot that climbs from a typically British village through trees to

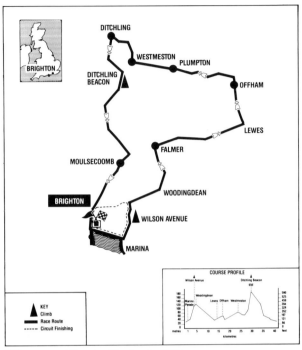

Wincanton Classic, England: 235km

For the third year running, victory in the Wincanton Classic was the result of a solo break — this time by Eric Van Lancker

Ditchling Beacon was the focal point of the day for the thousands of fans assembled there, although the less picturesque climb at Wilson Avenue saw the best racing

Rolf Sörensen, in his comeback from injury, was content to ride until the last ten miles and then abandon, secure in the knowledge that he would keep his World Cup leadership for another week at least

the stark outpost of the Beacon itself, was crammed with thousands of spectators, giving the race a continental atmosphere, and proved to be a challenging climb for the peloton.

The other main challenge was at Wilson Avenue, an unlikely-looking route that climbs away from the sea to the race course with residential housing on the left and wide open spaces to the right. Spectators there witnessed the best battles on each of the nine climbs, as riders tried to crack the field in a desperate attempt to break the race open.

In the end, no one succeeded until the last four finishing circuits, where strength alone took over and it came down to muscle power. Frenchman Marc Madiot (RMO), the brilliant winner of Paris-Roubaix in April and bronzed from his recent Tour efforts, went clear with Belgian Eric Van Lancker (Panasonic) along the avenue. This started a reaction and by the next lap the winning group had formed around them, including that

marvellous opportunist, Italian Claudio Chiappucci (Carrera), who likes nothing better than to annoy the other leading riders with his constant agitation.

Van Lancker, caught once, tried again half way up Wilson Avenue, and with one further climb to come, he was clear, racing to a typically lone win on a beautiful warm summer's day. In 1989, he had hung on to his lead to win the Amstel Gold race − his only win of the year − then last year he scored on home ground when he took the Liège-Bastogne-Liège classic, alone of course.

While Van Lancker was attacking in the last 20km, Rolf Sörensen decided to pull out. Despite this, it was a good return to racing for the World Cup holder, off the bike for 25 days and failing by only a few kilometres to reach the finish of a difficult race. 'I'm content. I went further than I expected and I only felt a bit of pain from my collar-bone, but that's natural after riding a bike for six hours,' said Sörensen, still the man to beat in this series.

RACE DETAILS

WEATHER *Sunshine all day; a moderate wind altered the race pattern a little on a course that changed direction frequently.*

COURSE *234.5km made up of five large circuits, each of 40.8km, with a finishing circuit of 7.6km. The revised route used the tough climb of Wilson Avenue on every circuit, giving nine climbs in all. The highlight, for the first five hours, was the ascent of 180 metre Ditchling Beacon.*

FIELD *172 started, 89 finished. 15 teams of 8 riders each. 4 teams, Z, Banesto, ONCE and Weinmann, raced only 6 riders each.*

RACE *Facing five climbs of Ditchling Beacon, riders did not try any early action, leaving Italian Bruno Cenghialta (Ariostea) and Belgian Richard Virenque (RMO) to fight for the mountains prize, which the Italian won ... 94km First solo attack by Spaniard Pello Ruiz Cabestany (Clas) ... 160km After gaining 2:15 he is caught on the fifth big circuit. During the*

next 20km, German Udo Bölts (Telekom), Mexican Miguel Arroyo (Z), Australian Stephen Hodge (ONCE), Italian Flavio Giupponi (Carrera), Belgian Frank Van Den Abbeele (Lotto) and Italian Roberto Conti (Ariostea) were all crash victims. At the start of the first of four small circuits, Spain's Eduardo Chozas (ONCE), Belgian Marc Sergeant (Panasonic) and Cenghialta led by 0:30. The field regrouped and with 15km to go Madiot and Van Lancker broke clear. Joined by a group of 13, Van Lancker attacked again on Wilson Avenue taking the last lap, by 0:29.

Kellogg's Tour of Britain: 6-10 August

To win a stage race by a second these days is no longer uncommon; professional riders are calculating animals and they usually know when they have won, or lost, whichever the case may be. Of course, Australian Phil Anderson could never be sure that the single second gained in an inspired sprint finish in Birmingham was enough to win the Kellogg's Tour, but with a strong Motorola team around him, he was in the mood to try and defend it to the end – which he did. The win was Anderson's 12th victory this season, complementing his record of 1985 when he had 15 wins, and 1981 when he became the first Aussie to wear the yellow jersey in the Tour de France. And as you get older and the competition inevitably gets harder, it is something of a relief when you show the young bucks that you can still spray mud in their faces.

Anderson was as good as he has ever been in this Kellogg's Tour and the only rider to offer a challenge was Switzerland's 29-year-old Heinz Imboden – another ageing rider from the Helvetia team. The second place of Belgian Rudy Verdonck offered his Weinmann team some consolation for the poor form of last year's winner, Michel Dernies, whose 'attacks' were made more in defence, and the Belgian was clearly unhappy when Anderson and Imboden engaged in jousting on the hills of the Pennines.

Imboden earned more than his third place, but sport has no heart and you get what the computer says you are entitled to. In his case it was third, a second behind Anderson, but on most days the lively Swiss could be said to be (briefly) the leader on the road.

Enjoying his best season for six years, Phil Anderson was in no mood to allow Lincoln's Steep Hill to spoil his perfect start on the first day

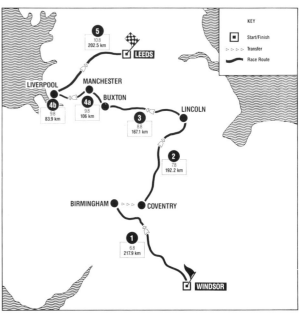

Kellogg's Tour of Britain: 969km

Only ten days after the Tour de France, and two days after a very hard Wincanton Classic, the assembled field were tired and jaded, so those who looked for the first-day escape automatically booked a high place in the finish at Leed's Roundhay Park five days later. This was an excellent course, based on five years' experience by the organisers, Sport for Television, but as with all races throughout the world, it is the riders who make or break the promotion and in this event, the professionals rode at their calculating best.

Every day the race charged along 10-15 minutes ahead of schedule, the Motorola team were obliged to chase and mark on every stage, and those who escaped did so more by the grace of a strong team than by the enthusiasm born from thoughts of winning. It is Anderson's first season with the new American Motorola team, and for the Melbourne professional it represented a breath of fresh air after riding for Peugeot, Panasonic and TVM, and he spent his winter 'riding more miles than ever in training'. Team-mates Sean Yates (GB), Brian Walton (Canada), fellow Americans Frankie Andreu, Ron Kiefel and a tired Andy Bishop, all raced to their limit to make sure that the opponents who mattered never strayed far from the wheels of Phil Anderson. Yates in particular lived up to his nickname of 'the Animal', causing widespread suffering by moving into the front line to keep up a tempo that discouraged all attacks. 'Everybody rode so well, but Yates rides like another person. I think he's schizophrenic, the way he gets up there and rides. I couldn't be happier with the way things went,' said Anderson as he contemplated his third big stage-race win of the year.

Jean-Luc Vandenbroucke's Lotto team looked on paper to be the best of the 16 teams, but the wedding the previous weekend of Johan Museeuw and his girlfriend of ten years, rapidly rearranged because of the imminent arrival of their first child, left most of the team – and certainly Johan – recovering from the celebrations.

After his success in Birmingham it was champagne all the way for Aussie Anderson. Chris Young (right) after his first day break, also took an early lead in the mountains. Rudy Verdonck (left) chased Anderson for five days to finish second

After his sprint win at Lincoln, the Belgian smiled ruefully and said: 'This is the type of race I can win overall, but I was too tired on the first stage after my marriage, so my chance has already gone'.

Indeed it had, but he continued to annoy the field along with team-mate and fellow countryman Hendrik Redant, who was unlucky not to win in Manchester (Stage 4a): the violence of his final attack brought his back wheel up into the frame and broke five spokes, and it was Italy's Gianluca Bortolami (Colnago-Lampere) who took first place, leaving Redant second. The race was welcomed in the city centre with fixed penalty parking tickets on official vehicles and motor bikes, and this from a city that had hoped to host the Olympic Games!

The race did give a chance to the new names for 1992 to show their not inconsiderable talent, so when Phil Anderson retires in two or three years' time, make a note to watch for Dutchman Eddy Bouwmans (Panasonic), his team-mate former East German Jens Heppner and Switzerland's Rolf Aldag (Helvetia), who won a bronze medal in the team time trial for Germany at last year's World Championships and this season finished third in the Tour Du Pont as well as taking the Liverpool stage in the Kellogg's.

Perhaps the most impressive was Bo Hamburger (TVM), who turned professional in June and seems set to be the next Danish star. On the last stage through the Pennines, Hamburger drove the break along, making most of the running on the steep climbs. And on the hardest day of the Tour, after a slow start in the rain, he earned congratulations from Heinz Imboden when Anderson, Imboden and Denmark's Brian Holm (Histor) caught up after the climb over Bleara Moor. It had been a hard chase, and everyone knew it.

Heading out towards a rendezvous with the slopes of Winnats Pass, Anderson keeps strongman Yates alongside him

Johan Museeuw lost his chance of victory on the first day when he struggled to recover from his wedding celebrations the previous weekend

Last year's winner Michel Dernies did not feature this time but Banana-Falcon's Rob Holden (left) did, finishing eighth overall and hoping for a move to Italy in 1992

The rain in the Pennines ruined the hopes of many. Here Anderson controls Heinz Imboden and Christophe Manin with more than a little help from Motorola team-mate Sean Yates

Realisation that he had lost the Kellogg's Tour dawned on Robert Millar after the second stage at Lincoln, when he missed a late breakaway that gained 16 seconds in the last five kilometres. On the previous day, the unpredictable Scot had read the move correctly and joined the nine-man escape that won over three minutes; even at this early stage in the race, the winner was certain to come from this group

RACE DETAILS

WEATHER *Pleasantly warm throughout the race, but the last two days through the Pennines were made very unpleasant by low cloud and rain, heavy at times. A strong westerly wind blew for the last two days, which helped keep the race ahead of schedule.*

COURSE *Five stages on a north-bound route from Windsor to Leeds. A compact course with just one short transfer. A flat first day followed by three days of climbs in the Peak district and over the Pennines.*

FIELD *96 starters in 16 professional teams. On the last day more than 30 riders retired, 50 finished.*

STAGE 1 – Windsor-Birmingham, 217.9km ... *16km Germany's Marcus Sleicher (Telekom) attacks first, but is quickly caught and unsponsored professional Chris Young breaks clear ... 120km Young is 14:0 ahead when the reaction begins, just before the day's main climb of Dovers Hill. By the top of the climb*

nine riders break clear and Young's lead is drastically reduced. These nine riders were to retain the top nine places overall throughout ... 152km Young becomes the first leader of both sprint and mountains competitions, but is caught and quickly dropped from the leading group. Anderson wins stage and becomes race leader by one second from Verdonck.

STAGE 2 – Coventry-Lincoln, 192.2km ... *74km Frenchman Richard Virenque (RMO) attacks and by Newark (137.7km) he leads by 5:36. On the hilly circuits in Lincoln, Virenque is steadily hauled in ... 187km After breaking a spoke, Virenque is caught; 18 riders break clear to gain 0:16 and Belgian Johan Museeuw (Lotto) wins sprint. Anderson retains lead.*

STAGE 3 – Lincoln-Buxton, 167.1km *Sleicher heads race with a lone 8km break, but he is not part of a group of six that attacks near Chesterfield ... 78km The sextet enter the difficult narrow roads in the Peak District with a 2-minute lead ...117km Yates tows the Anderson bunch but punctures soon after ... 130km Anderson*

attacks but is caught within 2km on the climb of Winnats Pass. Dane Kim Andersen (Z) attacks but is caught by Imboden and Anderson before the top, where Anderson passes over first. They are joined by Millar and Verdonck, bringing together the top four riders overall, and Anderson wins his second stage in Buxton, retaining the race lead.

STAGE 4A – Buxton-Manchester, 106km *In the rain and wind three riders, Dutchman Jan Van Loenhout (TVM), Frenchman Dante Rezze (RMO) and Andreu are the survivors of a seven-man attack that starts after the descent of Winnats Pass. On Holme Moss Andreu is replaced by Kim Andersen who leads with a 30-second advantage ... 101km A dogged defiance by the trio ends on the outskirts of Manchester. After van Der Poel and Germany's Remig Stumpf (Histor) crash in the wet, Redant's wheel gives way and Bortolami wins sprint. Anderson retains lead.*

STAGE 4B – Manchester-Liverpool, 83.9km *An attack by Redant and Sleicher stays away until the finishing circuit*

in Liverpool. Sean Yates, a full three lengths ahead approaching finish, sits up in the mistaken belief that he has led Anderson out for the sprint, but instead lets Aldag through to win the stage. Anderson retains lead.

STAGE 5 – Liverpool-Leeds, 202.5km *The climb of Wiggin Tree Hill near Parbold projects four leaders, Holland's Louis de Koning (Panasonic), America's Joe Parkin (Motorola) with team-mate 'policeman' Brian Walton and Hamburger, who gain over 2:0 on the climb of Knowley Brow. Here the race disintegrates and in the chaos, Millar punctures and loses a minute. On the Pennine hill Nick o' Pendle, Walton is dropped and Parkin soon follows, leaving Hamburger and de Koning in the lead. Parkin rejoins on the descent and the lead hovers at around 1:0. On Bleara Moor Anderson, Imboden and Holm catch Hamburger, they neutralise the attack and wait for a general regrouping. As the race enters Roundhay Park, van Der Poel attacks and wins stage. Anderson wins overall by one second.*

Clasicá San Sebastian: 10 August

Clasicá San Sebastian, Spain: 238km

Despite his top placings in the Tours of Italy and France and his victory in the Italian road championship, there was a feeling amongst cycling fans as the Clasicá San Sebastian approached that we had still to see the best of Gianni Bugno this season. Although he had been riding strongly, the 26-year-old Italian leader of the Gatorade team had seemed to lack the punch which last season won him fourteen races, the World Cup and top spot in the World FICP rankings.

However, that punch came back with a vengeance in the run up to the World Championships in Stuttgart, Germany. Bugno missed the Wincanton Classic, but signs that his winning form was returning came in the Spanish Tour of Burgos, where he was second overall to Spain's Pedro Delgado (Banesto). And two days later, Bugno stole what was intended to be a Basque and Spanish celebration of Miguel Indurain's Tour de France win with a magnificent win at San Sebastian.

In fact, Italian riders stole the entire show: not only did Bugno win with a lightning solo attack, but his third-placed compatriot Maurizio Fondriest (Panasonic) took over leadership in the World Cup – of which this

A small fishing fleet forms the backdrop for the peloton's progress in the early stages of the Clasicá San Sebastian

was the seventh round – from Denmark's Rolf Sörensen (Ariostea). It was Fondriest's most convincing performance since he won the World Championship in 1988; some would say, given the controversial circumstances of his win after front runners Steve Bauer and Claude Criquielion collided within sight of the finishing line, his performance at San Sebastian was the more impressive of the two.

For the thousands of Indurain fans who flocked to the Atlantic Ocean holiday town in the Basque country, the only consolation was to see Delgado finish a brave second. Like Bugno, he finished alone after trying to chase down the Italian with 11km to go, but he could get no closer to him than 0:55.

The Clasicá San Sebastian, now 11 years old and the only Spanish event in the World Cup calendar, was a significant race for many other reasons as well. Not only did it confirm Bugno's number one FICP ranking over his compatriot Claudio Chiappucci (Carrera), and the continuing momentum of Italy's two-year-long 'renaissance'. It also provided the first realistic indication of the front runners for the forthcoming World titles. The Wincanton Classic, although it earned winner Eric Van Lancker a place in the Belgian team for the Worlds despite his initial omission, was still too soon after the Tour de France to be regarded as a fair indication of form. Hence, Bugno's absence.

But at San Sebastian, where there is a menu of four climbs – including the testing nine kilometre Alto Jaizkibel with its summit at 209km – the best of the best are rested and ready to race to the limit. And it was no coincidence that from the selection of 30 or so leading riders at the foot of the Jaizkibel climb, the final protagonists were also key figures in the World titles. Bugno's attack, nearing the Jaizkibel summit, mirrored Indurain's last year, when the Pamplonan won. And by dropping Delgado and the Italian pair of Moreno Argentin (Ariostea) and Claudio Chiappucci (Carrera), Bugno secured a much-needed victory.

Bugno's triumphant arrival in San Sebastian was a forerunner of an upturn to his season

RACE DETAILS

WEATHER *Cloud cover in morning, sunny afternoon. Temperature between 25-28°C with gusty sea breezes.*

COURSE *Anti-clockwise route starts and finishes at San Sebastian. Four climbs, of which the last and most decisive is the first category Alto de Jaizkibel at 209km.*

FIELD *26 eight-man teams invited. 199 starters; 171 finishers.*
44km *Dutchman Dick Dekker (Paternina) attacks alone ... 71km He gets maximum lead of 8:25 ... 182 km Dekker's lead drops*

to 2:30 ... 189km Under PDM drive, Dekker is caught ...196km Italian Roberto Pagnin (Lotus-Festina) attacks ... 199km Pagnin caught on approach to Alto Jaizkibel. Group of about 30 riders, including Indurain, Chiappucci, Dutchman Eric Breukink (PDM), Delgado, Bugno, Argentin and American Andy Hampsten (Motorola), leads race ...
201km *Chiappucci attacks. Delgado and Bugno chase but are caught by group ...*
202km *Bugno attacks again and joins Chiappucci, as do Argentin and Delgado ...*
207km *Bugno attacks alone ... 208km Bugno still away as Delgado and Chiappucci attack each other, temporarily*

dropping Argentin ... 209km Bugno passes summit with 0:23 lead on Chiappucci, Delgado and Argentin ... 220km Just after Hondarribia and back on flat, Bugno has 0:32 on chase group of 30 which now includes Delgado, Chiappucci and Argentin ... 222km Soviet Piotr Ugrumov (Seur) attacks, taking Delgado, Fondriest, Spain's Iñaki Gaston (Clas), France's Gilles Delion (Helvetia) and Laurent Jalabert (Toshiba) and Italy's Bruno Cenghialta (Ariostea) ...227km Delgado counter-attacks alone on slight rise but is too late ... 238km Bugno wins by 0:55 on Delgado and 1:17 on six other chasers, led by Fondriest.

Championship of Zürich: 18 August

One of the most striking features of this year's Championship of Zürich was the boos and hisses of the spectators. They weren't because of a controversial crash, or an unfair result. Nor were they aimed at any particularly notorious rider. No, the object of their scorn was the entire peloton, which ambled through the first three of the five circuits of the race at a speed that any Sunday rider could have kept up with. So slowly did the peloton 'race' that the organisers even had to neutralise the amateur race, which began 30 minutes after the professionals, because it came so close to catching them!

So any hope that the Championship of Zürich might provide a last-minute insight into who to tip for the world professional road title a week away in Stuttgart was doomed to disappointment. Apart from the poor showing from American Greg LeMond (Z) who started the race suffering from a sore throat and soon abandoned, all we saw in the closing kilometres was simply confirmation of the strengths and weaknesses already revealed at San Sebastian. And the eventual win by Belgian Johan Museeuw (Lotto-Superclub) in the bunch sprint didn't affect his world title odds: immediately after his 'biggest win', Museeuw declared that he would ride only as a helper for Claude Criquielion. 'The course at Stuttgart is too hard,' he said.

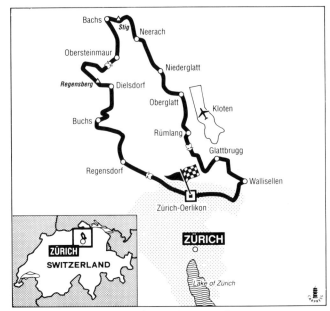

Championship of Zürich, Switzerland: 240km

Round eight of the Perrier World Cup, the race didn't really start firing up until the last circuit, which saw the end of the long solo break by Spaniard Federico Echave (Clas). He attacked after 64km, got a maximum lead of

Museeuw's victory in Zürich drew more emotion from the Belgian sprinter than the entire race managed to inspire in the unimpressed Swiss public

Echave's massive advantage at the midway point of the race seemed insurmountable ...

... but Fondriest, here leading Alcalá on the Regensberg, instigated the chase that eventually reeled him in

13:00 at 112km and then, only 25km from the finish, saw his near-victory become an exhausted defeat on the last twisting descent of the Regensberg. It was here that nine riders caught him, and the several chases and regroupments that subsequently took place constituted the most significant action of the race.

Nineteen riders formed the front group as the race passed the 220km mark. Up there were Australia's Phil Anderson (Motorola), Spain's Pedro Delgado (Banesto), Dutchmen Gert-Jan Theunisse (TVM) and Steven Rooks (Buckler), Mexico's Raúl Alcalá (PDM), Switzerland's Pascal Richard (Helvetia), Italy's Claudio Chiappucci (Carrera) and Maurizio Fondriest (Panasonic). But while it looked strong on paper, in reality it was never going to work: too many riders were looking to others to do the work, and with 11km to go they were caught by the main group.

Efforts were made in the dying kilometres. Anderson

and Delgado had a go, and even one of the contenders for the inevitable bunch sprint – Frenchman Laurent Jalabert (Toshiba) – threw his hat into the ring. But with the Lotto train chasing down every escape in order to set up Museeuw for victory, no attack was able to succeed.

And when Museeuw easily beat Jalabert and Italian Maximilian Sciandri (Carrera) in the sprint, his victory also seemed to have been inevitable. 'To win, all I had to do was follow Jalabert's wheel,' said Museeuw later. 'I knew he was the most dangerous. After that it was relatively easy to win.'

As for the World Cup rankings, Fondriest's first defence of his competition leader's jersey proved faultless. After his aggression on the final lap, which created the split, he still took fourth place and saw his points rise to 92, against the 83 of Jalabert, who scored his 11th second place of the season.

RACE DETAILS

WEATHER *Hot, but overcast in middle of day. Sunny afternoon.*

COURSE *Five 48km clockwise circuits, each including two climbs of which the most decisive is the first – the Regensberg at 16km, 64km, 112km, 160km and 208km. The second, the Stig, is at 24.5km, 72.5km, 120.5km, 168.5km, and 216.5km.*

FIELD *25 eight-man teams invited. 192 starters; 142 finishers.*

64km *After very slow start, on the second circuit Echave attacks alone on Regensberg ...* 112km *On third circuit, Echave's lead reaches a maximum of 13:00 at summit of Regensburg. Peloton's speed until now between 25-27km/h ...* 160km *On fourth circuit, Echave's lead at the Regensberg summit is down to 9:00 ...* 192km *At end of fourth circuit, gap is down to 4:30. Sammie Moreels (Lotto) of Belgium begins solo chase but is never more than 0:30 ahead ...* 208km *On fifth circuit, Echave still leads by 1:30 at Regensburg summit. Moreels is caught on climb as Fondriest, Rooks and Chiappucci force the pace, creating a split in*

the peloton. Up there too are Jalabert, Theunisse and Alcalá ... 209km *Echave is caught by chasers who are joined by others including Anderson, Soviet Dmitri Konyshev (TVM), and Belgium's Dirk De Wolf (Tonton Tapis) and then Italy's Gianni Bugno (Gatorade) and Franco Ballerini (Del Tongo), Delgado and Germany's Uwe Ampler (Histor) ...* 220km *After several regroupments, a lead group of 19 forms ...* 229km *Peloton catches break ...* 236km *Anderson and Austria's Harald Maier (PDM) attack but are chased down by Jalabert ...* 240km *Museeuw beats Jalabert and Sciandri in bunch sprint.*

NORBA Series: 25 May-18 August

Now in its fifth year, the NORBA National Championship series comprised six events designed to test the skill, endurance and tenacity of the best off-road riders over a broad range of terrain. And fittingly enough, it was world champions Ned Overend and Juli Furtado who won the national course, and demonstrated why they wear the rainbow jersey. Yeti's Furtado dominated the women's competition, winning five of the six events, including the prestigious double points final. Since each rider's worst result is dropped from the total tally, the all-conquering Furtado achieved a perfect score – the highest possible number of points. Second place went to Specialized's Sara Ballantyne, with 1990 national champion Susan DeMattei (Diamond Back) third.

Round 1: Durango, Colorado: 25-27 May
The series opener marked the return to American shores of most of the top riders, after two rounds of the Grundig/FIAC World Cup in Europe. The gruelling eight-mile circuit on the edge of Durango featured difficult climbs and long sections of technically demanding single-track over rocky terrain.

Grewal went on the offensive in the men's three-and-a-half lap race, but the Durango-resistant Tomac kept him in sight by maintaining a steady effort. Meanwhile, local favourite Overend was embroiled in a massive pile-up on the course's brutal descent, damaging his bike. But the valiant world champion came back at full power, passing 16 riders on his way to a remarkable fifth place. At the front a reserved Tomac accelerated with one lap to go, overtaking Grewal on a rock-strewn climb and then 'just started hauling ass' according to his rival, who finished 2:28 back. In third place was Grewal's GT team-mate Tom Rogers, with Wiens fourth.

The women's contest quickly became a two-lap duel between Furtado and Ballantyne, who took a two-and-a-half minute lead over DeMattei. And by pushing her advantage as a fearless descender on the ensuing rugged drop, world champion Furtado scored her first ever NORBA national win.

Round 2: Big Bear Lake, California: 15-16 June
A national series event has been held on the loose, dusty service roads and trails of Snow Summit for the past three years, making it a familiar venue for the experienced pros. The bone-dry, wide-open course featured the customary, punishing climb to the 8200-feet peak, and super-rough descents developed washboards of monstrous proportions – over nine inches deep in places.

Grewal dominated the men's race, never relinquishing the apparently easy lead he established on the first of five, 5.8-mile laps. Overend won the tight battle for second place, with Klein's unfortunate Tinker Juarez, who had double flatted in the closing moments of the race, third.

In the women's event, a potentially gut-wrenching battle between Furtado and her arch-rival Ballantyne evaporated when Ballantyne flatted three times on the final lap, leaving the masterful Furtado in absolute control of the race. Smooth-climbing DeMattei's took second place, with Darcy Dangremont-Wright (Fat Chance) third.

Round 3: Traverse City, Michigan: 29-30 June
Counting also as the fifth round of the Grundig/FIAC World Cup, the field for the third round of the NORBA series was strengthened by an influx of top European riders. The 100°F heat, combined with 90 per cent

Furtado proved worthy of her rainbow jersey with five wins from six rounds, but arch-rival Ballantyne gained her revenge with the World Cup title later in the season

Unbeatable mid season, Grewal fell victim to mechanical problems in the final and dropped from first to fifth overall

Two victories assured Tomac of a high overall position, but two rounds missed when road duty called meant the overall would remain out of reach

Overend's superbly consistent riding paid dividends and his third place in the double points final secured him the overall title

humidity and pervading shin-deep sand, pushed the riders to their physical limits, and about half the field failed to finish. But the extreme conditions produced an epic men's race – won in impressive style by Grewal. Ritchey's versatile Dane, Henrik Djernies, proved to be Grewal's toughest adversary, strongly countering his devastating attacks before falling off the pace on the final lap, but outsprinting the late-charging Polish *émigré*, Jan Wiejak (Ironhorse), for second place.

Meanwhile, Furtado torched the women's international field to win her third World Cup series in four tries, and make it three out of three in the NORBA series. Furtado rode through the infernal heat like a woman possessed, winning the 29-mile race with an astonishing nine-minute margin. 'That's the hardest thing I've ever done,' panted the world champion after crossing the line. Churning the sandy trails behind her in the battle for second place, Ballantyne just beat Germany's Regina Stiefl (Scott).

Round 4: Mammoth Lakes, California: 17-21 July

Situated in dramatic, chilly Sierra Nevada, with a base elevation of 9000 feet, and characterised by long, grinding climbs on service roads, flat gravelly descents and limited single-tracks, Mammoth is one of the least technically demanding courses on the circuit. Nonetheless, this cross-country is justifiably infamous for its extreme climbing challenge and its seriously thin air. A drastic shake-down occured in both men's and women's title races, the 'Rishi and Juli freight train' being finally derailed as both riders suffered a seriously 'off' day. In the men's event, Wiens rode a dream race, out-powering the international field and dropping second-placed Tomac by over four minutes with his inexorable climbing style. Overend again fell victim to mechanical troubles, but the tenacious world champion kept on the pressure to recover a third place finish. Grewal, in an unaccustomed fifth place, nevertheless maintained his overall NORBA lead and took the Grundig leadership from no-show Gerhard Zadrobilek.

The two-lap women's race yielded a surprise victory for Matthes, who outclimbed the more experienced Ballantyne to take her first off-road victory, with Giant's Tammy Jacques third. Furtado finished eighth, but remained in control of the NORBA series points, with Ballantyne closing in.

Round 5: Park City, Utah: 27-28 July

The last stop before heading east for the finale in Vermont, Park City presented a multi-dimensional course. Set in aspen groves around the ski resort of Deer Valley, the five mile loop contained steep climbs, twisting technical descents and plenty of forest single track for a well rounded-test. Overend claimed his first major victory of the season, confirming his reputation for reaching top form for the late season 'crunch' events. His swift climbing carried him to victory over Rogers, while the consistent Juarez was third. Early leader Tomac was eliminated for accepting aid with his second flat tyre; Grewal also suffered a disappointing puncture, but managed sixth place and kept the overall lead.

Furtado avenged her disappointment at Mammoth with yet another brilliant victory in the tough four-lap women's race. And Matthes proved her technical ability by streaking in second, ahead of the favoured Ballantyne.

Round 6: Mount Snow, Vermont: 14-18 August

With double points on offer, no less than ten men had a chance of ousting Grewal from the lead, making the muddy finale a tense duel. And while Tomac scored a convincing win over the seven-lap, 3-mile circuit, an even more fascinating drama was unfolding behind him.

Would-be national champions Juarez, Wiens and top-ranked Grewal all waxed and waned as the technically demanding race wore on. A wide-open 650-foot climb split the field early, and was followed by a hazardous, mile-long muddy single track descent – lined with slippery exposed tree roots – before returning to the start/finish area. Nerves jangled, spelling the eventual demise of Grewal (due to mechanical problems) and Juarez (who blew up trying to keep pace with Tomac) – to name but two. But one rider who calculated his position and put in a powerful, tactical ride was the wily Overend. Successfully defending his national crown for another year, the superbly fit Colorado rider advanced from third overall to clinch the NORBA title on the final, all-important day.

In the women's title race, Furtado posted the brilliant win her fans have come to expect. Ballantyne needed double points to keep any hope of a win, but Furtado held the symbolic white jersey from begining to end. The battle between the front runners carried them well clear of the fight for third place, taken by DeMattei.

World Championships: 13-25 August

The success, efficiency and friendly atmosphere of the 1990 World Championships in Japan was always going to be a hard act to follow. The location of the 1991 edition, Stuttgart – 'the Detroit of Germany' – was hardly endowed with the magic of Japan, or many another old European city for that matter. Not only was the surrounding vista of factories, offices, railway lines and car-parks uninspiring; for the competitors, the urban and road congestion that was so wrongly feared to exist in Japan's world title sites of Maebashi and Utsunomiya was like a nightmare come true in Stuttgart.

Nevertheless, the championships did go on – even if the legendary German efficiency seemed to be more myth than reality. And when the 20 championships were decided, Germany topped the medal table, winning six gold, five silver and one bronze. Eleven of their medals came from the track events, held from 13-18 August. In the road championships, held between 21 and 25 August, Italy proved to be the dominant nation, winning three medals, including two gold. But the award for consistent performance would have to go to the Netherlands, who finished second overall with three track and three road medals.

Will the balance of power change in 1992? We will have to look to Spain, host to the 1992 Olympic Games in Barcelona and World Championships in Benidorm, for the answer to that.

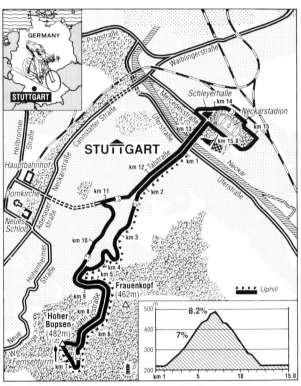

Road circuit, Stuttgart, Germany: 15.8km

Gianni Bugno's brilliant win in the professional road race championship endowed the World Championships with well-earned prestige

Between them, the Spanish and Italian teams shared control of the race to great effect. Here, Pedro Delgado leads the peloton in the first half of the race with Chioccioli to his right, and Alvaro Mejia, Raúl Alcalá and Laurent Fignon to his left

Road events

Men's professional road race: 25 August

It was almost inevitable that the blue-ribbon event of the 1991 World Championships would have an Italian flavour to it. Not only did the Italians have a team that, on paper, was head and shoulders above any other, plus an outstanding individual favourite in Gianni Bugno. There was also, following Italy's gold and silver in the men's team time trial and the amateur road race respectively, a feeling transcending hope in the Italian camp that they were impossible to beat.

Yet even so, Bugno's eventual win the 252.8km race from three fellow breakaways was still an inspiration. For it confirmed not only how well a good team can work, but also that the 27-year-old Bugno's billing as the next Italian *campionissimo* was justified. It was a testimony to Bugno's characteristic modesty that after outsprinting Dutch champion Steven Rooks and Spain's Tour de France champion Miguel Indurain to win the gold medal, world title and *arc en ciel* jersey, he was still unwilling to accept the honour. 'I know that to reach the level of *campionissimo* I still need to win the Tour de France and have that yellow jersey in Paris,' he said.

The Italian *tifosi* might argue with that. So too might many others around the world. For the black-haired, gimlet-eyed Gatorade leader has never disappointed public expectations since he first stunned everyone with his Giro d'Italia victory last year. In that season he won 14 races and the World Cup and hit the number one spot in the world FICP rankings. And in the World Championship road race he took the bronze medal. This year has seen him rise to the occasion just as impressively. His performances in the Italian and French national Tours were consistent, although they fell short

of revealing his best form; that started coming after the Tour de France with victory in the Clasicá San Sebastian and several smaller World Championship lead-ups.

But there is no doubt that his win at Stuttgart, in his eleventh season as a professional, was his greatest. And he revealed his own joy in winning by his uncharacteristic victory salute. 'I raised my arms because the occasion was too great to let it pass. Normally I don't do it, but how could I deprive myself of such a gesture of joy at the moment when I had the world title in my hands?', he said.

As always, the world title race was decided by the last few laps. With five riders in the decisive group of 34 which got away on lap 13, the Italians were always in control of events, despite efforts from the Spaniards, Dutch and French, the latter of whom also had five men up front. Sensing that any one of them had the form to win, Bugno's team-mates launched a barrage of attacks in the last two laps to make sure of a strong Italian presence in the finale. Hence the prominence of Maurizio Fondriest, Claudio Chiappucci, Davide Cassani and Franco Ballerini.

There were attempts to reduce the odds in Italy's favour. Defending World Champion Rudy Dhaenens of Belgium suddenly found the form that had eluded him all year, and he tried to make a move. Frenchman Gérard Rué was also in aggressive mood, as too was Denmark's Bjarne Riis and the Australian Neil Stephens, who surprised everyone when he set off on the last climb in pursuit of Fondriest and France's Marc Madiot. But their only rewards finally were the minor placings because, as the two-year-old Italian renaissance has shown us, when Bugno and the Italian *squadra* are on fire, nothing can put out the flames.

RACE DETAILS

WEATHER *Early morning cloud cleared; sunny by race start. Temperature 22°C.*

COURSE *16 laps of 15.8km circuit, totalling 252.8km. Circuit includes one 7.6km climb with maximum 8.2% gradient (average 4.23%).*

FIELD *27 nations represented. Each team allowed 12 riders, but nation of defending World Champion (Belgian Rudy Dhaenens) allowed 13 riders. 191 starters, 96 finishers.*
    Peloton holds steady pace for first eight laps. Highlights include ... Lap 1 American champion Davis Phinney abandons ... Lap 2 at 20km Italian Moreno Argentin crashes, but is not injured ... Lap 4 Pole Zenon Jaskula joins list of eight abandons ... Lap 7 Spaniards

Marino Alonso and Alberto Leanizbarrutia attempt first attack but fail.

Lap 9 (completes 142km) Attack by Denmark's John Carlsen, Frenchman Bruno Cornillet, Germany's Uwe Ampler, Spain's Eduardo Chozas and Italy's Franco Chioccioli. Chiappucci chases and peloton regroups. American Greg LeMond is at back of peloton.

Lap 10 (completes 158km) Bugno attacks on climb but is caught. 11-man group attacks with Chiappucci who accelerates at summit. He is joined by Germany's Rolf Aldag, Belgium's Edwig Van Hooydonck, Switzerland's Pascal Richard, Italy's Massimiliano Lelli, and French champion Armand De Las Cuevas. They finish lap with 0:17 on Colombian Alberto Camargo, 0:24 on

another group of six (including Frenchman Charly Mottet) and 0:42 on the peloton.

Lap 11 (completes 173km) Leaders chased by Spanish-led peloton. Ireland's Sean Kelly and Stephen Roche abandon ...
Lap 12 (completes 89km) Leaders caught soon into lap. At foot of climb Dutchman Eric Breukink attacks and is joined by Frenchman Thierry Claveyrolat. They get 0:20 lead but are caught on descent. Abandonees include LeMond and Denmark's Rolf Sörensen ... Lap 13 (completes 205km) Germany's Rolf Gölz attacks on climb. Fondriest and Belgium's Dirk De Wolf chase. Peloton splits because of crash; 34 riders in front group. At end of lap gap is 0:55.

Lap 14 (completes 221km) Gap widens to 1:57 between lead group and peloton ...
Lap 15 (completes 237km)

Spain's Pedro Delgado attacks. Rué and Gölz follow and group rejoins. Fondriest attacks on climb, followed by Madiot. At summit they have 0:15 on group; 0:28 at end of lap.

Lap 16 (completes 252km) On last ascent Stephens, Cassani and – by himself – Argentina's Daniel Castro chase Fondriest and Madiot. Delgado, Dutchman Gert-Jan Theunisse and Soviet Piotr Ugrumov force pace in group. Gölz attacks but is followed by Bugno who, when Fondriest and Madiot are caught, also attacks. With Bugno are Indurain, Rooks and Colombia's Alvaro Mejia. Their lead gets to 0:20, but drops under chase to 0:15 with 3km to go. Bugno leads out sprint with 300m to go and wins from Rooks (2nd) and Indurain (3rd).

Bugno leads Indurain and Mejia into the last four kilometres

Not even the most sophisticated technology could stop the German men's time trial team from losing to Italy

The French women produced a scorching ride to win the team time trial for the first time

Men's and women's team time trials: 21 August

The first two of the road titles to be held, the men's and women's team time trials saw contrasting wins by Italy and France respectively. Italy's victory in the men's 100km race over Germany and Norway produced a very convincing result, while France's win in the women's 50km event over the Netherlands and the Soviet Union was extremely close.

Italy, scoring their first world title win in the discipline since 1987 at Villach in Austria, clocked 1:54.48 for the two-lap race, against 1:57.21 of Germany and 1:57.39 of Norway, whose result was the biggest shock of the event – worth remembering come the 1992 Olympic Games. Yet while the race for the silver and bronze medals was close, Italy's authority was clearly too daunting to challenge, recording as they did the fastest time at every interval.

For the Germans, the pressure of carrying on where their track team left off was immense. And they did well to finish where they did. 'Though my riders are disappointed, I am happy. The pressure was so great,' said the German coach Peter Weibel. 'While we started fast, the Italians started very fast. They were always the great favourites for me.'

Meanwhile, in the women's race, only 0:37 separated the first three places. France's time of 1:02.14 was enough to see them take the gold and defeat last year's gold medallists, the Netherlands, this year without Leontien Van Moorsel, who clocked 1:02.41. And the Soviet Union won their third medal of the titles, with a bronze-medal-winning time of 1:02.51.

Certainly the disappointing performance of the United States had a bearing on this result. Last year's silver medallists dropped team-mate Maureen Manley in the first 10km and finally finished just out of a medal place – fourth with 1:03.03.

The team time trials, contested on a slightly rising out-and-back 25km course, were followed by a two-day break before the road programme resumed with the men's and women's amateur events.

Women's road race: 24 August

Leontien Van Moorsel never disguised her designs on the 78km women's world road race title. After failing to qualify for the 3000-metre pursuit which she won last year, the Dutchwoman quickly dismissed her lack-lustre performance by saying she was in Stuttgart only to win the road race.

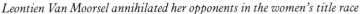

Leontien Van Moorsel annihilated her opponents in the women's title race

A late attack – or an early sprint – won the amateur title for Viktor Riaksinski of the Soviet Union

And putting all her eggs in that particular basket was a gamble that finally paid off when she crossed the finish line 1:54 clear of America's silver medallist Inga Thompson and 2:46 ahead of the peloton, led by Canada's Alison Sydor who took the bronze medal. And judging by the precision with which she attacked the field on the ascent halfway through the five-lap course, it was less of a gamble than it had seemed a week earlier, when her track performance had left everyone wondering what went wrong.

Van Moorsel's solo break was the first sign of aggression in a race that began under showers and was contested on a wet and slippery road surface that caused many crashes in the first two laps. And, barring Thompson's late chase, it was the only effective show of strength to be seen. Once more, the women's world road title was swamped by the domination of one rider and turned into a race for the minor placings. Without belittling Van Moorsel's undoubted class, determination and sheer strength, it was all the same a sad finale to a race that should have been hotly contested – especially in light of the on-paper strength of the French team, which boasted names like defending champion Catherine Marsal, American-born Marion Clignet and Cécile Odin. But once Van Moorsel's lead reached 0:20, the fight seemed to go out of the French riders.

Even had they tried, it is doubtful – given Van Moorsel's strength – whether they could have made any impact. As Van Moorsel said afterwards, 'The first lap was quite slow. When I saw the faces of the others who looked as if they had had it, I felt stronger than them,' she said. And then: 'I can't believe I am World Champion!' But deep down she probably asked herself could she have believed it were she not.

Men's amateur road race: 24 August

Raced almost immediately after the women's road race – although in warm and sunny conditions that left the road dry – the men's amateur world road title was full of electricity. The 11-lap, 178km race saw numerous solo and group attacks set off, before the decisive break got free on the final circuit.

The group, numbering eight riders, formed after several changes on lap 11 and came from a lead group of 13 that attacked on lap 6 and was split by a barrage of devastating attacks from Brazil's Magalhaes Azevedo that at one time looked like creating a major upset. But the Belgian-based Brazilian, whose aggression led to the final eight-man group forming and kept him in the running for a place in the finale, finally ran out of puff on the last circuit and was dropped.

In the winning group which finished 0:23 ahead of the chasing peloton were two Italians, two Soviets, and two Swiss, plus one Pole and a Frenchman. But the world title finally went to the Soviet 1991 Peace Race winner Viktor Riaksinki who jumped from the back of the group with 500 metres to go and led out the sprint.

Twenty-four year old Riaksinki's victory was even a surprise to the Soviets as he was originally the team's second leader, the first being Viatcheslav Djavanian, who was in the break as well and finally finished fourth. But as Riaksinki later said: 'I rode for him up until the 500 metres to go sign. Then, I knew the main group was coming behind and just as our group hesitated a bit, I knew the door was open to surprise everyone.'

That he certainly did. And as the image of Riaksinki and Djavanian hugging each other later proved, there was no ill-feeling that one's hopes were sacrificed for the other's. In fact, Riaksinki's win over Italy's Davide Rebellin and Switzerland's Beat Zberg was a most timely one for the Soviets, who were under immense psychological pressure because of the attempted *coup* of Mikhail Gorbachev back in the Soviet Union. It was also the Soviets' fourth and last medal for the entire championships. 'The situation in the Soviet Union did leave its mark on us,' he said afterwards. 'Such things can lead to psychological problems. But now I have won the world title ....!'

The well-used six-day velodrome of Hans-Martin Schleyer Halle hosted the opening week of the World Championships

Track events

The unification of East and West Germany may have led to political, social and economic turmoil, but in sporting terms it was an unqualified success. In this year's cycling, rowing and athletics world championships, Germany's first appearance as a united nation led to impressive and startling degrees of domination. It was only in swimming at the European titles that German strength saw any decline.

In cycling, German strength was particularly prominent in the track events of the World Championships, held from 13-18 August. From the fifteen track titles contested, the Germans walked off with six gold medals, four silver and one bronze. And whilst they were unable to repeat their outstanding performance for the road events, their supremacy on the track was the big talking point of the championships. The words of one Soviet coach best summed up the impact of bringing East and West Germanys together. 'Unification seems to be as good as doping for the Germans. They now ride with twice as much power,' he said, perhaps forgetting that it wasn't too long ago that most of the world was wondering the same thing about the Soviet Union. This year, the Soviets won only two track medals – Viatcheslav Ekimov's gold in the professional 50km points race and a silver in the amateur 4000-metre team pursuit.

The Soviets were not the only ones to be surprised by the Germans' ability to mould two strong teams into one formidable unit, dispensing in the process with speculation that the team would prove to be riddled with divisive rivalries. Everyone was surprised ... including some within the German team, such as Michael Hübner. The daunting former East German, defending champion in both professional sprint and keirin events, said: 'I was surprised with how unified the team

was, and how quickly it all came about.'

Sadly for Hübner, he was unable to win a back-to-back sprint title – an event marred by the drug scandal of two Australians, Carey Hall and Stephen Pate, who were stripped of their respective gold and bronze medals after being tested positive for the steroid stanozolol. Finally, first and third places were left vacant. But Hübner's chance for revenge came in the keirin; he beat Italy's Claudio Golinelli and French neo-professional, Fabrice Colas – the sprint silver medallist – to win Germany's fifth world title. The other German wins came in the women's individual pursuit (Petra Rossner) and the men's amateur 4000-metre individual pursuit (Jens Lehmann), the team pursuit, the sprint (Jens Fiedler) and the final championship to be decided, the tandem.

Arguably Germany's greatest performance was in pursuiting, or more precisely in the person of the former East German Jens Lehmann, who not only won the individual title from Stuttgart local, Michael Glockner, but teamed up with Glockner and two other former West Germans to win the team pursuit from the Soviets and Australians after setting a world record time for the 4000 metres in the qualifying heat. For Lehmann, and to a degree Glockner, it was a remarkable feat, and even more notable because they had also clocked world best times for the individual pursuit of 4:22.152 and 4:22.602 in the qualifying heat.

But in the team pursuit, riding their new carbon-fibre bicycles, they returned to clock 4:08.064 in the time trial-style qualifier. Then in the ensuing match races in the quarter- and semi-finals they bettered this with times of 4:07.07 and 4:06.244 respectively, before finishing with a 4:07.003 in the final against the Soviet Union, who fell in a heap to clock a demoralised 4:12.259. However, the statisticians' ink was allowed to dry as the latter German times were made in races against another team and as a result could not be considered for world record sanctioning by the UCI.

What then were the causes of such dominance? Having home crowd support of the extreme ear-piercing levels reached at Stuttgart was always going to favour the Germans. The nightly thunder and roar of nationalistic cheers was nothing less than inspiring for the German riders, and nothing less than terrifying for those who dared take them on. But other factors also played a part. Firstly, there was the benefit of having two sources of sports science, coaching and technology to draw upon. Then, for the amateurs and women, there was an overwhelming desire to perform; the wealth of cycling talent brought together by unification made the competition for an Olympic team berth for the 1992 Games all the more desperate. For the professionals, like Hübner, there was immense pressure to impress sponsors, who had invested US $3.52 million in advertising at the track events. On top of that, for all competitors, there was the very basic incentive of the financial bonuses offered by the German cycling federation – as they were by most other federations – to any cyclist becoming world champion.

Thankfully, other nations did get some of the pickings – albeit a rather minor share. After Germany in the track medal standings was the Netherlands, with three medals – two golds and a bronze. Then came France who won six medals – one gold, two silvers, and three bronze. The main highlights of the battle for the nine medals the Germans *didn't* win were Frenchman Francis Moreau's 5000-metre professional pursuit victory over the British pair of second-placed Shaun Wallace and third-placed Colin Sturgess; Australian Danny Clark's professional motor-paced victory, which marked his fourth career world title and his last world championship appearance – one week before his 40th birthday; and Spaniard José-Manuel Moreno's unexpected win in the 1000-metre amateur time trial, over the favoured German Jens Glücklich and Trinidad's biggest-ever cycling surprise Gene Samuel. Then there was Switzerland's Bruno Risi's win over defending champion, Steve McGlede of Australia, in the amateur 30km points race, and Austrian Roland Königshofer's third successive victory in the amateur motor-paced race.

But perhaps the greatest sensation of the 1991 Worlds was the 27-year-old policewoman Ingrid Haringa who – having started cycling only two months earlier after an ice-skating career – won the women's sprint and 30km points titles, becoming the only dual gold medallist this year. In the sprint she defeated Germany's Annette Neumann in two straight matches, while the race for the bronze medal saw defending champion Connie Paraskevin-Young triumph with a similar win over France's Felicia Ballanger. Then in the points race, Haringa pipped Belgium's Kristel Werckx and America's Janie Eickhoff, who were on equal points, by three points.

Haringa's winning streak made her this year's 'Queen of the Track', upstaging not only her compatriot Leontien Van Moorsel, who failed to get beyond the

Janie Eickhoff thought she was well on her way to a gold medal in the individual pursuit . . .

qualifying round of the women's pursuit she won in Japan last year, but also the German Rossner, who defeated Eickhoff in a most controversial pursuit final. The dispute that followed Rossner's narrow win over the American highlighted some of the ill-feeling that was brewing against the local stranglehold on the titles. For when the pursuit final was rescheduled 15 minutes earlier, so that the final – and Rossner's fancied victory – could be broadcast live on TV, everyone knew but Eickhoff's camp.

The plucky, stocky American rushed up to the velodrome in a fluster. And, when Rossner had nearly two seconds lead after 1000m, it looked as though Eickhoff was finished. Nobody thought she would fight back the way she did, and they certainly didn't expect her to hit the lead in the second kilometre and threaten to take the gold medal. That she nearly accomplished,

Viatcheslav Ekimov swopped his pursuit crown for the points title, and is seen here in company with Francis Moreau lapping the field for the second time during the 50-kilometre event

Jens Lehmann, seen here in the final of the 4000-metres pursuit, was the only double gold-medal winner of the championships

Ingrid Haringa shocked the host nation by beating German champion Annette Neumann in the sprint – then went out and won the 50-kilometre points race as well!

and certainly would have, had the home crowd not cheered Rossner on to race back from a 0:01 deficit with one lap to go and win by 0:111.

Eickhoff's despair was clear. So was the resentment amongst the visiting teams against the unpredictable and rather questionable scheduling of events throughout the titles. It was just unfortunate that it took a world title final and Eickhoff's arguable loss of a gold medal to provoke a protest. That came when head coaches from each team met on the final day of track events to set up a

coaches' body to 'find better ways of developing the sport of track cycling,' as one coach explained. Basically, it was designed to let all nations have a say in race programming and scheduling – in not only World Championship meetings, but in the Olympic Games as well. The lesson learnt by the rest of the world in the 1991 World Championships was that it is going to be hard enough to compete against a united Germany on an even playing field, without having to contend with administrative disadvantages as well.

After his victory in the individual pursuit, Lehmann powered the German team through a world record en route to winning the team pursuit

Francis Moreau became a very stylish professional pursuit champion, beating Britain's Shaun Wallace in the final

THE TRACK

Located inside Stuttgart's Hans-Martin Schleyer Halle, the 285m wooden velodrome was built in 1983 and is regarded as one of the fastest in Europe. And the speed is not simply because it is indoors, but also because of its long straights adjoining each bank. It is no coincidence that the track, the site of the annual Stuttgart six-day race in winter, was also where Italy's Francesco Moser followed up his world outdoor high-altitude hour record with the world indoor record of 50.644km/h as well. So you could say that the barrage of world records and world best times recorded at the 1991 World Championships was not that surprising.

The fully air-conditioned velodrome, situated only 300m from the finish line of the road events and only a few kilometres from the centre of Stuttgart, seats 5000 spectators and, like most multi-purpose sports halls, is equipped with bars, restaurants, cafes and – for the cyclists – showering facilities. If you count the standing room as well, the velodrome can accommodate up to 7000 people – and for many of the fifteen track events contested over six days, it did.

A rare sight: two Britons – Shaun Wallace and Colin Sturgess – share the winner's podium with professional pursuit champion Francis Moreau

Grundig World Cup Series: 27 April–8 September

1991 saw the establishment of a UCI-sanctioned World Cup series, sponsored by Grundig, that completed the 'mondialisation' of mountain biking in line with road racing. There was an equal split of events on both sides of the Atlantic and a double points final in Berlin just a few weeks before the World Championships in Italy. And what a series it proved to be! Seven different winners from the nine rounds – just John Tomac and Tim Gould managing to win two apiece – and an overall classification not decided until the final event!

Round 1: Bassano del Grappa, Italy: 27-28 April
First blood to the Europeans: Tim Gould scored an impressive victory in the northern Italian town that had played host to the World Road Championships in 1985. On the steep road climbs that linked the off-road sections the leading group of eight riders was whittled down to four – Gould, Tomac, Glazja and Grewal. First to crack was Grewal, then Tomac punctured out of the picture leaving Gould to deal with his Czech rival in a re-run of the Grundig round in Belgium the previous year. Then it was Glazja who dropped Gould on the last climb to win, but this year Gould gained his revenge, attacking when a bad gear change caused Glazja to lose momentum on a steep climb, and racing away to a 37-second victory and the first ever blue leader's jersey.

Juli Furtado showed her surprise world title in 1990 was no fluke, winning by nearly two minutes over Sara Ballantyne, who narrowly outsprinted Regina Steifl in a 1 hour, 28 minute race.

John Tomac clinched the World Cup with victory in the heavily weighted, double points final in Berlin

Round 2: Manosque, France: 4-5 May
What a difference a week makes! The story was not so much of the race but the non-qualification of series leader Gould due to a pair of snapped handlebars in the qualifying race, used to obtain a start line order for a main race. With the jersey up for grabs it was John Tomac who never lost the lead on the toughest course of the series to head an American top three placing, being followed by Tom Rogers and Mike Kloser who both overtook an unfortunate Glazja, delayed by a puncture; but his fourth place was good enough to take over in blue.

No change to the women's top three placings from the previous week's. The positions on this severe circuit underlined Furtado's early season form, although even she admitted to being 'out of control' on the fearsome descents. Ballantyne, 2:39 down, was again out of touch, but this time a straight 34 seconds clear of Steifl.

Round 3: Groesbeek, Holland: 25-26 May
With the Americans back across the pond contesting their first national series race, the flat sandy parkland of Groesbeek proved a cyclo-cross rider's dream. From the gun the line out of the top twenty riders flew around the circuit in a haze of dust, but out of sight straight away went Peter Hric from Czechoslovakia with a comfortable minute's lead, whilst behind him havoc reigned as the frantic pace snapped the string of riders. Out of the mêlée on the last lap came two of Germany's best 'cross men, Kluge and Kizukenbaum, just ahead of Gould, proving he is not just a mountain man, but failing by a single point to take the jersey. This passed from the non-finishing Glazja to the consistent Austrian Gerhard Zadrobilek.

The American women accompanied their male counterparts back home, leaving Steifl to outpace the Swiss duet of Chantal Daucourt and Sylvia Fürst and move into the overall lead.

Round 4: St Anne, Canada: 22-23 June
A new continent and a new winner – this time talented youngster Daryl Price stole the show from fellow-countryman Dave Wiens and an inspired Zadrobilek. Two rounds all and a European in blue, but the American courses loomed and Europe's domination looked to be in trouble – especially with ace climber Gould sidelined by a broken collar-bone.

Ballantyne finally got the win she deserved, but only just: Fürst caught the American with 500 metres to go, narrowly losing out in a tight sprint. Puncture victim Furtado was third and series leader Steifl fifth, holding onto the jersey by a slim two points over Furtado, with Ballantyne a single point behind.

Round 5: Traverse City, Michigan: 29-30 June
In incredible 100°F heat and 90% humidity, American Rishi Grewal rode to a suberb win over Danish 'cross star Hendrik Djernies. These two had left the rest for dead and attacked each other constantly until Grewal attacked once too often for Djernies, leaving him to salvage second in a sprint finish with Pole Jan Wiejak.

Sara Ballantyne leap-frogged arch-rival and fellow American Juli Furtado, the series-long leader, following her second place in Berlin − being beaten to first by DeMattei − and Furtado's collapse to a disappointing sixth

Dave Wiens only had to finish the Berlin final higher than ninth, if Tomac won, to secure the overall victory. An unsuitable circuit for his climbing talents, plus a crash at the start meant he came 12th, and lost the title

Zadrobilek showed amazing consistency to gain his fifth top ten placing of the series and hang on to the overall lead.

After the previous round's disappointment Furtado came back with a bang, thrashing her closest rival Ballantyne by nearly nine minutes, with third-placed Steifl over ten-and-a-half minutes down. 'The hardest thing I've ever done', Furtado was heard to say after the finish, but then wins of nine minutes never come easily!

Round 6: Mammoth Lakes, California: 20-21 July
The altitude of Mammoth hosted a crushing show of strength by Dave Wiens, who turned the screws on Tomac on the long dusty climbs to race to a clear four-minute victory. Third place went to reigning world champion Ned Overend − quiet so far this season, but starting to show signs of form as the major races loomed. With Zadrobilek back in Europe the jersey passed to Grewal, who was fifth on the day, but again consistently in the top ten throughout the series.

With her first ever off-road win, road star Ruthie Matthes changed the order for once with a clear victory over Ballantyne and Furtado out of the running in an unaccustomed eighth place. Series leader Furtado was stopped by her manager at the end of the first lap and instructed to put on the blue Grundig leader's jersey to avoid a time penalty, but the move obviously damaged her motivation and she finished nearly 14 minutes down.

Round 7: Park City, Utah: 27-28 July
The last round in the States before the entourage returned to Europe gave Overend his first win of the series, helped a little by punctures to Tomac − who led the race in its early stages − and series leader Grewal. Tomac was eliminated for accepting help with his second flat of the day, but Grewal managed to salvage sixth to keep his grip on the jersey.

Furtado bounced back to record her fourth win from six starts, helped by Ballantyne's first lap crash and the slower descending of Mammoth winner Matthes, who was unable to match her fearless downhill expertise on the final lap.

Round 8: Chateau d'Eux, Switzerland: 31 August-1 September
The biggest surprise of the series to date was the win by Canada's Alison Sydor, bronze medallist in the previous week's world road championships. Sydor was never out of the lead, with Ballantyne a minute adrift and her sprinting partner on home turf Fürst, running Ballantyne to a tight finish, in third place.

In the men's race Gould, back with a bang after his enforced lay-off, romped around the beautiful alpine resort to his second win of the series. He was delayed on the last two miles by a tangled chain which reduced his two-minute advantage to a handful of seconds over Europe-based American Mike Kloser, but Gould managed a nasty repair and put the hammer down to open the gap back up to half a minute at the end. Wiens overtook Tomac late in the race to claim third and wrest the jersey from Grewal. One race left, double points and all to play for!

Round 9: Berlin, Germany: 7-8 September
A small park in east Berlin might seem an incongruous setting for the last race in a fine series, especially with so much at stake, but sponsors' wishes must be accommodated, so with no mountains in sight the race was on.

Straight into a lead he was never to relinquish rode John Tomac, and that was simply that! A great race for the minor placings saw Tinker Juarez out-pace the ever present Zadrobilek, but the fast, demanding circuit saw the overall aspirations of Wiens and Grewal go out of the window and the double points meant a big change to the final overall. With the best five rounds plus the final to count Tomac scraped home by a single point from Zadrobilek, with a disappointed Wiens third, just four points behind Tomac.

The women's final ended as dramatically, with another new name on the podium, Susan DeMattei. DeMattei outsprinted Ballantyne, who had the consolation of taking the overall title from Furtado, who managed only sixth place in this crucial double-point finale. Consistent Chantal Daucourt chased hard all day to claim third place, ahead of Steifl who held on to third overall.

Grand Prix de la Liberation: 10 September

Team time trialling is one of the unsung disciplines of cycling – highly specialised, almost an art form, in which cohesion is a must. All the members of a team must pedal at a tempo everyone can follow: a team is as strong as its weakest member.

And we were treated to a copybook example of good team trialling by the Dutch Buckler team at this year's Grand Prix de la Liberation – the ninth round of the Perrier World Cup, counting for teams classification. Nineteen teams took part, but only the Spanish ONCE team threatened Buckler in their run to victory on the flat, 90km, two-lap course at Eindhoven in the Netherlands. Buckler, after having the fastest time by 0:18 at the half-way point, rode on to hold that lead and finish in 1:37.15 to ONCE's 1:37.33. Panasonic was third with 1:37.57, and fourth was last year's winner PDM who, on their home territory (Eindhoven is the base of PDM), clocked 1:38.40.

Buckler *directeur sportif* Jan Raas had a special reason to celebrate: his team achieved their victory at the expense of his Dutch rivals PDM – a highly satisfactory way to avenge their third place last year.

By contrast, ONCE's second place for the second year running – and by a margin as narrow as 0:18 – was a sour defeat for an exhausted team. While their shortfall was smaller this time round, ONCE's performance was not nearly as good as last year's. 'There was more spark in the team last year. There was more purpose to what we were doing. This year, several guys were exhausted before the start, Marino Lejarreta being one of them,' lamented ONCE's Australian team member Stephen Hodge afterwards.

Frustratingly, this diagnosis has been common to most of the events ONCE has contested in 1991. Their attempt to win all three major Tours, as they so nearly did in 1990, was unsuccessful, apart from Melchor Mauri's victory in the Vuelta – but it certainly took its toll on the riders. Many of them had found it hard enough to struggle through to the end of the season, let alone live up to the ambitions ONCE *directeur sportif* Manolo Saiz had been harbouring for them.

And alas, ONCE will not have another opportunity to avenge their defeat: not only will the Grand Prix de la Liberation not be a World Cup race next year, it will not even be contested. The reason is the lack of interest – by teams, sponsors and all the media. From all their points of view, Grand Prix de la Liberation suffers from numerous disadvantages. It only counts for World Cup

Second place, at only 0:18, rubbed salt into the ONCE wounds; they came second last year as well. Despite a promising start their exhaustion showed and spoilt what could have been

The pressure to race well on home ground was immense for PDM, especially after their disastrous Tour de France. Under the circumstances, it was an honourable fourth place

Team time trialling is one of cycling's most difficult disciplines. Yet Buckler produced a near-perfect display of precision, power and cohesion at the Grand Prix de la Liberation, proving how well it can be done

points as a team event, so individual riders have nothing to gain from it. In addition, coming right after the Grand Prix Lazio in Italy, in which many teams and riders compete, the time trial teams often lack their strongest riders. And from the point of view of the spectators and the media, it is a dull race contested in drab surroundings. Unlike 1991, it was not even covered live on television this year; all the local TV station could manage was a later broadcast of the final stages. And the lack of enthusiasm affected the racing at Eindhoven: many of the teams who are normally powerhouses in team time trialling − an element which is critical in races like the Tour de France − produced lacklustre performances. The results were proof enough.

Under grey clouds that released rainfalls in the morning, it was always Buckler, PDM, Panasonic and ONCE who controlled affairs, although dark horses Motorola and Tulip caused the leaders a few anxious moments with their quick first lap times. After the first circuit, Buckler and ONCE had the two best times of 47:06 and 47:22 respectively, but Motorola were third fastest in 47:36 and Tulip were fourth in 47:52.

Panasonic and PDM were only fifth and seventh respectively, split by 1989 winners TVM.

Desperation to impress proved decisive in the race for minor placings; Motorola and Tulip both faded to finish sixth and seventh at 2:02 and 2:34 respectively, whereas the Dutch units wound up their speeds. PDM's ability to fight back, after their troubles in July, was particularly encouraging. And while they were only fourth this year, this performance boosted their morale for the remaining end of season races.

Interestingly, all of the top teams bar Tulip finished with their complement of six riders still intact. Although the course at Eindhoven was windy, it was dead flat and ideal for team time trialling.

On the World Cup team standings, Buckler's victory was not good enough to topple their rivals Panasonic from the number one spot: Panasonic's tally moved up to 87 points against Buckler's 78. The main change was PDM's move up to third with 44 points, ousting Ariostea who did not take part at Eindhoven. Whereas Motorola rose from 17th to equal 12th place with RMO, their team score rising eight points to 19.

Paris-Brussels: 18 September

Like Ghent-Wevelgem, Paris-Brussels is a race that now faces an uncertain future. And like its spring counterpart, the 1991 edition of the mid-week 'Race of the Two Capitals' was only saved from oblivion by an historic result. While Ghent-Wevelgem produced its first Soviet winner in Djamolidin Abdujaparov (Carrera), Brian Holm (Histor) become the first Dane ever to win Paris-Brussels.

The blond 28-year-old's attack 8km from the finish – at the entrance to Brussels' Bois de la Cambre – went unchallenged by the teams with sprinters like Abdujaparov, Belgium's Johan Museeuw (Lotto), and Germany's Olaf Ludwig (Panasonic), who might reasonably have been expected to chase down his escape. And without trying to detract from Holm's effort, the apathy only further dulled the already tarnished image of the event, which for local residents causes more headaches than entertainment.

As it does every year, the race's peak hour arrival on city-centre Avenue Emile Jacqmain created mammoth traffic jams, making entering and leaving the European capital a near-impossible feat. Then, due to a shortage of money, the traditional live television coverage was scrapped and replaced by a broadcast that evening of race highlights, sandwiched between the first and second halves of that night's European Cup soccer match. The final straw was when the Belgian police, ever keen to make their presence felt, confiscated race radio scanners (strictly illegal in Belgium, but nonetheless permitted during every spring classic) from team, press and official cars as the race passed the French-Belgian border. Hardly surprising, then, that without adequate radio or television coverage, public interest was waning by the time the race approached Brussels.

Notorious for its dull first half, because of the wide, straight roads that take the race from the start at Noyon to the French/Belgian border at 150km, there were nevertheless several spirited attempts – besides Holm's successful effort – to avoid the 'inevitability' of a bunch sprint. A 60km break attack by Poland's Marck Kulas (La William) and Italy's Fabio Roscioli (Del Tongo) just before the border crossing broke the deadlock of calm in the peloton. Then when that attack was caught there came another series of attempted attacks until Italian Claudio Chiappucci (Carrera) tried his luck by attacking on the côte d'Alsemberg, between Braine-l'Alleud and Mont Saint Pont (224km). With him went Denmark's

Paris-Brussels: 253km

Rolf Sörensen (Ariostea), Dutchman Johan Lammerts (Z), Soviet Dmitri Konyshev (TVM), Australia's Dean Woods (Telekom), Italy's Giovanni Fidanza (Gatorade), and Switzerland's Kurt Steinmann (Weinmann).

They were caught 10km from the finish, just as suburban Brussels came into focus. But that didn't stop Chiappucci, who attacked again – but was caught with 8km to go, thus opening the door for Holm's move.

'I really came here to win,' said Holm later. 'I have the reputation of being an attacker but in this race I didn't have any choice. I am not a fast sprinter. Today I knew I would attack, but not when. But with seven kilometres to go, the chance was open.'

Holm's attempt succeeded because the peloton hesitated before chasing, and he made it to the finish with 0:07 on the peloton, led by Ludwig, with Museeuw in third place.

For Holm, it didn't matter that Paris-Brussels has its critics. It was still his biggest career win to date. And, for his future employers, Tulip, it was a vindication of their decision to pluck him from Histor's pool of jobless riders for their 1992 team.

RACE DETAILS

WEATHER *Sunny and warm. Slight tail-wind.*

COURSE *Mainly flat route of 253km from Noyons to Brussels. Wide, straight roads up to the French/Belgian border at 150kms. Several small hills in last 40km.*

FIELD *198 starters, 119 finishers. Peloton rides calmly for first two hours* *(33-35km/h)... 146km First attack of the day by Kulas and Roscioli just before border crossing ... 150km At Quevy, Kulas and Roscioli get more than 4:00 lead ... 161km Peloton starts chase ... 169km At Binche, two leaders have only 2:20 lead ... 207km Break caught and at same time peloton splits.*

219km At Ophain five riders attack: Chiappucci, Dutchman Wilco Zuyderwijk (Buckler), Lammerts, Fidanza, and *Sörensen. Breaks gets 0:30 before Fidanza is dropped and, like the others, soon caught by peloton ... 224km Chiappucci attacks on côte d'Alsemberg, taking with him Lammerts, Konyshev, Woods, Fidanza and Steinmann ... 243km Break is caught in the Bois de la Cambre, but Chiappucci tries one more break alone ... 245km As Chiappucci is caught, Holm attacks alone ... 253km Holm wins by 0:07 on peloton led by Ludwig.*

A solo attack in the last kilometres paid off for Brian Holm, who became the first ever Danish winner of Paris-Brussels

Nissan Classic: 25-29 September

There are many stage races around the world – national tours like the Nissan Classic in Ireland and the Kellogg's Tour of Britain – which mean just as much to the country concerned as the Tour de France does to the wider world of international cycling.

Over the last few years, professional riders – many of them anyway – have become highly paid performers in a sport that is undoubtedly as hard as any other, and harder than most. But the combination of this new professionalism with the importance now attached to world-ranking FICP points means that, outside the Classics and the Tour de France, the racing has become too calculated and clinical to remain the heart-stirring spectacle it used to be. Gone are the days when riders won races by hours. That is to be expected – top-class equipment and highly experienced service crews are bound to reduce time differences. But are the riders so closely matched that races can now only be decided by seconds – or are they carefully calculating their efforts, husbanding their resources so they live to race another day elsewhere?

A few results illustrate the trend: in 1988, the Tour of Britain was won by 0:18; in 1989 by 0:08; in 1990 by 0:04; in 1991 by 0:01. And this is not an isolated example. It is a trend which indicates that the riders have decided that the best man wins – but only on time bonuses, or on the last 50km, and that they are only going to expend just as much energy as they need to, and it can lead to boring, predictable racing.

The competition for time bonuses dictated the pattern of racing and produced some exciting sprints at the numerous Hot Spot locations along the route. John Talen won this, the first of the race, and later on that day became race leader

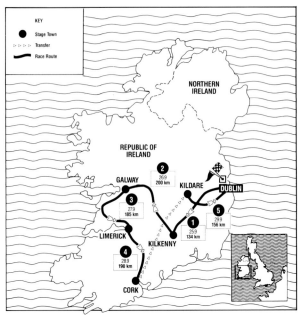

Nissan Classic, Ireland: 865km

The 1991 Nissan Classic was saved from this fate, and transformed into an outstanding race, by the activities of two Seans, Ireland's Sean Kelly (PDM) and Englishman Sean Yates (Motorola). Until they took control, the Nissan was just another race in a long string of races for the big names of the world circuit and, like the good professionals they are, they tried to calculate it every inch of the way. The first three stages hardly gripped the imagination, with small time bonuses at the rate of three a day deciding who should wear the yellow jersey.

Plenty of forgettable shadow boxing took place on the three stages before Limerick, but it would be wrong to forget those who tried – and often enough managed – to attract attention. On the opening day Italian Maurizio Fondriest (Panasonic) tried and failed, then next day Ireland's Stephen Roche (Tonton Tapis) set off on a magnificent suicide mission but was caught before the finish. New Danish professional Bo Hamburger (TVM), as impressive as he was during the Kellogg's Tour, earned his final under-23 award, but he was never allowed his head for long.

In the early stages, the young Irish amateur team thoroughly embarassed the professionals because in their naivety they failed to grasp that they should go slow at first then ride like hell at the end. Paul Slane won the first climb from team-mate Robert Power, and that gave the Belfast national champion the incentive to try again at the next, where he was third; an early lead in the mountains was his reward. Under new FICP rules, amateur racers will be barred from professional races next year; a shame, as it will mean long days of inactivity in some of the major races. But the eagerness of this young team, whose oldest member is 22, justified hopes that one day another Kelly or Roche might emerge from this small country of only four million people.

By the time the Nissan reached Limerick, 12 seconds covered the first 73 riders, and the field was tense – any break of a few seconds could change the course of the race. The next morning, 28 September, dawned wet, very windy and with all the appearance of winter. For days, the television weather reports had forecast storm conditions; already a boat was in distress off the nearby coastline. It was Sean Kelly weather, and the riders knew it. A hard man, reared in a corner of Ireland where the weather is often bad, but work in the fields goes on nonetheless, Kelly arrived at the Limerick start with a smile.

At 35, Kelly had not won a race for 13 months. He had not won a stage of the Nissan since 1985 – the first edition of the race – although he won it three times overall. He was having contractual problems and needed a good result, but so far he had had a season characterised by injury, ill-luck and personal tragedy. According to the form book, he had nothing to offer now. So much for form books.

The day started fast as Belgian Etienne De Wilde (Histor) loosened up with a lone win in the first sprint, being caught soon afterwards by German Rolf Aldag (Helvetia), as together they climbed the wet and dreary Glen of Aherlow. Aldag was first over the top and soon afterwards the race regrouped, but overall leader Belgian Johan Museeuw (Lotto) had seen all of his team fall behind when he punctured, putting him under pressure from which he struggled to recover.

On the Vee, Sean Kelly told his Mexican team-mate Raúl Alcalá to go with an eight-man attack which included Yates; confirmation, perhaps, of the word he had put about in the morning that Alcalá would be the man to beat. On the descent of the Vee, its roads running with flood water, a tree had been brought down by the

Stephen Roche rediscovered some of his previous form with a magnificent solo breakaway on Stage 2

high winds, completely blocking the route. But the arrival of helpers and a chain saw from a nearby hamlet saved the day, and the trunk was pulled away two minutes before the race arrived at the spot.

Thanks to his sprint gains, John Talen spent two days in the race-leader's jersey, but lost the lead to Johan Museeuw in Limerick on Stage 3

Adrie van Der Poel, attacking on Gallows Hill on the run-in to Limerick, enjoyed his best form for years. His efforts earned him the Mountains competition

Like the Kelly of old: Sean Kelly's face says it all as he takes Patricks Hill by storm during his race-winning attack with Sean Yates

As the race reformed one of the original eight escapers, French champion Armand De Las Cuevas, took the sprint at Fermoy before a bedraggled bunch of around 50 regrouped. Then, just a few miles later, Yates jumped clear. 'I saw Yates go and thought to myself, you can't let him go, he is too strong − so I went after him,' said Kelly. Once together, the pair formed a perfect alliance as they sought to open a gap.

With a typical display of brute strength, Yates powered the train, while behind them Museeuw, who had had

further mechanical trouble, returned to the lead bunch only to find his most dangerous rival had gone. 'I didn't know Museeuw was in trouble,' said Kelly afterwards. 'I saw the Lotto team manager tell Sammie Moreels to stop riding at the front, but didn't know why, and then I went after Yates.'

Kelly and Yates in tandem was a formidable sight. On the hills Kelly was stronger, but on the treacherous descents he had problems holding the Englishman, who was attracted to the bottom like a falling stone. These

RACE DETAILS

WEATHER *Autumn chills in the air at the start from Dublin, but the opening three days were sunny and pleasant although the forecast for the last two days was poor. On the penultimate day, gale-force winds brought a tree down on the course, and heavy rain made conditions among the worst the race has experienced. The last day was again sunny, but with temperatures down to 10°C.*

COURSE *Five stages taking the race anti-clockwise round Ireland, starting and finishing in Dublin.*

FIELD *18 professional teams and one Irish national team, each of five men. 94 starters from 95 entered; 76 finished.*

STAGE 1 − Dublin-Kilkenny, 134km *The seventh Nissan Classic became a battle in the early stages for three-second time bonuses at the hot spot sprint points ... 22km On this stage, Dutchman John Talen (PDM) became the first leader when he won the first match at Naas ... 32km The warming sunshine and lush green countryside did not inspire the field to break up until Kilcullen when Talen was again the winner, both times ahead of Dutchman Adrie van Der Poel (Tulip).*

The only attack of the day came from Fondriest who gained almost two minutes. The Italian was caught on the finishing circuit with 2km to go. Belgian Eric Vanderaerden (Buckler) won the sprint to give him a record six stage wins this race. Talen became the overall leader, as no time bonuses were offered to the stage winner each day. Ireland toasted a new name in Paul Slane, a 20-year-old amateur from Belfast who took the lead in the King of the Mountains competition.

STAGE 2 − Kilkenny-Galway, 200km *Talen started the day equal on time with van Der Poel and three seconds*

ahead of Fondriest, with the field all covered by a scant six seconds ... 32km Talen increased his lead at Abbeyleix where he won the sprint. On the first category climb of the mountain road in the Slieve Broom mountains, Roche pedalled away from the lethargic field to take the prime and build a lead of almost six minutes ... 142km The change of wind direction at Loughrea broke the Irishman and he was caught on the finishing circuits of Galway on Taylor's Hill. German Olaf Ludwig (Panasonic) beat Museeuw in a close sprint finish which went in favour of the Belgian until the photo finish was consulted.

*'I wouldn't have liked people to think I'd won this race on time bonuses,' said Kelly at the post-race press call.
'They can't think that now'*

two veteran professionals, who between them have spent 24 years on the pro circuit, oozed determination to break the grip of those riders who were determined to keep the race together for the time bonus sprints. They arrived at the finish line in Cork with 29 seconds in hand and four 5km circuits to go. Kelly thundered through the finish line to the cheers of a small crowd. Most spectators had gathered on the steep slopes of Patricks Hill, although many missed the finish because the strong tailwinds had put the race an hour ahead of schedule. But thousands had braved the terrible weather to cheer on their hero

with the chant they know best: 'Kelly Kelly Kelly'.

Museeuw, it must be said, was magnificent as he fought back in the streets of Cork. In the end he proved that Kelly had made the right decision to attack out on the open road: had the race arrived in Cork together, Museeuw would have held Kelly and won the race. In the event, it was Yates who produced the best sprint and won the stage, but Kelly took the lead by a second – a second that had been hotly contested every inch of the way. And in Dublin twenty-four hours later, Kelly was king of the Nissan for the fourth time in seven years.

STAGE 3 – Galway-Limerick, 185km *Only nine seconds covered the field and Talen led by a single second from van Der Poel. Paul Slane was proving quite troublesome to the professionals and he proved his opening day's lead was not just an opportunistic fluke by holding an 11 point advantage over Roche by the end of the stage. Slane won the climbs of Corkscrew Hill and the cliffs of Moher, but on the severe test of Gallows Hill after 156km he was literally caught with his trousers down and failed to catch the field for a long time having taken a natural break. Museeuw won the sprint from most of the field again, but there had*

been plenty of attacking.

STAGE 4 – Limerick-Cork, 190km *This was the day that everyone had predicted would decide the race, and the weather made certain of it. Strong winds, cross and tail, heavy rain and attacks from the start, turned the stage into a classic to befit the race's name ... 93km By the Vee climb Alcalá was forcing the pace in atrocious conditions and the field was splitting up in pieces for the first time since leaving Dublin. A long attack by Yates and a group of eight riders including Alcalá and van Der Poel ended after 64km. The winning attack came after Fermoy when Yates*

went again and was quickly followed by Kelly. The pair entered Cork for four climbs of the 25 per cent Patricks Hill with a lead of 0:29. The field, led by Museeuw and van Der Poel, became smaller each lap, reducing from 45 to just five, but in the finish Yates beat Kelly while van Der Poel led the yellow jersey home 0:44 later. Kelly took the lead by one second from Yates. Slane, who finished 28:30 behind, lost his lead in the mountains to van Der Poel by two points.

STAGE 5 – Kildare-Dublin, 156km *Slane stunned van Der Poel by winning the first climb on Ballymore Eustace to put him back in the lead, but van*

Der Poel finalised the jersey on the next climb at Sally Gap, where the Irish amateur champion was third ... 93km The one-second margin in the Classic remained until the race arrived at Deansgrange. Here Kelly – helped by Talen – won the three seconds bonus to take a four-second lead. From this point Yates surrendered and never attacked Kelly to the finish. In O'Connell Street, the race ended in a charge of the sprinters, Ludwig again proving faster than Museeuw.

Johan Museeuw could do little to counter Kelly's attack in Cork, but rode strongly on the climb of Patricks Hill in a last-ditch effort to retain his race lead

In Dublin Olaf Ludwig won his second stage of the 1991 Nissan, repeating his stage success of 1990

Clad in his race-leader's jersey, Kelly raced through the streets of Dublin a proud man on the final day

World Mountain Bike Championships: 29 September - 6 October

Il Ciocco in Italy played host to the second world mountain bike championships, following the inaugural race at the dizzy heights of Purgatory, Colorado in 1990, and for the time being the Americans continued to reign supreme in the major cross-country events. But unlike past major races the Europeans didn't let them have it all their own way and made significant inroads into the medal table.

This championship showed the need for a road racing background and although the course chosen, high on the wooded slopes above the Gafagnana Valley, was anything but 'roadie-friendly' the high fitness levels road racing offers, plus some necessary technical skills, proved the recipe for success for John Tomac and Ruthie Matthes.

It was a conclusive victory for Tomac. He trounced the most complete field ever assembled, and after a hectic

John Tomac made up for the disappointment of his second place in the downhill title race, with a conclusive victory in the cross-country race the following day

season on the road with the high powered Motorola team combined with a limited off-road campaign of major world cup and NORBA races, proved that the form which gave him victory in the final World Cup race in Berlin some four weeks previously was no fluke.

From the start on the running track and into the initial climb Tomac showed he meant business by going straight to the front with pre-race favourite Tim Gould happy to sit on, as the field stretched out and the first gaps appeared. The initial five-kilometre middle chainring climb was followed by a rapid descent which led to the major obstacle of the circuit; a very steep, narrow and loosely surfaced climb which wound its way upwards for the best part of two kilometres before the gravity-assisted plunge down to the stadium over washboard tracks – rutted from constant rain and training during the run up to the race.

It was the second severe climb that was to make or break the major contenders: for Tomac it was the springboard to his victory. As he put his strength and technical climbing ability – the ability to climb at little more than walking pace on a very low gear without having to dismount – to great effect, riding the entire climb and putting over half a minute into Gould, world cyclo-cross champion Thomas Frischknecht, 1990 victor Ned Overend, and a rejuvenated Don Myrah on the first lap.

The descent back to the stadium to complete the first of four laps gave Tomac the chance to extend his lead, as Gould – realising the danger – gave chase, dropping Overend and Frischknecht, but never coming close to the flying American.

The second lap saw only two significant changes: Tomac's lead increasing again after the severe climb and Gould being dropped by the Myrah-driven train, with Overend and Frischknecht happy to mark time.

Into lap three, it was Frischknecht's turn to suffer on the climb, leaving the Americans in the top three places, with Tomac's lead hovering around two minutes. And the crowd and a lot of other riders wondered if he hadn't perhaps done too much too soon. By the climb on the final lap it was obvious he hadn't; but one that had was Myrah, left by Overend and caught by a flying Frischknecht – over his bad patch and determined to salvage some European pride with a medal. As it turned out, he got a silver medal, his running legs having proved too much for the 36-year-old Overend on the steepest part of the final climb.

Another on a fourth lap charge was American Mike Kloser. He caught a dejected Gould soon after the start of the lap and picked up Myrah further up on the climb, only to puncture on the final descent, allowing Myrah back into a deserved fourth spot.

But the day belonged to John Tomac: for once the puncture bug that has so often cost him high placings stayed away and after missing a downhill title by seconds the day before, he was a man on a mission.

The women's race held later the same day was again won by a dominant display of aggressive riding. Ruthie Matthes had started her off-road season late and the interruption of the World Road Championships and

Tour of the EEC had left little time to show her form to the more established women over the final rounds of the World Cup circuit. But with obvious quality racing in her legs and tunnel vision for the title race only, it would have taken an exceptional talent to beat her. That talent was also present; with more off-road experience a major upset of the championships could have occurred. 20-year-old Czechoslovakian Eva Orvosova, riding her first race on a mountain bike, proved to be the only challenger to Matthes. She led up the first climb from the start before losing the lead on the severe climb and the descent – the likes of which she had never seen and which were the major reason behind the growing gap. By the end of lap one Matthes and Orvosova were well clear and it was the Swiss duet of Fürst and Daucourt together in third and fourth, proving the once all-conquering American women were no longer to be feared.

Orvosova continued to limit her losses on the climb only to lose more time on the way back down and Matthes came into the stadium to a great reception nearly two minutes clear after an incident-free third lap. Silvia Fürst dropped her compatriot to finish a superb third with pre-race favourites Juli Furtado and Sara Ballantyne never showing any signs of their normal unbeatable form, Furtado retiring on the second lap and Ballantyne finishing a disappointing sixth nearly ten minutes down.

The call of the Olympics road race is beckoning Matthes, Orvosova and fifth-placed Alison Sydor in 1992, but with that out of the way the latter part of the season should see some fascinating battles between the mountain bike specialists and 'cross over' road stars.

Third in the 1990 Cross-Country, second in the 1990 Road Worlds, Ruthie Matthes at last made it to the top of a worlds podium following her victory over Eva Orvosova

The setting of Il Ciocco in Tuscany provided a beautiful backdrop to the Worlds, but the size and layout of the resort caused major headaches to teams and spectators alike

Montreal Grand Prix: 6 October

There was a bewildered look on the face of Italian Maurizio Fondriest when he crossed the finish line, in seventh place, at the end of a hectic fourth edition of Canada's Montreal Grand Prix. A few moments earlier, Fondriest looked as though he had the race in the bag, but his attack from a seven-strong break, 600 metres from the line, was chased down, and it was his Panasonic team-mate, Eric Van Lancker, who came through to win the race, two lengths ahead of Buckler's Steven Rooks (Holland), with PDM's Martin Earley (Ireland) third.

The Montreal Grand Prix is the tenth round of the Perrier World Cup, and if Fondriest's late attack *had* been successful, he would have wrapped up the 1991 World Cup title; instead, there were still half a dozen riders − including Van Lancker − capable of overtaking him before the end of the series. 'I knew I was taking a risk,' Fondriest told reporters after the race. 'But usually when there is a small group like that, no one wants to chase down a rider who attacks in the final kilometre. It's easy to say, now, that I made a mistake'.

Fondriest wasn't the only rider who gambled − and lost − on this blustery, showery day in Montreal. A long-range effort was started on only the second of 14 laps of the 16km Mount Royal circuit, by a group of a dozen riders, headed by local favourite Steve Bauer and his Motorola team-mate Australian Phil Anderson. Also in the group was Earley − who had a remarkable race − five French riders, and the enterprising Colombian star, Alvaro Mejia (Ryalcao-Postobon). By the time the rain stopped, 80km into the race, this group was 2:46 clear.

As the day warmed up so did the pace, in an event that would see a new record speed of almost 38km/h. The pack began to close, and when it was only half minute behind the leaders Bauer attacked, over the top of the 3km-long Mount Royal climb, on lap 7. He was joined on the descent by Italian Carrera rider Alessandro Giannelli and the strong-looking Frenchman Martial Gayant (Toshiba). But this wasn't going to be Bauer's day, and the trio was reeled in after extending their attack for a further 30km.

Van Lancker's late charge earned him victory over Rooks (left), Earley, Gianetti, Rominger and Millar

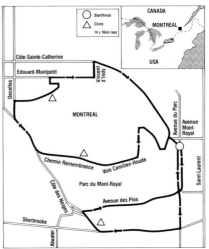

Montreal Grand Prix, Canada: 224km

After a general regroupment, Bauer's team-mate Dag-Otto Lauritzen of Norway set the race going again, on the tenth lap. He gained 30 seconds, but was losing time when he was joined by the amazing Earley − on his way to his best-ever showing in a one-day classic. The Irishman's help allowed Lauritzen to stay away for another lap, but there was still 30km to go when he and Earley were caught, midway up the 13th climb of Mount Royal. In this aggressive race, there was no shortage of willing gamblers, and the next to try his luck was Belgian Sammie Moreels (Lotto), third here in 1990. Putting everything into his effort, Moreels topped the climb ten seconds ahead of a group of four − Fondriest, Rooks, Holland's Adri Van Der Poel (Tulip) and Frenchman Marc Madiot (RMO) − with the pack at 0:20.

Moreels was still clear of the chasers heading into the final lap, but he was caught just as the chasers were reeled in by the 50-strong bunch. This regroupment didn't deter the ambitious Fondriest, who immediately counter-attacked with Rooks. They took five others with them: Earley (of course); Scotland's canny Robert Millar (Z); Swiss riders Tony Rominger (Toshiba) and Mauro Giannetti (Helvetia); and Van Lancker. With only 13km to go, this would prove to be the winning combination. Rooks, however, was not ready to accept that verdict. Riding in his best form, the gangling Dutchman shot away from the front on the 1-in-8 gradient of the course's second climb, the Polytechnique, and came through the start/finish area, with 7km to go, with a lead of 10 seconds. Rooks was still clear over the final hill, but a strong chase by Van Lancker towed up the other six, with a kilometre left, and everything was set for a seven-man sprint finish.

The rapid Fondriest could have been expected to win that sprint, but with 600 metres still remaining, he decided that a surprise attack was his best weapon. Then with 200 metres still left, Rooks galloped by the Italian. He looked sure to win, but his last-lap attack had probably taken the edge off his sprint, and it was the patient Van Lancker who managed to find the necessary momentum, flying through in the final ten metres to take his second World Cup win in two months.

The strongest riders in the early breakaway were Giannelli, Bauer and Gayant, here climbing Mount Royal

RACE DETAILS

WEATHER *Cool, wet and windy in early laps, giving way to clear sunny skies by finish.*

COURSE *14 laps of 16km Mount Royal circuit, containing two steep hills (of 1-in-10 and 1-in-8) on first loop, and one shorter climb on second loop of figure-8 course.*

FIELD *150 starters (from 18 teams), 58 finishers.*

Lap 1 *The peloton stays together ... Lap 2 12 riders break clear: Anderson, Bauer, Mejia, Colombian Efrain Rico (Ryalcao), Gayant and Frenchman Laurent Bezault (Toshiba), Earley, Frenchmen Bruno Cornillet (Z), Richard Virenque (RMO) and Laurent Pillon (Tonton Tapis); Italian Alessandro Giannelli (Carrera); and Holland's Peter Meinert (TVM). They are 0:54 ahead at the lap end.*

Lap 3 *With Motorola, Postobon and Toshiba riders working the hardest, break moves 1:30 clear ...Lap 4 Gap grows to 2:00 ... Lap 5 Break reaches its maximum lead of 2:46, after 80km ... Lap 6 A sharp acceleration by the peloton closes gap to 0:57.*

Lap 7 *Bauer attacks at top of main climb, and is chased and caught by Giannelli and Gayant. At the lap end, these three riders are 0:50 ahead of solo chaser Meinert, 1:07 ahead of the rest of the break, and 1:23 ahead of the peloton ... Lap 8 Peloton closes in on the chasers, leaving Bauer, Giannelli and Gayant dangling off the front ... Lap 9 Break is caught, and a bunch of about 60 regroups at the front.*

Lap 10 *At 152km, halfway through the lap, a lone attack is made by Lauritzen who gains 0:30 ... Lap 11 Lauritzen pursues his attack, but is only 0:03 ahead by the lap end ... Lap 12 With a renewed effort,*

Lauritzen moves away on the main climb, and is joined by Earley. The pair gains 0:20, with 32km to race.

Lap 13 – *On the Mount Royal climb, the two leaders are absorbed: Moreels counter-attacks and reaches the summit 0:10 ahead of four chasers – Fondriest, Rooks, Van der Poel and Madiot – and 0:20 ahead of 25-strong group. Moreels is a similar distance ahead of the chasers as he starts the final lap.*

Lap 14 *Moreels is caught on the main climb, where a counter-attack comes from Fondriest and Van Lancker, Rooks, Millar, Rominger, Gianetti and Earley. From this group Rooks attacks on the next climb and goes into the final 7km loop with chasers at 0:10 lead, and main group at 0:50. Rooks is caught with 1km to go, and Fondriest leads out in the sprint. Rooks comes by with 200m left, while Van Lancker overtakes the Dutchman in the final 10m to win by two lengths.*

The Panasonic team controlled the race, with Fondriest in his white World Cup leader's jersey always prominent on the climbs

Paris-Tours: 13 October

As in 1990, when a four-man break dented the tradition that Paris-Tours was always won in a bunch sprint, so this year's edition reminded cycling followers to expect the unexpected. In the end, it was a bunch sprint which led to victory for 27-year-old Belgian TVM rider Johan Capiot, but the race did not arrive at this result without exploring every other possible scenario on the way.

Firstly, there was a solo attack by Frenchman Christophe Lavainne (Castorama) after only eight kilometres. It was a planned manoeuvre, but as he said after riding away to a maximum lead of 27:30 before being caught a painful 245km later: 'I didn't think I would be away so long by myself like that.' Such a move was never likely to work, but then that's what they said during Stage 6 of this year's Tour de France, when Lavainne's team-mate Thierry Marie won the leg and took the leader's yellow jersey with a 237km solo attack. And while Lavainne's longer break was not quite so profitable, he still made sure his efforts were worthwhile, with £8500 in primes on the way!

Then at 200km there was the 21-man chase group, which split to ten on the second of two hills near the finish, the côte du Crochu with 20km to go. Sure, in the strong headwinds and grey clouds which later turned to rain, such a group was to be expected: but not that it would contain such a high proportion of top-class sprinters, nor that PDM and Panasonic would completely miss the boat.

The peloton's anxiety was quickly revealed as, led by PDM and Sean Kelly, it started the chase well before the break caught Lavainne at 253km. Yet the chase failed to prevent the barrage of attempted breaks within the sprinters' group, which included Belgians Johan Museeuw (Lotto), Carlo Bomans (Weinmann) and Johnny Dauwe (Tulip); Dutchman Jelle Nijdam

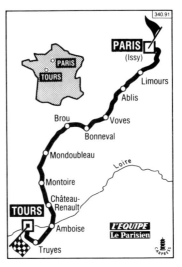

Paris-Tours,
France: 286km

(Buckler), Soviet Djamolidin Abdujaparov (Carrera) and up-and-coming speedster Rolf Aldag (Toshiba) of Germany.

Contrary to accepted sprinter's behaviour, throughout the last 20km these men concentrated on trying to form a winning break. As Museeuw had said in the days leading up to Paris-Tours, 'You just can't gamble on there being a bunch sprint any more. These days you have to be open to take some risks.' And he, Nijdam and Abdujaparov certainly did that: all three were involved in as many as four attacks each in the last 20km. On one occasion, all three riders figured in one four-man break! And they continually tried their hands with solo attacks, which were countered every time.

Museeuw's last chance came with three kilometres to go and the peloton at 0:15, after being 0:43 before all the action began 17km earlier at the côte du Crochu. He

'The gambler': Christophe Lavainne spent a lonely 245km ahead of the peloton, but thanks to successive sprint and hill primes, earned £35 per kilometre. He was caught with 35km to go

'The sprinter': Abdujaparov's presence in the 21-man escape group enticed other sprinters to join this unexpected move, but their recapture within a few kilometres of the finish handed the race on a plate to less notable sprinters

'The chase': alarmed at completely missing the big break, the PDM and Panasonic squads began to chase furiously with 70km to go, but their efforts failed to prevent a TVM victory

bolted away, only to be followed by Dane Kim Andersen (Z) and then by Frenchman Bruno Cornillet (Z) who for a moment looked like becoming the first Frenchman to win since 1956, when Albert Bouvet triumphed. But it was not to be: they were all reeled in, and everything was set for a bunch sprint. And ironically, most of the true sprinters would be too exhausted to deal with it.

Not a prolific winner (Flèche Brabançonne in 1988 and '89, and Het Volk in 1990) Johan Capiot was the best equipped to take advantage of the circumstances. Although he can be a gifted sprinter, with some strong showings in the lead-up round of *kermesses* in Belgium,

his chances in this sprinter's grand finale were never even rated beforehand. And later, even he admitted to being a little lucky. 'In the finale, it was a bit my good luck that I found myself in front. I didn't look to take the wheel of Olaf Ludwig, Abdujaparov or Museeuw as I would normally do. For a start I didn't even see them. Instead I found myself on Adri Van Der Poel's wheel and I quickly saw that he was riding strongly so I stayed there,' said Capiot who surged passed Van Der Poel and his lead-out man, Dutchman Peter Pieters, to win with a bike length on Ludwig and third-placed Dutchman Nico Verhoeven (PDM).

RACE DETAILS

WEATHER *Sunny and brisk first half. Then rain and strong headwinds.*

COURSE *Mostly flat. Principal difficulties were headwinds, long distance and two hills near the finish, at 264km and 280km.*

FIELD *Twenty-five eight-man teams invited. 189 starters; 167 finishers.*

8km *Solo attack by Lavainne at foot of côte de la Mine goes unchallenged ...* 124km *At first feed station at Brou, Lavainne leads by 24:00 ...*135km *Swiss Thomas Wegmüller*

(Weinmann) counterattacks alone ... 144km *Lavainne gets maximum lead of 25:00 on Wegmüller and 27:30 on peloton ...* 178km *Wegmüller is caught by peloton.*

200km *Peloton splits into three and 21 riders get away in pursuit of Lavainne. Amongst them are Abdujaparov, Museeuw, Nijdam, Italian Franco Ballerini (Del Tongo), Andersen, Sörensen, Australian Stephen Hodge (ONCE), Aldag and Dauwe. No Panasonic, PDM or Motorola riders are in the break ...* 202km *Chase group and peloton split by 0:30 at second feed station. Amongst abandonees are*

American Greg LeMond (Z).

215km *Lavainne has 14:00 on chase group, and 14:20 and 15:00 on next two groups ...* 253km *Lavainne is caught by chasers, now numbering 18 ...* 255km *Lavainne is dropped ...* 263km *At foot of côte du Crochu peloton is at 0:43; then 0:34 at summit; then 0:43 again. Lead group now only 10 men ...* 276km *After attacks by Nijdam, Museeuw, Andersen, and Abdujaparov, leaders are caught at foot of côte de Joué-les-Tours. Immediately, Italy's Fabio Roscioli (Del Tongo) and Museeuw attack and are caught by Cornillet ...* 286km *Peloton regroups and Capiot wins.*

'The break': Jelle Nijdam was one of the most aggressive riders in the large breakaway, launching several solo attacks as the chasers closed in on the run-in to Tours

'The winner': Johan Capiot streaks home ahead of a posse of fast men: (left to right) Ludwig, Van Der Poel, Pieters, American Frankie Andreu (Motorola) and Museeuw

Tour of Lombardy: 19 October

Sean Kelly's name has occupied a regular place in the story of the 1991 season, but more as a result of his ill-luck than his racing successes. So of all the headlines proclaiming all the victories this season, there was none so gladly written, nor so emotionally satisfying, as Kelly's win in the season's last major classic: the Tour of Lombardy.

The 35-year-old Irishman's season-long injuries, sickness and most recently personal tragedy – the death of his brother Joe in a cycling accident – have been well-documented. So when he won the Nissan Classic on home territory the previous month, the hearts of cycling fans everywhere rejoiced for him. But when he won this 85th Tour of Lombardy it was clear how deeply his brother's death had affected him. 'If it wasn't for Joe I probably wouldn't have been a bicycle racer today,' lamented a misty-eyed Kelly, who said he planned to lay the race-winner's flowers on his brother's grave in dedication.

However, the joy at Kelly's win was not just an emotional reaction. In racing terms, it was a victory that

Tour of Lombardy, Italy: 249km

With distant snows indicating the approach of winter, the peloton skirts Lake Lecco before turning onto the first climb of the day, the Esino Lario

everyone in the sport would celebrate. For Kelly to win a major classic was just what cycling needed, after several years of upheavals caused by the creation of the World Cup points system, a more crowded calendar, greater commercialisation and a deliberate policy on the part of those who control the sport to 'modernise' professional cycling. Like Italian Moreno Argentin, with his win in Liège-Bastogne-Liège and Frenchman Marc Madiot who took Paris-Roubaix this year, Kelly – *il vecchio* ('the old one'), as the Italians respectfully call him with affection and veneration – is one of the last champions of cycling's old school. And his win at Lombardy re-affirmed the qualities that cycling used to stand for – courage, endurance and a 'never-say-die' spirit. All this came back to us as 'King Kelly' surged across the line with his arms aloft in a V for victory, his chest sticking out like a prize fighter, eyes glaring and blowing like a steam train.

The fact that this year's 'Race of the Falling Leaves' was the penultimate round of the World Cup cut no ice at all with the traditionalists, even though it intensified the battle for overall victory between Italian leader Maurizio Fondriest (Panasonic) and Frenchman Laurent Jalabert (Toshiba), who went into the final round – the

Grand Prix des Nations time trial – with only four points between them.

Historically, Kelly's win was also significant. It made him one of only four riders to win the Tour of Lombardy three times. After previous wins in 1983 and 1985, Kelly is now in the company of Italians Costante Girardengo (1919-21-22) and Gino Bartali (1936-39-40), and Frenchman Henri Pelissier (1911-13-20). Ahead of him on the all-time stakes are Italy's four-time winner Alfredo Binda (1925-26-27-31) and the record holder Fausto Coppi, with five wins (1946-47-48-49-54).

So Kelly's six hours, 10 minutes and 38 seconds in the saddle certainly entitled him to bask in the applause he received, even from the begrudging Italian press and public, who felt that if any year was going to halt the run of home losses since Argentin's win in 1987 this year was it. And from 'yer man's' own point of view, it was a triumph. It was his first win in a major classic since Liège-Bastogne-Liège in 1989, and as he later reflected: 'After all my troubles this year, this is a very important win for me. It proves I am still a winner. Ever since the season began, journalists have asked me if I think I can still win a classic. I have always said "yes": I never ever doubted that. And this proves I was right.' Although he

Tony Rominger set a brutal pace on the unscheduled climb nicknamed 'Super Ghisallo' by the hopeful organisers. Here leading Venezuela's Leonardo Sierra, Rominger's acceleration only played into the hands of his team-mate Gayant who attacked as soon as Rominger conceded

On the ensuing descent Fondriest suffered his second puncture and subsequent fall, and needed all the speed of Viatcheslav Ekimov to get him back to the leading bunch: but by then Sörensen had taken off in company with Kelly, Ballerini and others ...

Thierry Gouvenou leads his two-up breakaway alongside Lake Lecco, but will soon take off alone on the Esino Lario climb

Looking full of confidence here, and with the knowledge that he'd left Fondriest far behind, Sörensen cruises along at the head of the leading break on the approach to the Colle Brianza, where the Danish rider unhappily began to lose contact

revealed later that before the race began, under crisp, blue autumn skies, he was fearful of not finishing at all – a training crash on the Wednesday between Milan-Turin on Tuesday and the Tour of Piedmont on the Thursday had left him with a sore and swelling right knee.

While one can't deny that the absence of the 1,336km Valico di Valcava made the race easier – even Kelly said 'without a doubt' – those who believed the Irishman would not have been a contender if the mountain had been included in the route should think again. In past Tours of Lombardy, in which the Valcava was one of the seven or eight climbs in the route, Kelly was always up with the leaders, in the first eight or ten, watching every move like a hawk. And judging by the form he showed here and in Milan-Turin, where he was fourth, and his instinct for how the race would be played, this year's race would not have been any different.

'It did make a difference to the race with the Valcava not being there – definitely – but what counts is who wins. And my name will be there as the 1991 winner. When people look back in ten years' time, they won't be talking about the Valcava, but the winner. And that is me', maintained Kelly. 'In any case, I knew the race would be won or lost on the Ghisallo instead. I knew that a break would go there,' he added, referring to the fourth of seven climbs in this year's route, also a hallmark of the Tour of Lombardy route. 'That's why I said to my team-mates that we have to have a man in every break. We did, and in the end I was in the right break.'

As the first 80km of the race from Monza were flat, serious early attacks were unlikely. And by the time the steep, twisting 'corkscrew' up the Valico di Esino Lario arrived, the only objective for the peloton as it left the picturesque blue waters of Lake Lecco for the climb was to start making inroads into the lead of early attackers, Frenchman Thierry Gouvenou (Z) and Jan Svorada (Colnago) of Czechoslovakia. A seven-man chase group took care of Gouvenou, now alone, after 135km, and was itself then caught by the peloton on the Madonna del Ghisallo. It was only on the narrow Pian Rancio climb, just after the Ghisallo and inserted into the route at the last minute because of roadworks blocking the original route, that the race was ready for any serious action.

It was initiated by Italian Davide Cassani (Ariostea) and last year's winner Switzerland's Tony Rominger (Toshiba), but Frenchman Martial Gayant (Toshiba) made the important move with his attack at 175km on the ascent of the Pian Rancio climb, nicknamed 'Super Ghisallo' because of its proximity to the Ghisallo, which forms part of its descent.

'Up until the Ghisallo the race was pretty easy. It was quiet, so something had to go on the [Super] Ghisallo,' said Kelly. Away after Gayant went Kelly, Frenchmen Dante Rezze (RMO) and Bruno Cornillet (Z), Denmark's Rolf Sörensen (Ariostea), Italians Franco Ballerini (Del Tongo) and Alberto Volpi (Gatorade). Plummeting down the Pian Rancio climb, back onto the Ghisallo at 180km and down further towards the foot of the sixth climb of the day, they caught Gayant with

60km to go. It was clearly a dangerous seven-man group, especially in World Cup terms – Sörensen was equal third and only 24 points short of Fondriest's lead.

Fondriest's last chance to win a major classic and clinch the World Cup was frustrated. Two punctures – one on the ascent of the Super Ghisallo and another on its descent – were rapidly converted by his rivals into opportunities to attack. And after he missed the winning break there, Fondriest accused his rivals of breaking cycling's 'gentleman's agreement' and taking advantage of another rider's mechanical problems to attack. In the end, he was lucky to have even his four points on Jalabert and 14 on Sörensen, who picked up 13 and 16 points respectively with their 13th and fifth places.

But the sandy-haired Italian was not the only one with problems. Italian Claudio Chiappucci (Carrera), unable to find his competitive form, abandoned at the 120km feed station, as did many others including 1988 winner Frenchman Charly Mottet (RMO) and Australia's Phil Anderson (Motorola).

Many of the big names who would normally have been billed as contenders didn't even make it to the start, most of them having opted for an early end to the season. Foremost amongst these were American

Fondriest had an unhappy day, and had to settle for a lowly place after two punctures. Perhaps his late-season form was ebbing away just when he needed it most ...

Ballerini set a fast pace up the Colle Brianza with 30 kilometres to go

In a style reminiscent of his best years, Kelly steamed towards Monza in the last twenty kilometres

Greg LeMond (Z), who returned to the US after the first of two lead-ups to Lombardy, Milan-Turin, four days before. Others included Italy's World Champion Gianni Bugno (Gatorade) because of tendinitis; Italian Moreno Argentin (Ariostea); Spaniards Miguel Indurain, Pedro Delgado (both Banesto) and Marino Lejarreta (ONCE); France's Laurent Fignon (Castorama), last year's winner Gilles Delion (Helvetia) and his team-mate and 1990 runner-up Pascal Richard.

The absence of so many leading riders gave rise to some criticism. For while Kelly's end of season strength may have owed something to his absence from the racing earlier in the season, the decision by so many of his peers to cut their seasons so short cast doubt on both their grit and their commitment to the racing calendar. Had Kelly not been kept out of the racing by injury and sickness, one can't help but feel that he would still have been at Lombardy with victory in mind.

Did such absences affect the race as well? Perhaps, but then again the 'Kelly seven' were world-class riders, and it was indicative of their calibre that they stayed away as they did despite the reluctance of Gayant − anxious for his leader Jalabert to catch up − to work in the break.

Once they were away, the process of elimination was provoked by 28-year-old Cornillet, who came so close to pulling off a surprise win at Paris-Tours the week before. He led the descent down the Colle Brianza at 210km, at

one moment only finding Volpi on his wheel and the others slightly adrift. He then tried to go away on the final climb, the 7% Lissolo, but was caught by Gayant and Kelly just before the summit at 220km. And then he even fought back after being dropped when Ballerini, having slipped behind under the force of Cornillet's charge, joined him on the last flat stretches towards Monza for aspirited chase of the leading pair − Kelly and Gayant.

That chase was Kelly's one big fear as the final 20km sped under his wheels. 'I was always worried about Ballerini coming back. He is a strong rider, a great chaser and in a sprint he can be a danger too,' he said, adding that as soon as a sprint against Gayant became inevitable, he was confident the day would be his.

More confident, perhaps, of his future as well. A season bedevilled by injury and sickness for a rider in the twilight of his career had not improved Sean Kelly's chances of negotiating a lucrative contract for 1992, but whether PDM find a co-sponsor to cover his salary or he heads back to Spain instead, the market worth of a major classic like the Tour of Lombardy can only have enhanced his prospects. Maybe next year will, as he says, be his last, and there will certainly be people asking him if he can still win a classic. But Kelly has learned to live with doubts, and as he has just showed us, he can overcome them like nobody else can.

'My greatest victory in Lombardy'. Kelly easily won the sprint, leaving Gayant five lengths behind

RACE DETAILS

WEATHER *Sunny, but cold winds from the north. Slight cloud cover.*

COURSE *Started and finished at Monza. First 80km flat, followed by seven climbs but not including the 1,336m Valico di Valcava which normally comes two-thirds of the way through the race. Route includes new passages of the Madonna del Ghisallo at 160km, and inclusion of Pian Rancio climb (nicknamed Super Ghisallo as its descent passes through the town of Madonna Del Ghisallo) at 170km. Last climb, the Lissolo, is 29km from the finish.*

FIELD *Invited field of 27 eight-man teams. 196 starters, 105 finishers.*

7km Svorada and Gouvenou attack ... 37km Two leaders have 3:00 on peloton ... 66km At Mandello Lario, break gets maximum lead of 6:50 ... 80km At foot of Valico di Esino Lario, the first climb, Gouvenou drops Svorada ... 94km At summit of Esino Lario (altitude 1182m) Gouvenou has 3:20 on peloton. Amongst dropped riders are Anderson, Germany's

Rolf Gölz (Ariostea) and Canada's Steve Bauer (Motorola) at 4:00, Belgium's Edwig Van Hooydonck (Buckler) at 4:50, and Mottet and Chiappucci at 6:20.

120km At feed station Chiappucci, Anderson and America's Andy Hampsten (Motorola) are amongst abandonees ... 135km Just past summit of third climb, the Galbiate, Gouvenou is caught by seven chasers: Germany's Jens Heppner (Panasonic), Austria's Harald Maier (PDM), Italians Alberto Elli (Ariostea), Luigi Furlan (Helvetia) and Valerio Tebaldi and Frenchman Christophe Manin (RMO). Spain's José-Ramon Uriarte (Banesto) chases leaders, with peloton at 1:10 ... 155km On Madonna del Ghisallo peloton regroups and passes summit together.

175km On Pian Rancio climb (the 'Super Ghisallo'), Cassani and Rominger begin attacks; Fondriest and Cassani puncture. Near summit, Gayant attacks alone. Six others go with him on descent: Kelly, Ballerini, Volpi, Sörensen, Rezze and Cornillet ... 199km After descent – on

which Fondriest punctures again – seven leaders have 0:25 lead ... 210km Going up climb six, the Colle Brianza, attackers have 1:20 lead and 3:00 near summit ... 217km Cornillet and Volpi force pace on descent to Perego ... 218km Cornillet attacks on the Lissolo (climb seven) and gets up to 0:10 lead on Gayant, Kelly and Ballerini as Volpi, Rezze and Sörensen are dropped. Peloton is at 3:05 ... 220km Near Lissolo summit Gayant and Kelly catch and drop Cornillet. At top Cornillet is 0:20 behind, Ballerini is at 0:28, Volpi at 0:45, Sörensen and Rezze at 0:57. Rominger, after attacking from peloton, is at 2:50 while main group is at 3:06.

232km Ballerini catches Cornillet and two continue chase of Kelly and Gayant ... 235km Leaders still have 0:35 on Ballerini and Cornillet and 1:20 on Volpi, Rezze and Sörensen ... 241km Kelly and Gayant have 0:52 on Ballerini and Cornillet ... 248km Gayant leads out sprint, but Kelly easily wins. The two attackers finish 0:35 ahead of Ballerini and Cornillet, 2:09 on Sörensen, Volpi and Rezze, and 2:19 on main peloton of 54 riders led by Jalabert.

World Cup Final: 26 October

After twelve of the thirteen World Cup events 14 points separated the top three riders, and it looked as if the FICP might actually get the World Cup finale they wanted − a decisive cliff-hanger of a race worthy of everybody's attention. But sadly the 64km 'race of truth' at Bergamo in northern Italy, the relocated Grand Prix des Nations time trial, mirrored the uneventful display at Lunel, France in 1990: many of the top riders absented themselves, no impact was made on the World Cup standings and interest in general veered towards off-season vacations and the winter round of cyclo-cross and six-day track racing.

In fact, the Grand Prix des Nations was doomed as a race in its own right once the FICP decided that it should move from its traditional battleground of hilly Provence in the south of France and double up as the finale of the World Cup. 'Nations' was a race with a heritage − notoriously testing terrain, length (80-140km) and a fine pedigree of past winners − that had hitherto guaranteed its prestige value. And a strong body of opinion felt it should have stayed that way.

Tony Rominger's unimpressive style belied the effort he made in the Nations and reminded us all of his talent at time-trialling. It was the first major win for the Swiss rider since Paris-Nice in March, when he won all three time trial stages of the French race

Laurent Jalabert knew he had lost his World Cup chances the previous week in Lombardy and barely bestirred himself for Nations, coming a dismal tenth. His indifference to this charade of a finale seemed to be shared by the majority of his colleagues

In a last attempt to snatch the World Cup from Fondriest, Sörensen knuckled down to put time and placings between himself and the Italian. His eventual seventh place at Bergamo was testimony to what might have been but for Sörensen's Tour de France crash

But their protests fell on deaf ears. And the organisers' hopes of a worthwhile race faded when most of the season's big names started to drop off the start list as quickly as the autumn leaves from the trees. With such a wastage rate, one could suddenly understand why the FICP had such broad criteria for qualification: all winners of a World Cup race; the winners of the French, Spanish and Italian national tours; the top 20 in the World Cup competition and FICP world rankings, plus three 'wild cards'. Thirty-eight riders qualified; of a planned field of only twenty, nineteen actually raced.

Amongst those who declined to take part were Italy's Gianni Bugno (Gatorade), the current world champion, number one ranked FICP rider and the winner at San Sebastian; Belgium's Eric Van Lancker (Panasonic) who won the Wincanton Classic and Grand Prix of Montreal, but then broke his collar-bone in a training crash; Spain's Miguel Indurain (Banesto) winner of the Tour de France, and his team-mate Pedro Delgado, who were both on holiday; Ireland's Sean Kelly (PDM), winner of the Tour of Lombardy seven days before; plus America's Greg LeMond (Z), Italian Franco Chioccioli (Del Tongo), Holland's Steven Rooks, and Spain's Marino Lejarreta (ONCE).

Then in the race itself, the anticipated tussle between front-runners Fondriest, Jalabert and Sörensen never materialised, although Sörensen − third in the competition, with 100 points to Fondriest's 114 − did put up a spirited attempt in the first 30km. But after that mark, Fondriest summoned up his last reserves of energy to come back from eighth place at 24.5km, where the Dane was fifth, to fourth place against Sörensen's eventual seventh. Whereas Jalabert, who started the day placed second in the World Cup with 110 points, never looked like threatening Fondriest − in fact, never looked like intending to, if his decision not to wear a helmet − thus losing vital seconds − was anything to go by.

Switzerland's Tony Rominger (Toshiba) put in a splendid ride, his average speed of 47.603km/h beating the Eddy Merckx Grand Prix winner Eric Breukink (PDM) of Holland by 0:58 and Swiss Thomas Wegmüller (Weinmann), last year's Nations winner, by a massive 2:08. But on Italian soil and with an Italian

Home and dry: Fondriest's World Cup victory was clearly a relief, especially as he had failed to win any of the qualifying events: his second place at the Amstel Gold in April was his best performance of the year

World Cup winner, his victory was outshone by Fondriest's effort.

It was a result that made the purists shudder. The Grand Prix des Nations is intended to be a celebration of the best that time trialling can offer, not a 'middle of the field' contest between three riders like Fondriest, Jalabert and Sörensen, who are far from being notable time triallists. But as the 1991 cycling year has showed us, cycling can no longer rest on its feather bed of laurels. For better or worse, 'modernisation' is now firmly entrenched as a force to be reckoned with.

RACE DETAILS	COURSE 64km, starting and finishing in Bergamo. First half mostly flat, but then undulating to the finish with four hills, the last with eight kilometres to go.	FIELD Twenty riders selected from 38 qualifiers. 19 starters; all finished.
WEATHER Cold, 8-10° C. Heavy mist. Headwind for last eight kilometres.		

INTERMEDIATE TIMES FOR TOP 10					
AT 24.5KM		AT 43.5KM		AT 64KM (FINISH)	
1 Rominger	30:10	Rominger	56:03	Rominger	1:20.40
2 Hodge	at 0:23	Breukink	at 1:00	Breukink	at 0:58
3 Wegmüller	at 0:29	Maassen	at 1:20	Wegmüller	at 2:08
4 Breukink	at 0:34	Fondriest	at 1:24	Fondriest	at 2:12
5 Sörensen	at 0:37	Sörensen	at 1:26	Echave	at 2:16
6 Echave	at 0:40	Wegmüller	at 1:26	Maassen	at 2:22
7 Mauri	at 0:46	Hodge	at 1:27	Sörensen	at 2:24
8 Fondriest	at 0:49	Echave	at 1:33	Hodge	at 2:25
9 Maassen	at 0:51	Mauri	at 1:53	Mauri	at 2:44
10 Van Hooydonck	at 0:56	Van Hooydonck	at 2:09	Jalabert	at 3:20

Team Listings

AUSTRIA

VARTA-ELK
Sponsor: Battery manufacturer.
Bicycles: Pinarello. Directeur
sportif: Gerhard Schönebacher.
Assistant: Günther Greimel.
Austrians
Johann Lienhart
Alois Pfleger
Paul Popp
Petr Privara
Bernhard Rassinger
Foreigner
Ludek Styks (Cz)

BELGIUM

COLLSTROP-ISOGLASS
Sponsors: Garden fence post
manufacturer and home
insulation company. Bicycles:
Rossin. Directeurs sportifs:
Paul Debaeremacker and Luc
Landuyt.
Belgians
Edwin Bafcop
Jan Bogaert
Nick Botteldoorn
Philippe Cottennies
Corneille Daems
Stefan De Beleyr
Geert Decorte
Alain De Schacht
Ferdi Dierickx Pascal Elaut
Edwin Hendrickx
Peter Naessens
Franky Pattyn
Frank Van Himst
Peter Van Impe
Peter Verbeken
Willy Willems
Foreigners
Harry Lodge (GB)
Stephan Rakers (Hol)

HISTOR-SIGMA
Sponsor: Paint manufacturer.
Bicycles: Basso. Directeur
sportif: Willy Teirlinck.
Assistant: Frans Van Looy.
Belgians
Luc Colijn
Patrick De Wael
Pierre Dewailly
Etienne De Wilde
Herman Frison
Kurt Huygens
Wilfried Peeters
Wim Sels
Benjamin Van Itterbeck
Johan Verstreppen
Foreigners
Uwe Ampler (Ger)
Brian Holm (Den)
Kai Hundertmarck (Ger)
Andreas Kappes (Ger)
Raimund Lehnert (Ger)
Sören Lilholt (Den)
Remig Stumpf (Ger)
Marc Thevenin (Fr)
Didier Virvaleix (Fr)

LA WILLIAM
Sponsor: Liquor distillery.
Bicycles: Colnago. Directeur
sportif: Rudy Pevenage.
Assistant: Willy Geukens.
Belgians
Jean-François Brasseur
Eric De Clercq
Ludo Giesberts
Yves Godimus
Frank Hoste
Peter Huyghe
Mark Macharis
Jan Mattheus
Danny Neskens
Michel Stasse
Stan Tourné Roger Van Den
Bossche
Patrick Van Roosbroeck
Koen Van Rooy
Foreigners
Michel Cornelisse (Hol)
Marek Kulas (Pol)

LOTTO-SUPERCLUB
Sponsor: National lottery.
Bicycles: MBK. Directeur
sportif: Jean-Luc
Vandenbroucke. Assistant:
Jef Braeckevelt.
Belgians
Serge Baguet
Thierry Bock
Johan Bruyneel
Claude Criquielion
Peter De Clercq
Dirk DeMol
Patrick Deneut
Jos Haex
Bart Leysen
Sammie Moreels
Johan Museeuw
Fabrice Naessens
Jan Nevens
Hendrick Redant
Peter Roes
Frank Van Den Abbeele
Wim Van Eynde
Rik Van Slycke
Patrick Verschueren
Marc Wauters

SEFB
Sponsor: Savings bank.
Bicycles: Look. Directeur
sportif: Walter Dalgal.
Assistant: Gérard Bulens.
Belgians
Daniel Beelen
Jerry Cooman
Danny De Bie
Paul De Brauwer
Johan Devos
Bruno Geuens
Paul Haghedooren
Dirk Heirweg
Benny Heylen
Wim Lambrechts
Marnix Lameire
Peter Spaenhoven
Benny Van Brabant
Koen Vekemans
Marc Verbeeck
Jan Wijnants
Foreigners
Andrei Tchmil (USSR)
Frank Van Bakel (Hol)

TONTON TAPIS
Sponsor: Carpet manufacture.
Bicycles: Gios. Directeur
sportif: Roger De Vlaeminck.
Assistant: Marcel Van der
Slagmolen.
Belgians
Erwin Biets
Marc Bouillon
Gino De Backer
Klaus De Muynck
Dirk De Wolf
Rudi Dexters
Patrick Jacobs
Didier Priem
Patrick Roelandt
Noël Szostek
Jan Van Camp
Kurt Van Keirsbulck
Foreigners
Laurent Biondi (Fr)
John Carlsen (Den)
Jean-Claude Colotti (Fr)
Vincent Lacressonniaire (Fr)
Francis Moreau (Fr)
Atle Pedersen (Nor)
William Pirard (Fr)
Laurent Pillon (Fr)
Laurence Roche (Ire)
Stephen Roche (Ire)

TULIP
Sponsor: Computer company.
Bicycles: Koga-Miyata.
Directeur sportif: José De
Cauwer. Assistant: Dirk
Wayenberg.
Belgians
Johnny Dauwe
Tom Desmet
Roland Liboton
Kurt Onclin

Rudy Patry
Johan Remels
Rudy Rogiers
Luc Roosen
Wim Van De Laer
Ronny Van Holen
Stefan Van Leeuwe
Flip Van Vooren
Foreigners
Dietmar Hauer (Austria)
Olaf Jentsch (Ger)
Adri Kools (Hol)
Joe Parkin (USA)
Allan Peiper (Aus)
Peter Pieters (Hol)
Colin Sturgess (GB)
Adri Van Der Poel (Hol)
Jac Van Der Poel (Hol)
Michel Zanoli (Hol)

WEINMANN
Sponsor: Bicycle components
manufacturer. Bicycles: Eddy
Merckx. Directeur sportif:
Walter Godefroot. Assistants:
Patrick Lefevere and Jules De
Wever.
Belgians
Carlo Bomans
Michel Dernies
Marc Dierickx
Peter Farazijn
Jan Goessens
Laurenzo Lapage
Wilfried Nelissen
Rudy Verdonck
Ludwig Willems
Foreigners
Alfred Achermann (Swi)
Rolf Järmann (Swi)
Stephan Joho (Swi)
Kurt Steinmann (Swi)
Werner Stutz (Swi)
Thomas Wegmüller (Swi)

COLOMBIA

PONY MALTA-AVIANCA
Sponsors: Soft drink producer
and national airline. Bicycles:
Battaglin. Directeur sportif:
Jorge Tenjo. Assistant: Hector
Mayorga.
Colombians
Juan-Carlos Arias
Luciano Bonilla
Marco Carreno
German Castillo
Demetrio Cuspoca
Luis Gonzalez
Alvaro Lozano
Edilberto Marino
Ruban Ramirez
Fabio Rodriguez
Francisco Rodriguez
Nelson Rodriguez
Celio Roncancio
Angel-Miguel Sanabria
Rafaël Tolosa
Pablo Wilches

POSTOBON
Sponsor: Soft drinks producer.
Bicycles: Pinarello.
Directeur sportif: Raul Meza.
Assistant: Elkin Rondon.
Colombians
Raul Acosta
Hector Betancourt
Alberto Camargo
Henry Cardenas
Juan Castillo
Arsenio Chaparro
Omar Hernandez
Luis Herrera
Carlos Jaramillo
Fabio Jaramillo
Alvaro Mejia
Gerardo Moncada
Reynel Montoya
Luis Mosquera
Federico Muñoz
Victor-Hugo Olarte
Jorge Otalvaro
Julio-Cesar Ortegon

William Palacio
Hector Patarroyo
William Pulido
Efrain Rico
Alvaro Sierra
Oscar Vargas
Gustavo Wilches

FRANCE

CASTORAMA
Sponsor: Hardware store chain.
Bicycles: Raleigh.
Directeurs sportifs: Cyrille
Guimard and Bernard Quilfen.
Assistant: Jacques Cadiou.
French
Dominique Arnould
Jean-Claude Bagot
Jacky Durant
Laurent Fignon
Dominique Garde
Christophe Lavainne
Luc Leblanc
Yvon Ledanois
Thierry Marie
Patrick Moncassin
Eric Pichon
Jean-Cyril Robin
Jean-Philippe Rouxel
François Simon
Pascal Simon
Didier Thueux
Frédéric Vichot
Foreigner
Bjarne Riijs (Den)

RMO
Sponsor: Temporary
employment agency.
Bicycles: Liberia-Mavic.
Directeur sportif: Bruno
Roussel. Assistant: Christian
Rumeau.
French
Philippe Bouvatier
Frederic Brun
Eric Caritoux
Philippe Chevalier
Thierry Claveyrolat
Jean-Philippe Dowja
Jean-Luc Jonrond
Thierry Laurent
Pascal Lino
Marc Madiot
Yvon Madiot
Christophe Manin
Charly Mottet
Dante Rezze
Richard Virenque
Foreigners
Mauro Ribeiro (Br)
Clayton Stevenson (Aus)
Michel Vermote (B)
Marcel Wüst (Ger)

TOSHIBA
Sponsor: Electronics
manufacturer. Bicycles: Look.
Directeur sportif: Bernard
Vallet. Assistant: Marc Durant.
French
Henri Abadie
Laurent Bezault
Thierry Bourguignon
Pascal Chanteur
Christian Chaubet
Christophe Faudot
Sebastian Flicher
Martial Gayant
Laurent Jalabert
Pascal Lance
Philippe Louviot
Laurent Madouas
Denis Roux
Foreigners
Hans Kindberg (Sweden)
Olaf Lurvik (Nor)
Tony Rominger (Swi)

Z
Sponsor: Children's clothing
manufacturer. Bicycles:
LeMond. Directeurs sportifs:
Roger Legeay and Michel
Laurent. Assistant: Serge
Beucherie.

French
Bruno Bonnet
Eric Boyer
Christophe Capelle
Philippe Casado
Bruno Cornillet
Gilbert Duclos-Lassalle
Robert Forest
Thierry Gouvenou
François Lemarchand
Jérôme Simon
Foreigners
Kim Andersen (Den)
Miguel Arroyo (Mex)
Wayne Bennington (GB)
Atle Kvalsvoll (Nor)
Johan Lammerts (Hol)
Greg LeMond (USA)
Robert Millar (GB)
Paul Willerton (USA)

GERMANY

TELEKOM
Sponsor: Telephone company.
Bicycles: Eddy Merckx.
Directeur sportif: Hennie
Kuiper. Assistant: Hermann
Snoeynk.
Germans
Hartmut Bölts
Udo Bölts
Gerd Derich
Guido Eickelbeck
Peter Gansler
Bernd Gröne
Markus Hess
Josef Holzmann
Robert Matwew
Uwe Nepp
Marcus Schleicher
Carsten Wolf
Werner Wüller
Foreigners
Marcel Arntz (Hol)
Urs Freuler (Swi)
Dariusz Kajzer (Pol)
Erwin Nijboer (Hol)
Gerard Veldscholten (Hol)
Ad Wijnands (Hol)
Dean Woods (Aus)

GREAT BRITAIN

BANANA-FALCON
Sponsors: Fruit marketing
group and bicycle
manufacturer. Bicycles:
Falcon. Directeur sportif:
Keith Lambert.
British
Jon Clay
Rob Holden
Chris Lillywhite
Keith Reynolds
Chris Walker
Foreigner
Shane Sutton (Aus)

HOLLAND

BUCKLER
Sponsor: Brewers of low
alcohol beer. Bicycles:
Colnago. Directeur sportif: Jan
Raas. Assistant: Hilaire Van der
Schueren.
Dutch
Gerrit De Vries
Patrick Eyeck
Antoine Goense
Martien Kokkelkoren
Frans Maassen
Jelle Nijdam
Twan Poels
Steven Rooks
Gerrit Solleveld
Patrick Tolhoek
Marco Van der Hulst
Wiebren Veenstra
Peter Winnen
Wilco Zuyderwijk

Foreigners
Hans De Clercq (B)
Ludo De Keulenaer (B)
David Rayner (GB)
Patrick Robeet (B)
Noël Segers (B)
Eric Vanderaerden (B)
Edwig Van Hooydonck (B)
Gino Van Hooydonck (B)

PANASONIC-SPORTLIFE
Sponsors: Electronics
manufacturer and chewing
gum producer. Bicycles:
Panasonic. Directeur sportif:
Peter Post. Assistants: Walter
Planckaert and Theo De Rooy.
Dutch
Eddy Bouwmans
Louis De Koning
Jacques Hanegraaf
Eric Knuvers
Michel Le Grand
Henk Lubberding
Harry Rozendal
Patrick Strouken
Robert Van De Vin
Marc Van Orsouw
Menno Vink
Foreigners
Rudy Dhaenens (B)
Viatcheslav Ekimov (USSR)
Maurizio Fondriest (It)
Jens Heppner (Ger)
Jef Lieckens (B)
Olaf Ludwig (Ger)
Guy Nulens (B)
Eddy Planckaert (B)
Marc Sergeant (B)
Eric Van Lancker (B)
Jean-Marie Wampers (B)
Marco Zen (It)
Dmitri Zhdanov (USSR)

PDM
Sponsor: Video and audio tape
manufacturer. Bicycles:
Concorde. Directeur sportif:
Jan Gisbers. Assistant: Ferdi
Van den Haute.
Dutch
Eric Breukink
Tom Cordes
Marten Den Bakker
Gert Jakobs
Danny Nelissen
John Talen
Jos Van Aert
John Van Den Akker
Jean-Paul Van Poppel
Nico Verhoeven
John Vos
Foreigners
Raúl Alcalá (Mex)
Falk Boden (Ger)
Thomas Dürst (Ger)
Martin Earley (Ire)
Sean Kelly (Ire)
Harald Maier (Austria)
Uwe Raab (Ger)

TVM-SANYO
Sponsors: Trucking company
and electronics manufacturer.
Bicycles: Zunu. Directeur
sportif: Cees Priem.
Dutch
Maarten Ducrot
Rob Harmeling
Martin Schalkers
Eddy Schurer
Jan Siemons
Marcel Siemons
Gert-Jan Theunisse
Jos Van der Pas
Willem Van Loenhout
Foreigners
Thomas Barth (Ger)
Johan Capiot (B)
Dmitri Konyshev (USSR)
Januus Kuum (Nor)
Jörg Müller (Swi)
Peter Meinart Nielsen (Ger)
Jesper Skibby (Den)
Scott Sunderland (Aus)

Sergei Uslamine (USSR)
Alain Van Den Bossche (B)

ITALY

AMORE E VITA-FANINI
Sponsor: Bicycle manufacturer.
Bicycles: Fanini.
Directeur sportif: Giorgio
Vanucci. Assistant: Giuseppe
Lanzoni.
Italians
Florido Barale
Walter Brugna
Franco Cavallini
Andrea Chiurato
Fabrizio Conalle
Stefano Della-Santa
Pierino Gavazzi
Stefano Giraldi
Fabrizio Margon
Maurizio Molinari
Ottavio Paccagnella
Roberto Pelliconi
Foreigners
Marcelo Alexandre (Arg)
Daniel Castro (Arg)
Brian Petersen (Den)
Eddie Salas (Aus)

ARIOSTEA
Sponsor: Ceramics
manufacturer. Bicycles: De
Rosa. Directeur sportif:
Giancarlo Ferretti. Assistant:
Alfio Vandi.
Italians
Moreno Argentin
Adriano Baffi
Davide Cassani
Bruno Cenghialta
Roberto Conti
Alberto Elli
Andrea Ferrigato
Giorgio Furlan
Federico Ghiotto
Massimiliano Lelli
Marco Lietti
Dario Mariuzzo
Rodolfo Massi
Valerio Piva
Marco Saligari
Foreigners
Rolf Gölz (Ger)
Rolf Sörensen (Den)
Micheal Wilson (Aus)

CARRERA
Sponsor: Jeans manufacturer.
Bicycles: Battaglin. Directeur
sportif: Davide Boifava.
Assistants: Sandro Quintarelli
and Giuseppe Martinelli.
Italians
Guido Bontempi
Claudio Chiappucci
Mario Chiesa
Massimo Ghirotto
Alessandro Giannelli
Flavio Giupponi
Giancarlo Perini
Felice Puttini
Max Sciandri
Enrico Zaina
Foreigners
Djamolidin Abdujaparov
(USSR)
Christian Henn (Ger)
Erich Mächler (Swi)
Jure Pavlic (Yug)
Vladimir Pulnikov (USSR)

COLNAGO-LAMPRE
Sponsor: Bicycle manufacturer.
Bicycles: Colnago. Directeur
sportif: Pietro Algeri.
Italians
Sandro Bono
Fabrizio Bontempi
Gianluca Bortolami
Luigi Botteon
Davide Bramati
Luca Bramati
Stefano Cortinovis
Gianvito Martinelli

Dario Nicolletti
Oscar Pellicioli
Maurizio Piovani
Foreigners
Lech Piasecki (Pol)
Jan Svorada (Cz)
Marek Szerszynski (Pol)

DEL TONGO-MG BOYS
Sponsors: Fitted kitchen
manufacturer and childrens
clothing manufacturer.
Bicycles: Pinarello.
Directeur sportif: Enrico
Paolini. Assistant:
Czeslaw Lang.
Italians
Fabio Baldato
Franco Ballerini
Luigi Bielli
Francesco Cesarini
Franco Chioccioli
Mario Cipollini
Luca Gelfi
Angelo Lecchi
Eros Poli
Fabio Roscioli
Foreigners
Joachim Halupczok (Pol)
Zenon Jaskula (Pol)

**GATORADE-CHATEAU
D'AX**
Sponsors: Sports drink
manufacturer and furniture
manufacturer.
Bicycles: Moser. Directeur
sportif: Gianluigi Stanga.
Assistants: Vittorio Algeri and
Claudio Corti.
Italians
Emanuele Bombini
Gianni Bugno
Giuseppe Calcaterra
Giovanni Fidanza
Marco Giovannetti
Ivan Gotti
Roberto Gusmeroli
Mario Mansoni
Camillo Passera
Mauro-Antonio Santaromita
Mario Scirea
Valerio Tebaldi
Alberto Volpi
Stefano Zanatta
Foreigners
Mario Kummer (Ger)
Jan Schur (Ger)

GIS-BALLAN
Sponsors: Ice cream
manufacturer and bicycle
manufacturer. Bicycles:
Benotto. Directeur sportif:
Franco Gini. Assistant:
Antonio Salutini.
Italians
Antonio Berardi
Orio Berardi
Fabio Bernardi
Fabio Bordonali
Dario Bottaro
Angelo Canzonieri
Enrico Cacchetto
Daniele Ceraretti
Salvatore Criscione
Enrico Galleschi
Nicola Gasperi
Mauro Giancecchi
Settimio Guidi
Pier Imola
Bruno Leali
Walter Magnago
Silvio Martinello
Settimio Mini
Ettore Pastorelli
Giuseppe Petito
Germano Pierdomenico
Pier Rosti
Alessandro Santi
Paolo Stefanelli
Roberto Tomassini
Maurizio Vandelli
Pier Venerucci
Sergio Zarrerani
Silvio Zonzini

**ITALBONIFICA-
NAVIGARE**
Bicycles: Conti. Directeur
sportif: Bruno Reverberi.
Assistant: Greziano Rossi.
Italians
Stefano Allocchio
Gianluca Bordignon
Sergio Carcano
Michele Coppolitto
William Dazzani
Fabiano Fontanelli
Danilo Gioia
Michele Moro
Massimo Podenzana
Fabrizio Settambrini
Stefano Zanini

JOLLY-CLUB 88
Sponsors: Kitchenware
manufacturer and travel group
Bicycles: Pinarello
Directeur sportif: Enrico
Paolini
Assistant: Pietro Abetoni
Italians
Gianluigi Barnotelli
Paolo Botarelli
Claudio Brandini
Stefano Cattai
Stefano Giuliani
Endrio Leoni
Eduardo Rocchi
Massimo Strazzer
Marco Toffali
Marco Vitali
Sandro Vitali
Franco Vona
Foreigner
Daniel Steiger (Swi)

SELLE ITALIA-VETTA
Sponsors: Saddle manufacturer
and hard-shell helmet
manufacturer. Bicycles: Moser.
Directeur sportif: Domenico
Cavallo.
Italians
Roberto Caruso
Stefano Casagrande
Andrea De Mitri
Marino Marcozzi
Andrea Michelucci
Andrea Tafi
Raimondo Valretti
Foreigners
Manuel Guevarra (Ven)
Alexis Mendez (Ven)
Richard Parra (Ven)
Leonardo Sierra (Ven)
Arno Wohlfahrter (Austrian)
Daniel Wyder (Swi)

ZG-BOTTECCHIA
Sponsors: Furniture
manufacturer and bicycle
manufacturer. Bicycles:
Bottecchia. Directeur sportif:
Dino Zandegu. Assistant:
Enrico Guadrini.
Italians
Giuseppe Citterio
Stefano Colage
Mauro Consonni
Antonio Fanelli
Gianni Faresin
Gian Paolo Fregonese
Silvano Lorenzon
Mario Mantovan
Michele Mara
Davide Petrona
Gianluca Pierobon
Gianluca Tonetti
Diego Trepin
Flavio Vanzella
Foreigner
Andrea Guidotti (Swi)

JAPAN

**JAPAN PROROAD
PROJECT**
Japanese
Akira Asada
Kazuya Hashizume
Kyoshi Miura

Yukiharu Mori
Masahiro Yasuhara

SPAIN

AMAYA SEGUROS
Sponsor: Insurance company.
Bicycles: BH. Directeur
sportif: Javier Minguez.
Assistant: José-Luis Lopez-
Cerron
Spanish
Eladio Ambite
Francisco-José Antequera
Vicente Aparicio
Santiago Crespo
Laudelino Cubino
José-Luis Diaz
Juan-Carlos Garcia
Enrique Guerricagoitia
Juan-Carlos Martinez
Jesus Montoya
Javier Murguialday
Asencio Navarro
Fernando Quevedo
Juan Romero
Antonio Sanchez
Miguel Zarrabeitia
Foreigners
Patrice Esnault (Fr)
Roland Le Clerc (Fr)
Fabio Parra (Col)
Per Pedersen (Den)

ARTIACH
Sponsor: Cereal foods
company. Bicycles: Orbea.
Directeur sportif: Francisco
Giner. Assistant: Jesus
Cuzman.
Spanish
Miguel Anton
Juan-Carlos Arribas
Jon Arrospide
Joaquim Llach
Joaquim Martinez
José Merenciano
Carmelo Miranda
Vicente Ridaura
Eduardo Ruiz
Antonio Sanchez
Mariano Sanchez
Foreigner
Americo-José Da Silva-Neves
(Por)

BANESTO
Sponsor: Banking corporation.
Bicycles: Banesto.
Directeur sportif: José-Miguel
Echévarri. Assistant: Eusebio
Unzue. Manager: Francis
Lafargue
Spanish
Marino Alonso
Pedro Delgado
José-Luis De Santos
Aitor Garmendia
Julian Gorospe
Ruben Gorospe
Miguel Indurain
Prudencio Indurain
Javier Lazpiur
Roberto Lezaun
Javier Luquin
Juan Martinez-Oliver
Jokin Mujika
José-Fernando Pacheco
Jesus Rodriguez-Magro
Francesco San Roman
José-Luis Santamaria
José-Ramon Uriarte
Foreigners
Dominique Arnaud (Fr)
Jean-François Bernard (Fr)
Armand De Las Cuevas (Fr)
Fabian Fuchs (Swi)
Fabrice Philipot (Fr)
Abelardo Rondon (Col)

CLAS
Sponsor: Cooperative dairy.
Bicycles: Colnago. Directeur
sportif: Juan Fernandez.
Assistant: Jesus Suarez-Cueva.

Spanish
Guillermo Arenas
Angel Camarillo
Manuel-Jorge Dominguez
Javier Duch-Ballester
Federico Echave
Fernando Escartin
Francisco Espinosa
Iñaki Gaston
Arsenio Gonzales
Manuel Gonzalo
Victor Gonzalo
Alberto Leanizbarrutia
Pedro Marquina
Francisco Mauleon
Casimiro Moreda
José-Manuel Oliveira
Vicente Prado
Pello Ruiz-Cabestany
Juan-Carlos Sevilla
Roberto Sierra
Foreigner
Nico Emonds (B)

KELME-IBEXPRESS
Sponsors: Shoe manufacturer
and parcels service.
Bicycles: Eddy Merckx.
Directeur sportif: Rafael
Carrasco.
Assistant: Juan Suñol.
Spanish
Francisco Cabello
Xavier Claramunt
Antonio Diaz
Antonio Espejo
Ignacio Garcia
José-Maria Genesca
Bernardo Gonzalez
Mario Lara
Alvaro Pino
Juan Reina
Jesus Rosado
Ramon-Antonio Rota
Foreigners
Marco Bernal (Col)
Hernan Buenahora (Col)
Julio-Cesar Cadena (Col)
José-Martin Farfan (Col)
Nestor Mora (Col)
Pedro-Saul Morales (Col)
Luis-Felipe Moreno (Col)
Carlos Revelo (Col)
Oliveiro Rincon (Col)
Augusto Triana (Col)

LOTUS-FESTINA
Sponsor: Watch manufacturer.
Bicycles: Macario. Directeur
sportif: Miguel Moreno.
Assistant: Manuel Carrera.
Spanish
Enrique Alonso
Josaba Berrojalbiz
Jesus Blanco-Villar
Carlos Galarreta
Pedro Garcia
Ramon Gonzalez
Carlos Hernandez
Juan-Ramon Martin

Manuel Martinez-Costa
Juan-Tomas Martinez
Luis Perez
Fernando Pinero
Santiago Portillo
Josaba Ruiz-Martinez
Agualin Sebastian-Alvarez
Roberto Torres
Juan Valbuena
Foreigners
Theo Akkermans (Hol)
Vadim Chablkine (USSR)
Acacio Da Silva (Por)
Romes Gaynetdinov (USSR)
Mathieu Hermans (Hol)
Yuri Manouylov (USSR)
Joaquim Marques (Por)
Roberto Pagnin (It)
Luc Suykerbuyk (Hol)
Dmitri Vassilichenko (USSR)
Andrei Zoubov (USSR)

ONCE
Sponsor: Society of the blind,
vendors of state lottery tickets.
Bicycles: Otero and Look.
Directeur sportif: Manolo Saiz.
Assistant: Santiago Garcia.
Spanish
José Ahedo
Xavier Aldanondo
Eduardo Chozas
Luis-Maria Diaz De Otazu
Herminio Diaz-Zabala
Pedro Diaz-Zabala
Anselmo Fuerte
Santos Hernandez
Juan-Carlos Jusado
Marino Lejarreta
Juan Llaneras
Miguel Martinez
Melchor Mauri
José-Luis Villanueva
Foreigners
Stephen Hodge (Aus)
Alex Pedersen (Den)
Johnny Weltz (Den)
Kenneth Weltz (Den)

PUERTAS MAVISA
Sponsor: Wooden door
manufacturer. Bicycles: Ocaña.
Directeur sportif: Faustino
Ruperez.
Spanish
Juan-Carlos Alonso
Emilio Cuadrado
Manuel Delgado
Juan-Carlos Gonzales
Manuel Guijarro
Miguel-Angel Iglesias
Rafaël Lorenzana
Fernando Martinez De
Guerenu
José-Luis Moran
Alejandro Muñoz
José-Luis Otero
José Pedrero
Jesus Rodriguez

SEUR
Sponsor: Overnight parcels
service. Bicycles: Macario.
Directeur sportif: José-Antonio
Gonzales-Linares. Assistant:
José Garcia
Spanish
Ivan Alemany
Eleuterio Anguita
José-Juan Cano
Roque De La Cruz
Federico Garcia
Joaquim Hernandez
Pablo Moreno
Francisco Perez
José Recio
José Rodriguez
José-Salvador Sanchis
Juan Unzaga
José Urea
Foreigners
Luis Barroso (Ven)
Malcolm Elliott (GB)
Jean-Pierre Heynderickx (B)
Peter Hilse (Ger)
Ivan Ivanov (USSR)
Viktor Klimov (USSR)
Ronan Pensec (Fr)
Piotr Ugrumov (USSR)

SWITZERLAND

HELVETIA
Sponsor: Insurance company.
Bicycles: Villiger. Directeur
sportif: Paul Köchli.
Assistants: Jean-François Rault
and Alain Vigneron
Swiss
Serge Demierre
Laurent Dufaux
Mauro Gianetti
Heinz Imboden
Roman Jeker
Hans-Rudi Marki
Pascal Richard
Guido Winterberg
Foreigners
Rolf Aldag (Ger)
Gilles Delion (Fr)
Dominik Krieger (Ger)
Jean-Claude Leclercq (Fr)
Henri Manders (Hol)
Luigi Furlan (It)
Gérard Rué (Fr)
Peter Stevenhaagen (Hol)

USA

COORS LIGHT
Sponsor: Brewer. Bicycles:
Serotta. Directeur sportif: Len
Pettyjohn.
Americans
Mike Engleman
David Farmer
Alexi Grewal

Chris Huber
Roy Knickman
Scott Moninger
Greg Oravetz
Davis Phinney
Clark Sheehan
Foreigners
Roberto Gaggioli (It)
Stephen Swart (NZ)

MOTOROLA
Sponsor: Multinational
electronics manufacturer.
Bicycles: Eddy Merckx.
Directeur sportif: Jim
Ochowicz. Assistant: Noel
Dejonckheere.
Americans
Norman Alvis
Frankie Andreu
Andy Bishop
Michael Carter
Andy Hampsten
Ron Kiefel
Scott McKinley
Bob Roll
John Tomac
Foreigners
Phil Anderson (Aus)
Steve Bauer (Can)
Nathan Dahlberg (NZ)
Dag-Otto Lauritzen (Nor)
Brian Walton (Can)
Sean Yates (GB)

SPAGO
Sponsor: Restauranteurs.
Bicycles: Giordana. Directeur
sportif: Tom Kaplan.
Americans
Kenny Adams
Peter Davis
Tommy Matush
Mark Southard
Oliver Starr
Foreigners
Radisa Cubric (Yug)
Peter Gylling (Den)
Arjan Jagt (Hol)

SUBARU-MONTGOMERY
Sponsors: Auto manufacturer
and financial investment
company. Bicycles: Merlin.
Directeur sportif: Eddie
Borysewicz.
Americans
Bart Bowen
Jim Copeland
Todd Gogulski
Steve Hegg
Mike McCarthy
Gary Mulder
Nate Reiss
Thurlow Rogers
Craig Schommer
Foreigners
Andrzej Mierzejewski (Pol)
Krystof Wiatr (Pol)
Cezary Zamana (Pol)

Perrier World Cup Classification

Individual classification

#	Rider	Milan-San Remo	Tour of Flanders	Paris-Roubaix	Liège-Bastogne-Liège	Amstel Gold	Wincanton Classic	Clasicá San Sebastian	Championship of Zürich	Grand Prix Montreal	Paris-Tours	Tour of Lombardy	World Cup Final	Total
1	Maurizio Fondriest (It), Panasonic	9	6	0	1	22	16	20	18	14	0	8	18	**132**
2	Laurent Jalabert (Fr), Toshiba	4	12	3	10	14	0	18	22	0	14	13	11	**121**
3	Rolf Sörensen (Den), Ariostea	22	20	0	20	6	0	0	0	0	16	16	14	**114**
4	Edwig Van Hooydonck (B), Buckler	8	25	4	12	7	0	0	16	12	0	0	10	**94**
5	Johan Museeuw (B), Lotto	0	22	5	0	11	0	0	25	0	12	0	7	**82**
6	Marc Madiot (Fr), RMO	0	15	25	0	0	14	0	0	11	0	0	6	**71**
7	Frans Maassen (Hol), Buckler	0	16	0	3	25	11	0	0	0	0	0	15	**70**
8	Eric Van Lancker (B), Panasonic	0	0	0	16	0	25	1	0	25	0	0	0	**67**
9	Franco Ballerini (It), Del Tongo	0	13	16	0	2	10	0	0	0	0	20	5	**66**
10	Adri Van Der Poel (Hol), Tulip	0	0	0	0	8	0	0	0	13	18	10	8	**57**
11	Dirk De Wolf (B), Tonton Tapis	0	10	0	11	20	0	0	11	0	0	0	0	**52**
12	Phil Anderson (Aus), Motorola	14	3	0	6	10	0	0	14	0	0	0	4	**51**
13	Olaf Ludwig (Ger), Panasonic	0	0	12	0	15	0	0	0	0	22	0	0	**49**
13	Carlo Bowmans (B), Weinmann	0	9	20	7	13	0	0	0	0	0	0	0	**49**
15	Marc Sergeant (B), Panasonic	0	11	0	13	0	9	6	8	0	0	0	0	**47**
16	Steven Rooks (Hol), Buckler	0	0	0	0	0	15	6	0	22	0	3	0	**46**
16	Tony Rominger (Swi), Toshiba	0	0	0	0	0	0	0	0	15	0	6	25	**46**
18	Rolf Gölz (Ger), Ariostea	0	18	0	5	0	22	0	0	0	0	0	0	**45**
19	Nico Verhoeven (Hol), PDM	0	0	14	8	0	0	0	0	0	20	0	0	**42**
20	Eric Vanderaerden (B), Buckler	20	2	0	0	16	0	0	0	0	0	0	0	**38**
21	Moreno Argentin (It), Ariostea	0	0	0	25	0	0	9	0	0	0	0	0	**34**
22	Gilles Delion (Fr), Helvetia	0	0	0	0	0	18	15	0	0	0	0	0	**33**
22	Wilfried Peeters (B), Histor	0	0	15	0	0	0	5	5	0	8	0	0	33
22	Andreas Kappes (Ger), Histor	11	0	0	0	0	0	12	0	10	0	0	0	33
25	Martial Gayant (Fr), Toshiba	0	0	0	0	0	0	0	0	0	0	22	9	**31**
26	Maximillian Sciandri (It), Carrera	0	0	0	0	0	0	0	20	0	10	0	0	**30**
27	Gianni Bugno (It), Gatorade	0	0	0	4	0	0	25	0	0	0	0	0	**29**
27	Martin Earley (Ire), PDM	0	0	0	0	0	0	0	0	20	0	9	0	**29**
29	Sean Kelly (Ire), PDM	0	0	0	0	0	0	0	0	0	3	25	0	**28**
30	Jean-Claude Colotti (Fr), Tonton Tapis	0	0	22	5	0	0	0	0	0	0	0	0	**27**
30	Johan Capiot (B), TVM	0	0	0	0	0	0	0	0	0	25	0	2	**27**
32	Miguel Indurain (Sp), Banesto	0	0	0	18	0	0	7	0	0	0	0	0	**25**
33	Jan Goessens (B), Weinmann	0	0	0	0	3	20	0	0	0	0	0	0	**23**
34	Claude Criquielion (B), Lotto	0	0	0	22	0	0	0	0	0	0	0	0	**22**
34	Pedro Delgado (Sp), Banesto	0	0	0	0	0	0	22	0	0	0	0	0	**22**
34	Raúl Alcalá (Mex), PDM	0	0	0	15	0	0	0	0	7	0	0	0	**22**
34	Bruno Cenghialta (It), Ariostea	0	0	0	0	0	8	14	0	0	0	0	0	**22**
34	Rudy Verdonck (B), Weinmann	0	0	0	0	0	5	0	6	0	11	0	0	**22**
39	Iñaki Gaston (Sp), Clas	5	0	0	0	0	0	16	0	0	0	0	0	**21**
40	Bruno Cornillet (Fr), Z	0	0	0	0	0	0	3	0	0	0	0	18	**21**

Team classification

#	Team	Milan-San Remo	Tour of Flanders	Paris-Roubaix	Liège-Bastogne-Liège	Amstel Gold	Wincanton Classic	Clasicá San Sebastian	Championship of Zürich	Grand Prix de la Liberation	Grand Prix Montreal	Paris-Tours	Tour of Lombardy	Total
1	Panasonic (Hol)	7	6	12	7	9	12	12	8	14	12	3	5	**107**
2	Buckler (Hol)	8	12	1	9	12	7	1	9	18	9	0	0	**86**
3	PDM (Hol)	0	2	8	8	0	2	0	12	13	8	4	9	**66**
4	Ariostea (It)	0	7	0	12	0	9	9	2	0	0	5	6	**50**
5	Lotto (B)	0	8	9	4	4	1	0	5	0	7	7	1	**46**
6	ONCE (Sp)	6	0	0	6	0	0	3	0	15	0	0	4	**34**
6	Weinmann (B)	0	3	3	3	8	8	0	0	8	2	0	0	**35**
8	RMO (Fr)	0	9	7	0	3	0	1	0	0	6	0	8	**34**
9	Toshiba (Fr)	1	0	5	0	0	0	0	3	0	4	8	12	**33**
10	TVM-Sanyo (Hol)	0	4	3	0	0	0	0	0	12	1	12	0	**32**
11	Histor (B)	12	0	0	0	0	3	8	0	7	1	0	0	**31**
12	Tulip (B)	0	0	4	0	7	0	0	0	10	0	9	0	**30**
13	Motorola (USA)	3	0	0	0	5	0	0	0	11	3	6	0	**28**
14	Carrera (Fr)	9	0	0	0	1	0	0	7	0	5	2	0	**24**
15	Tonton Tapis (B)	0	5	6	5	6	0	0	1	0	0	0	0	**23**
16	Helvetia (Swi)	2	0	0	2	0	6	7	4	0	0	0	0	**21**

Results

Professional
1	Radomir Simunek (Cz)	1:4.22
2	Adri Van Der Poel (Hol)	st
3	Bruno Lebras (Fr)	at 0:06
4	Henk Baars (Hol)	at 0:24
5	Wim Lambrechts (B)	at 0:28
6	Frank Van Bakel (Hol)	at 0:33
7	Roger Honneger (Swi)	at 0:37
8	Martin Hendriks (Hol)	at 0:46
9	Dominique Arnaud (Fr)	at 1:06
10	Christophe Lavainne (Fr)	at 1:40

Amateur
1	Thomas Frischknecht (Swi)	50:19
2	Henrik Djernis (Den)	at 0:23
3	Daniele Pontoni (It)	st
4	Marcel Gerritson (Hol)	at 0:25
5	Edward Kuyper (Hol)	at 0:30
6	Timo Berner (Ger)	at 0:31
7	Rudy Thielemans (B)	at 0:44
8	Beat Wabel (Swi)	st
9	Radovan Fort (Cz)	at 0:54
10	Pavel Elsnic (Cz)	at 0:58

Junior
1	Ondrej Lukes (Cz)	45:47
2	Jiri Pospisil (Cz)	st
3	Dariusz Gil (Pol)	st
4	Vaclan Vetlicka (Cz)	at 0:01
5	Jan Ulrich (Ger)	st
6	Jan Faltynek (Cz)	at 0:04
7	Marcel Vrogten (Hol)	at 0:21
8	Tomasz Bukowski (Pol)	at 0:36
9	Roman Joerdens (Ger)	at 0:45
10	Patrick Flame (Ger)	at 0:48

SIX DAY RACING
Dortmund, Germany: 25-30 October
1	Olaf Ludwig (Ger) and Urs Freuler (Swi)	461 pts
2	Andreas Kappes (Ger) and Danny Clark (Aus)	450pts
3	(at 1 lap) Konstantin Krabsov (USSR) and Marat Ganeev (USSR)	231pts
4	(at 4 laps) Roland Gunther (Ger) and Stan Tourné (B)	176pts
5	(at 5 laps) Torsten Rellensmann (Ger) and Tony Doyle (GB)	184pts

Grenoble, France: 1-6 November
1	Laurent Fignon (Fr) and Laurent Biondi (Fr)	117pts
2	(at 1 lap) Pierangelo Bincoletto (It) and Adriano Baffi (It)	171pts
3	(at 1 lap) Gilbert Duclos-Lassalle (Fr) and Philippe Louviot (Fr)	112 pts
4	(at 2 laps) Tony Doyle (GB) and Rik Van Slycke (B)	52 pts
5	(at 3 laps) Olaf Ludwig (Ger) and Volker Diehl (Ger)	63pts

Munich, Germany: 8-13 November
1	Tony Doyle (GB) and Danny Clark (Aus)	303 pts
2	(at 1 lap) Pierangelo Bincoletto (It) and Adriano Baffi (It)	447pts
3	(at 1 lap) Urs Freuler (Swi) and Olaf Ludwig (Ger)	430pts
4	(at 1 lap) Andreas Kappes (Ger) and Etienne De Wilde (B)	369pts
5	(at 2 laps) Stan Tourné (B) and Jens Veggerby (Den)	248pts

Bordeaux, France: 14-19 November
1	Gilbert Duclos-Lassalle (Fr) and Etienne De Wilde (B)	219 pts
2	Pascal Lino (Fr) and Tony Doyle (GB)	74pts
3	(at 1 lap) Laurent Biondi (Fr) and Pierangelo Bincoletto (It)	175pts
4	(at 2 laps) Marc Meilleur (Fr) and Volker Diehl (Ger)	106pts
5	(at 4 laps) Konstantin Krabzov (USSR) and Marat Ganeev (USSR)	138pts

Ghent, Belgium: 20-25 November
1	Danny Clark (Aus) and Roland Gunther (Ger)	555pts
2	(at 2 laps) Konstantin Krabsov (USSR) and Marat Ganeev (USSR)	535pts
3	(at 2 laps) Urs Freuler (Swi) and Hans-Rudi Marki (Swi)	489pts
4	(at 2 laps) Tony Doyle (GB) and Stan Tourné (B)	217pts
5	(at 3 laps) Jens Veggerby (Den) and Rik Van Slycke (B)	350pts

Zürich, Switzerland: 26 November-2 December
1	Adriano Baffi (It) and Pierangelo Bincoletto (It)	259pts
2	(at 1 lap) Urs Freuler (Swi) and Hans-Rudi Marki (Swi)	259pts

3	(at 1 lap) Stefan Joho (Swi) and Werner Stutz (Swi)	245pts
4	(at 2 laps) Laurent Biondi (Fr) and Gilbert Duclos-Lassalle (Fr)	130pts
5	(at 3 laps) Tony Doyle (GB) and Bruno Holenweger (Swi)	164pts

Cologne, Germany: 27 December-1 January
1	Andreas Kappes (Ger) and Etienne De Wilde (B)	594pts
2	(at 1 lap)Bruno Holenweger (Swi) and Pierangelo Bincoletto (It)	622pts
3	(at 1 lap) Jens Veggerby (Den) and Stan Tourné (B)	465pts
4	(at 15 laps) Volker Diehl (Ger) and Roland Gunther (Ger)	314pts
5	(at 20 laps) Carsten Wolf (Ger) and Laurent Biondi (Fr)	334pts

Bremen, Germany: 10-15 January
1	Etienne De Wilde (B) and Andreas Kappes (Ger)	707pts
2	(at 1 lap) Danny Clark (Aus) and Urs Freuler (Swi)	740pts
3	(at 2 laps) Volker Diehl (Ger) and Bruno Holenweger (Swi)	539pts
4	(at 2 laps) Roland Gunther (Ger) and Remig Stumpf (Ger)	454pts
5	(at 7 laps) Rudy Dhaenens (B) and Pierangelo Bincoletto (It)	398pts

Stuttgart, Germany: 18-23 January
1	Etienne De Wilde (B) and Andreas Kappes (Ger)	387pts
2	(at 1 lap) Jens Veggerby (Den) and Stan Tourné (B)	239pts
3	(at 2 laps) Danny Clark (Aus) and Roland Gunther (Ger)	367pts
4	(at 4 laps) Urs Freuler (Swi) and Tony Doyle (GB)	233pts
5	(at 5 laps) Remig Stumpf (Ger) and Carsten Wolf (Ger)	410pts

Antwerp, Belgium: 25-30 January
1	Rudy Dhaenens (B) and Etienne De Wilde (B)	354pts
2	Stan Tourné (B) and Jens Veggerby (Den)	339pts
3	(at 1 lap) Danny Clark (Aus) and Johan Bruyneel (B)	332pts
4	(at 2 laps) Pierangelo Bincoletto (It) and Rolf Sörensen (Den)	226pts
5	(at 5 laps) Tony Doyle (GB) and Eric Vanderaerden (B)	146pts

Copenhagen, Denmark: 1-6 February
1	Jens Veggerby (Den) and Danny Clark (Aus)	487pts
2	Pierangelo Bincoletto (It) and Bruno Holenweger (Swi)	384pts
3	(at 1 lap) Adriano Baffi (It) and Rolf Sörensen (Den)	417pts
4	(at 2 laps) Urs Freuler (Swi) and Jesper Worre (Den)	302pts
5	(at 6 laps) Etienne De Wilde (B) and Brian Holm (Den)	241pts

EUROPEAN TRACK CHAMPIONSHIPS
Grenoble, France: 7-9 December
Omnium
Points: Konstantin Krabsov (USSR)
1000m: Konstantin Krabsov (USSR)
Pursuit: Konstantin Krabsov (USSR)
Elimination: Carsten Wolf (Ger)
Overall
1	Konstantin Krabsov (USSR)	11pts
2	Jens Veggerby (Den)	11pts
3	Guy Tarantini (Fr)	13pts
4	Carsten Wolf (Ger)	15pts
5	Pierangelo Bincoletto (It)	16pts

Derny
1	Stan Tourné (B)	at 62.161km/h
2	Laurent Biondi (Fr)	at 0:01
3	Luc Colyn (B)	at 0:03
4	Torsten Rellensman (Ger)	at 2 laps
5	Vincent Lavenu (Fr)	

Madison
1	Pierangelo Bincoletto (It) and Jens Veggerby (Den)	22pts
2	Guy Tarantini (Fr) and Laurent Biondi (Fr)	
3	(at 1 lap) Carsten Wolf (Ger) and Roland Gunther (Ger)	33pts
4	(at 1 lap) Konstantin Krabsov (USSR) and Stan Tourné (B)	24pts
5	(at 1 lap) Markus Hess (Ger) and Gerd Dorich (Ger)	9pts

Motor-paced
Title originally cancelled − not enough motor bikes available. But then title re-scheduled to 23 December and contested at Dortmund, Germany. Torsten Rellensman (Ger) won.

1	Andreas Kappes (Ger), Histor	4:46.30
2	Carlo Bomans (B), Weinmann	st
3	Edwig Van Hooydonck (B), Buckler	st
4	Peter Huyghe (Hol), La William	st
5	Jelle Nijdam (Hol), Buckler	st
6	Johan Museeuw (B), Lotto	st
7	Danny Nelissen (Hol), PDM	st
8	Marc Sergeant (B), Panasonic	st
9	Thierry Gouvenou (Fr), Z	st
10	Etienne De Wilde (B), Histor	st

1	Tony Rominger (Swi), Toshiba	24:09.19
2	Laurent Jalabert (Fr), Toshiba	at 1:55
3	Martial Gayant (Fr), Toshiba	at 2:27
4	Stephen Roche (Ire), Tonton Tapis	at 2:39.5
5	Andy Hampsten (USA), Motorola	at 2:41.6
6	Jérôme Simon (Fr), Z	at 2:53
7	Claude Criquielion (B), Lotto	at 3:16
8	Eric Caritoux (Fr), RMO	at 3:20
9	Atle Kvalsvoll (Hol), Z	at 3:49
10	Laurent Fignon (Fr), Castorama	at 4:16

Stage winners
Stage 1: Thierry Marie (Fr), Castorama
Stage 2 (TTT): Toshiba (Fr)
Stage 3: Andreas Kappes (Ger), Histor
Stage 4: Viktor Klimov (USSR), Seur
Stage 5: Jean-Paul Van Poppel (Hol), PDM
Stage 6: Tony Rominger (Swi), Toshiba
Stage 7: Uwe Ampler (Ger), Histor
Stage 8: Tony Rominger (Swi), Toshiba

1	Herminio Diaz-Zabala (Sp), ONCE	35:12.46
2	Federico Ghiotto (It), Ariostea	at 0:04
3	Raúl Alcalá (Mex), PDM	at 0:52
4	Thomas Wegmüller (Swi), Weinmann	st
5	Maarten Den Bakker (Hol), PDM	at 2:01
6	Jesper Skibby (Den), TVM	at 2:45
7	Gérard Rué (Fr), Helvetia	st
8	Giuseppe Petito (It), Gis-Ballan	at 3:22
9	Scott Sunderland (Aus), TVM	at 3:32
10	Luc Leblanc (Fr), Castorama	at 3:35

Stage winners
Stage 1: Federico Ghiotto (It), Ariostea
Stage 2: Pascal Richard (Swi), Helvetia
Stage 3: Dmitri Konyshev (USSR), TVM
Stage 4: Silvio Martinello (It), Gis-Ballan
Stage 5: Gérard Rué (Fr), Castorama
Stage 6: Dirk De Wolf (B), PDM
Stage 7: Jesper Skibby (Den), TVM
Stage 8 (TT): Eric Breukink (Hol), PDM

1	Claudio Chiappucci (It), Carrera	6:56.36
2	Rolf Sörensen (Den), Ariostea	at 0:45
3	Eric Vanderaerden (B), Buckler	at 0:57
4	Djamolidin Abdujaparov (USSR), Carrera	st
5	Eddy Planckaert (B), Panasonic	st
6	Gérard Rué (Fr), Helvetia	st
7	Phil Anderson (Aus), Motorola	st
8	Uwe Raab (Ger), PDM	st
9	Johnny Weltz (Den), ONCE	st
10	Andreas Kappes (Ger), Histor	st

1	Stephen Roche (Ire), Tonton Tapis	7:56.55
2	Gérard Rué (Fr), Helvetia	at 0:18
3	Charly Mottet (Fr), RMO	at 0:26
4	Johan Bruyneel (B), Lotto	at 0:40
5	Eric Breukink (Hol), PDM	at 0:59
6	Dmitri Zhdanov (USSR), Panasonic	at 1:08
7	Pascal Lance (Fr), RMO	at 1:18
8	Dmitri Konyshev (USSR), TVM	at 1:25
9	Jérôme Simon (Fr), Z	at 1:27
10	Fabian Jeker (Swi), Helvetia	at 1:30

Stage winners
Stage 1: Jean-Claude Leclercq (Fr), Helvetia
Stage 2: Charly Mottet (Fr), RMO
Stage 3 (TT): Viatcheslav Ekimov (USSR), Panasonic

1	Edwin Van Hooydonck (B), Buckler	7:2.0
2	Johan Museeuw (B), Lotto	at 0:45
3	Rolf Sörensen (Den), Ariostea	st
4	Rolf Gölz (Ger), Ariostea	st
5	Frans Maassen (Hol), Buckler	at 1:43
6	Marc Madiot (Fr), RMO	at 1:48
7	Jesper Skibby (Den), TVM	st
8	Franco Ballerini (It), Del Tongo	st
9	Laurent Jalabert (Fr), Toshiba	st
10	Marc Sergeant (B), Panasonic	st

GHENT-WEVELGEM *page 32*
1 Djamolidin Abdujaparov (USSR), Carrera 5:16.38
2 Mario Cipollini (It), Del Tongo st
3 Olaf Ludwig (Ger), Panasonic st
4 Eric Vanderaerden (B), Buckler st
5 Kurt Onclin (B), Tulip st
6 Marc Sergeant (B), Panasonic st
7 Jean-Claude Colotti (Fr), Tonton Tapis st
8 Johan Museeuw (B), Lotto st
9 Didier Priem (B), Tonton Tapis st
10 Allan Peiper (Aus), Tulip st

PARIS-ROUBAIX *page 34*
1 Marc Madiot (Fr), RMO 7:08.19
2 Jean-Claude Colotti (Fr), Tonton Tapis at 1:07
3 Carlo Bomans (B), Weinmann st
4 Steve Bauer (Can), Motorola st
5 Franco Ballerini (It), Del Tongo st
6 Wilfried Peeters (B), Histor st
7 Nico Verhoeven (Hol), PDM st
8 Marc Sergeant (B), Panasonic st
9 Olaf Ludwig (Ger), Panasonic at 1:41
10 Hendrik Redant (B), Lotto st

FLÈCHE WALLONNE *page 38*
1 Moreno Argentin (It), Ariostea 5:13.14
2 Claude Criquielion (B), Lotto at 2:20
3 Claudio Chiappucci (It), Carrera at 2:31
4 Jean-François Bernard (Fr), Banesto at 2:39
5 Dmitri Konyshev (USSR), TVM at 3:02
6 Johan Bruyneel (B), Lotto at 4:19
7 Eric Van Lancker (B), Panasonic at 4:26
8 Marino Lejarreta (Sp), ONCE at 4:53
9 Iñaki Gaston (Sp), Clas at 4:58
10 Benny Heylen (B), SEFB st

LIÈGE-BASTOGNE-LIÈGE *page 40*
1 Moreno Argentin (It), Ariostea 7:15.00
2 Claude Criquielion (B), Lotto st
3 Rolf Sörensen (Den), Ariostea st
4 Miguel Indurain (Sp), Banesto st
5 Eric Van Lancker (B), Panasonic at 0:10
6 Raúl Alcalá (Mex), PDM st
7 Marino Lejarreta (Sp), ONCE st
8 Stephen Roche (Ire), Tonton Tapis st
9 Edwig Van Hooydonck (B), Buckler at 2:30
10 Dirk De Wolf (B), Tonton Tapis at 2:36

AMSTEL GOLD RACE *page 44*
1 Frans Maassen (Hol), Buckler 6:04.46
2 Maurizio Fondriest (It), Ariostea st
3 Dirk De Wolf (B), Tonton Tapis st
4 Thierry Laurent (Fr), RMO at 0:10
5 Eric Vanderaerden (B), Buckler st
6 Olaf Ludwig (Ger), Panasonic st
7 Laurent Jalabert (Fr), Toshiba st
8 Carlo Bomans (B), Weinmann st
9 Jelle Nijdam (Hol), Buckler st
10 Johan Museeuw (B), Lotto st

FOUR DAYS OF DUNKIRK *page 46*
1 Charly Mottet (Fr), RMO 24:18.54
2 Laurent Jalabert (Fr), Toshiba at 0:14
3 Johan Museeuw (B), Lotto at 0:16
4 Frans Maassen (Hol), Buckler at 0:24
5 Thierry Marie (Fr), Castorama at 0:46
6 Dmitri Zhdanov (USSR), Panasonic at 0:47
7 Viatcheslav Ekimov (USSR), Panasonic at 0:53
8 Jean-Claude Colotti (Fr), Tonton Tapis at 1:07
9 Peter De Clercq (B), Lotto at 1:14
10 Thierry Laurent (Fr), RMO at 1:16
Stage winners
Stage 1: Remig Stumpf (Ger), Toshiba
Stage 2: Laurent Jalabert (Fr), Toshiba
Stage 3 (TT): Frans Maassen (Hol), Buckler
Stage 4: Paul Haghedooren (B), SEFB
Stage 5: Johan Museeuw (B), Lotto
Stage 6 (TT): Frans Maassen (Hol), Buckler
Stage 7: Charly Mottet (Fr), RMO
Stage 8: Johan Capiot (B), TVM

TOUR DE ROMANDIE *page 48*
1 Tony Rominger (Swi), Toshiba 21:00.19
2 Robert Millar (GB), Z at 1:31
3 Michael Carter (USA), Motorola at 2:52
4 Stephen Hodge (Aus), ONCE at 3:00
5 Laurent Dufaux (Swi), Helvetia at 3:27
6 Uwe Ampler (Ger), Histor at 3:52
7 Zenon Jaskula (Pol), Del Tongo at 4:06
8 Denis Roux (Fr), Toshiba at 4:50
9 Gianni Bugno (It), Gatorade at 5:12
10 Pedro Delgado (Sp), Banesto at 5:38
Stage winners
Prologue: Pascal Richard (Swi), Helvetia
Stage 1: Jean-Claude Leclercq (Fr), Helvetia

Stage 2: Tony Rominger (Swi), Toshiba
Stage 3: Stephen Hodge (Aus), ONCE
Stage 4a: Serge Demierre (Swi), Helvetia
Stage 4b (TT): Tony Rominger (Swi), Toshiba
Stage 5: Pascal Richard (Swi), Helvetia

CLASSIQUE DES ALPES *page 50*
1 Charly Mottet (Fr), RMO 6:18.03
2 Robert Millar (GB), Z at 0:02
3 Luc Leblanc (Fr), Castorama at 2:53
4 Michael Carter (USA), Motorola at 2:56
5 Claude Criquielion (B), Lotto at 4:12
6 Alfred Achermann (Swi), Weinmann st
7 Mauro Gianetti (Swi), Helvetia st
8 Laurent Dufaux (Swi), Helvetia at 4:19
9 Harry Lodge (GB), Collstrop-Isoglass at 7:00
10 Johan Bruyneel (B), Lotto at 7:57

TOUR DU PONT *page 54*
1 Eric Breukink (Hol), PDM 48:56.53
2 Atle Kvalsvoll (Nor), Z at 0:12
3 Rolf Aldag (Ger), Helvetia at 1:07
4 Alexi Grewal (USA), Coors Light at 1:56
5 Bobby Julich, US amateur at 2:06
6 Steve Bauer (Can), Motorola at 2:09
7 Ronan Pensec (Fr), Seur at 2:29
8 Mike Engelman (USA), Coors Light at 2:34
9 Fabian Jeker (Swi), Helvetia at 3:02
10 Vladislav Bobrik, USSR amateur at 3:56
Stage winners
Prologue (TT): Eric Breukink (Hol), PDM
Stage 1: Davis Phinney (USA), Coors Light
Stage 2: Patrick Roelandt (B), Tonton Tapis
Stage 3: Rolf Aldag (Ger), Helvetia
Stage 4: Phil Anderson (Aus), Motorola
Stage 5: Nathan Sheafor, US amateur
Stage 6: Atle Kvalsvoll (Nor), Z
Stage 7: Steve Bauer (Can), Motorola
Stage 8: Rolf Aldag (Ger), Helvetia
Stage 9: Eladio Ambite (Sp), Amaya
Stage 10: Steve Bauer (Can), Motorola
Stage 11 (TT): Eric Breukink (Hol), PDM

VUELTA A ESPAÑA *page 58*
1 Melchor Mauri (Sp), ONCE 82:48.07
2 Miguel Indurain (Sp), Banesto at 2:52
3 Marino Lejarreta (Sp), ONCE at 3:11
4 Federico Echave (Sp), Clas at 3:54
5 Fabio Parra (Col), Amaya at 5:38
6 Pello Ruiz Cabestany (Sp), Clas at 6:50
7 Raúl Alcalá (Mex), PDM at 6:57
8 Piotr Ugrumov (USSR), Seur at 10:43
9 Steven Rooks (Hol), Buckler at 12:09
10 Oliveiro Rincon (Col), Kelme at 12:11
11 Eduardo Chozas (Sp), ONCE at 14:07
12 Tom Cordes (Hol), PDM at 14:35
13 Luis Herrera (Col), Ryalcao-Postobon at 16:36
14 Iñaki Gaston (Sp), Clas at 17:06
15 Laudelino Cubino (Sp), Amaya at 17:12
16 Jon Unzaga (Sp), Seur at 20:54
17 Udo Bölts (Ger), Telekom at 22:09
18 Marco Giovannetti (It), Gatorade at 22:57
19 Ivan Ivanov (USSR), Seur at 24:57
20 Fernando Martinez de Guerenu (Sp), Puertas Mavisa at 25:30
21 Francisco-Javier Mauleon (Sp), Clas at 27:42
22 Alvaro Mejia (Col), Ryalcao-Postobon at 28:00
23 Jesus Montoya (Sp), Amaya at 28:54
24 Fabrice Philipot (Fr), Banesto at 29:27
25 Gerardo Moncada (Col), Ryalcao-Postobon at 30:05
26 Henry Cardenas (Col), Ryalcao-Postobon at 31:11
27 Santos Hernandez (Sp), ONCE at 32:26
28 Jesper Skibby (Den), TVM at 32:55
29 Nestor Mora (Col), Kelme at 32:56
30 Gerrit De Vries (Hol), Buckler at 34:46
31 José Rodriguez (Sp), Seur at 35:29
32 Jim Van Der Laer (B), Tulip at 35:56
33 Alvaro Sierra (Col), Ryalcao-Postobon at 36:14
34 Juan-Tomas Martinez (Sp), Lotus-Festina at 38:03
35 Pascal Lino (Fr), RMO at 42:15
36 Jesus Blanco Villar (Sp), Lotus-Festina at 43:02
37 Luc Roosen (B), Tulip at 44:22
38 Abelardo Rondon (Col), Banesto at 45:48
39 Jesus Rodriguez (Sp), Puertas Mavisa at 47:03
40 Jesus Rodriguez Magro (Sp), Banesto at 48:46
41 Eddy Bouwmans (Hol), Panasonic at 49:13
42 Herminio Diaz-Zabala (Sp), ONCE at 49:33
43 Uwe Raab (Ger), PDM at 52:33
44 Alberto Leanizbarrutia (Sp), Clas at 53:11
45 Cassio Freitas (Bra), Sicasal at 56:40
46 Christophe Manin (Fr), RMO at 56:53
47 Guido Bontempi (It), Carrera at 57:06
48 Johnny Weltz (Den), ONCE at 58:43
49 Carmelo Miranda (Sp), Artiach-Royal at 59:23
50 Marc Van Orsouw (Hol), Panasonic at 1:02.30

Stage winners
Stage 1 (Three man TTT): Melchor Mauri, Anselmo Fuerte, Herminio Diaz Zabala (Sp), ONCE
Stage 2a: Michel Zanoli (Hol), Tulip
Stage 2b (TTT): ONCE (Sp)
Stage 3: Jesper Skibby (Den), TVM
Stage 4: Jesus Cruz Martin (Sp), Wigarma
Stage 5: Uwe Raab (Ger), PDM
Stage 6: Jean-Paul Van Poppel (Hol), PDM
Stage 7: Jesper Skibby (Den), TVM
Stage 8 (TT): Melchor Mauri (Sp), ONCE
Stage 9: Jean-Paul Van Poppel (Hol), PDM
Stage 10: Guido Bontempi (It), Carrera
Stage 11: Cancelled
Stage 12: Ivan Ivanov (USSR), Seur
Stage 13: Jean-Paul Van Poppel (Hol), PDM
Stage 14 (TT): Fabio Parra (Col), Amaya
Stage 15: Guido Bontempi (It), Carrera
Stage 16: Luis Herrera (Col), Ryalcao-Postobon
Stage 17: Laudelino Cubino (Sp), Amaya
Stage 18: Antonio Miguel Diaz (Sp), Kelme
Stage 19 (TT): Melchor Mauri (Sp), ONCE
Stage 20: Jesus Montoya (Sp), Amaya
Stage 21: Jean-Paul Van Poppel (Hol), PDM
Teams classification
ONCE (Sp)
Mountains prize
Luis Herrera (Col), Ryalcao-Postobon
Best sprinter
Uwe Raab (Ger), PDM
Flying sprint
Miguel Angel Iglesias (Sp), Puertas Mavisa
Special sprint
Acacio Da Silva (Port), Lotus-Festina
Combined points jersey
Federico Echave (Sp), Clas
Neo-professional
Oliveiro Rincon (Col), Kelme

MILK RACE *page 64*
1 Chris Walker (GB), Banana-Falcon 45:33.21
2 Simeon Hempsall, Great Britain am at 0:22
3 Keith Reynolds (GB), Banana-Falcon at 0:25
4 Harry Lodge (GB), Collstrop-Isoglass at 0:51
5 Rob Holden (GB), Banana-Falcon at 0:56
6 Paul Curran (GB), Great Britain am at 1:02
7 Darren Baker, United States am at 1:58
8 Zbigniew Piatek, Poland am at 2:07
9 Bob Rasenberg, Holland am at 2:11
10 Steve Douce (GB), British Professionals at 2:13
Stage winners
Prologue: Jonny Clay (GB), Banana-Falcon
Stage 1a: Chris Walker (GB), Banana-Falcon
Stage 1b: Jan Bogaert (B), Collstrop-Isoglass
Stage 2: Simeon Hempsall, Great Britain am
Stage 3: Mark Walsham (GB), British Professionals
Stage 4: Johan Van den Dries, Belgium am
Stage 5: Darren Lawson, Australia am
Stage 6: Mark Gornall, Great Britain am
Stage 7: Patrick Jonker, Australia am
Stage 8: Chris Walker (GB), Banana-Falcon
Stage 9: Kevin Kimmage, Ireland am
Stage 10: Chris Walker (GB), Banana-Falcon
Stage 11: Jerry Cooman (B), SEFB-Saxon
Stage 12: Jerry Cooman (B), SEFB-Saxon
King of the Mountains
Tom Bamford
Points
Chris Walker
Combined competition
Chris Walker
Hot spot sprint competition
Jon Walshaw
Most aggressive rider overall
Steve Douce
Most unfortunate rider overall
Daniel Beelen

DAUPHINÉ LIBÉRÉ *page 68*
1 Luis Herrera (Col), Ryalcao-Postobon 28:38.09
2 Laudelino Cubino (Sp), Amaya at 0:46
3 Tony Rominger (Swi), Toshiba at 1:18
4 Robert Millar (GB), Z at 4:20
5 Oliveiro Rincon (Col), Kelme at 4:50
6 Eddy Bouwmans (Hol), Panasonic at 5:17
7 Andy Hampsten (USA), Motorola at 5:24
8 Luc Leblanc (Fr), Castorama at 5:35
9 Martin Farfán (Col), Kelme at 6:13
10 Alvaro Mejia (Col), Kelme at 7:52

CORESTATES CHAMPIONSHIP *page 70*
1 Michel Zanoli (Hol), Tulip 6:15.15
2 Davis Phinney (USA), Coors Light st
3 Phil Anderson (Aus), Motorola st
4 Kurt Stockton (USA), Chevrolet-LA Sheriffs st

5	Adri Van Der Poel (Hol), Tulip	st
6	Ettore Pastorelli (It), Gis-Ballan	st
7	Greg Oravetz (USA), Coors Light	st
8	Matt Eaton (USA), Poland Spring-Tommasini	st
9	Derin Stockton (USA), Chevrolet-LA Sheriffs	st
10	Paul Haghedooren (B), SEFB	st

GIRO D'ITALIA *page 72*

1	Franco Chioccioli (It), Del Tongo	99:35.43
2	Claudio Chiappucci (It), Carrera	at 3:48
3	Massimiliano Lelli (It), Ariostea	at 6:56
4	Gianni Bugno (It), Gatorade	at 7:49
5	Marino Lejarreta (Sp), ONCE	at 10:23
6	Eric Boyer (Fr), Z	at 11:09
7	Leonardo Sierra (Ven), Selle Italia	at 11:56
8	Marco Giovannetti (It), Gatorade	at 13:09
9	Zenon Jaskula (Pol), Del Tongo	at 18:22
10	Eduardo Chozas (Sp), ONCE	at 23:42
11	Vladimir Pulnikov (USSR), Carrera	at 24:36
12	Nelson Rodriguez (Col), Pony Malta	at 24:57
13	Federico Echave (Sp), Clas	st
14	Jean-François Bernard (Fr), Banesto	at 29:32
15	Pedro Delgado (Sp), Banesto	at 30:03
16	Gianluca Bortolami (It), Colnago	at 34:32
17	Gianni Faresin (It), ZG Mobili	at 35:44
18	Franco Vona (It), Jolly-Club 88	at 40:05
19	Juan Tomas Martinez (Sp), Lotus-Festina	at 43:47
20	Santos Hernandez (Sp), ONCE	at 43:49
21	Fabian Fuchs (Swi), Banesto	at 56:37
22	Stefano Della Santa (It), Amore E Vita	at 1:02.12
23	Iñaki Gaston (Sp), Clas	at 1:04.15
24	Michele Moro (It), Italbonifica	at 1:07.34
25	Miguel Arroyo (Mex), Z	at 1:08.10
26	Stephen Hodge (Aus), ONCE	at 1:11.30
27	Alessandro Giannelli (It), Carrera	at 1:14.04
28	Jean Claude Bagot (Fr), Castorama	at 1:14.10
29	Dominique Arnould (Fr), Castorama	at 1:18.03
30	Atle Kvalsvoll (Nor), Z	at 1:18.42
31	Roberto Gusmeroli (It), Gatorade	at 1:22.13
32	Ronan Pensec (Fr), Seur	at 1:24.31
33	Dominique Arnould (Fr), Banesto	at 1:27.05
34	Viktor Klimov (USSR), Seur	at 1:31.31
35	Federico Garcia (Sp), Seur	at 1:31.50
36	Gilbert Duclos-Lassalle (Fr), Z	at 1:33.36
37	Marco Vitali (It), Jolly-Club 88	at 1:33.56
38	Maurizio Piovani (It), Colnago	at 1:34.37
39	Germano Pierdomenico (It), Gis-Ballan,	at 1:35.01
40	Ruben Gorospe (Sp), Banesto	at 1:35.35
41	Juan Valbuena Roset (Sp), Lotus-Festina	at 1:36.51
42	Roberto Conti (It), Ariostea	at 1:39.46
43	Bjarne Rijs (Den), Castorama,	at 1:39.58
44	Demetrio Cuspoca (Col), Pony Malta	at 1:45.37
45	Enrico Zaina (It), Carrera	at 1:47.37
46	Sergio Carcano (It), Italbonifica	at 1:53.12
47	Valerio Tebaldi (It), Gatorade	at 1:54.52
48	Marek Szerszynski (Pol), Colnago	at 1:58.43
49	François Lemarchand (Fr), Z	at 2:02.55
50	Alvaro Lonzano (Col), Pony Malta	at 2:05.34

Stage winners
Stage 1: Philippe Casado (Fr), Z
Stage 2a: Gianni Bugno (It), Gatorade
Stage 2b (TT): Gianluca Pierobon (It), ZG-Mobili
Stage 3: Mario Cipollini (It), Del Tongo
Stage 4: Eric Boyer (Fr), Z
Stage 5: Marino Lejarretta (Sp), ONCE
Stage 6: Vladimir Pulnikov (USSR), Carrera
Stage 7: Mario Cipollini (It), Del Tongo
Stage 8: Davide Cassani (It), Ariostea
Stage 9: Massimo Ghirotto (It), Carrera
Stage 10 (TT): Gianni Bugno (It), Gatorade
Stage 11: Maximilan Sciandri (It), Carrera
Stage 12: Massimiliano Lelli (It), Ariostea
Stage 13: Eduardo Chozas (Sp), ONCE
Stage 14: Franco Ballerini (It), Del Tongo
Stage 15: Franco Chioccioli (It), Del Tongo
Stage 16: Massimiliano Lelli (It), Ariostea
Stage 17: Franco Chioccioli (It), Del Tongo
Stage 18: Silvio Martinello (It), Gis
Stage 19: Gianni Bugno (It), Gatorade
Stage 20 (TT): Franco Chioccioli (It), Del Tongo
Stage 21: Mario Cipollini (It), Del Tongo
Best team
Carrera
Best climber
Iñaki Gaston (Sp), Clas
Best young rider
Massimiliano Lelli (It), Ariostea
Points
Claudio Chiappucci (It), Carrera
Intergiro
Alberto Leanizbarrutia (Sp), Clas

TOUR OF SWITZERLAND *page 80*

1	Luc Roosen (B), Tulip	50:18.20
2	Pascal Richard (Swi), Helvetia	at 0:33

3	Andy Hampsten (USA), Motorola	at 2:33
4	Miguel Arroyo (Mex), Z	at 4:11
5	Robert Millar (GB), Z	at 6:33
6	Eddy Bouwmans (Hol), Panasonic	at 9:25
7	Giorgio Furlan (It), Ariostea	at 10:42
8	Bruno Cornillet (Fr), Z	at 13:00
9	Jérôme Simon (Fr), Z	at 14:12
10	Udo Bölts (Ger), Telekom	at 14:42

Stage winners
Prologue: Jean-Claude Leclerq (Fr), Helvetia
Stage 1: Heinz Imboden (Swi), Helvetia
Stage 2: Luc Roosen (B), Tulip
Stage 3: Heinz Imboden (Swi), Helvetia
Stage 4: Jan Nevens (B), Lotto
Stage 5 (TT): Robert Millar (GB), Z
Stage 6: Franco Vona (It), Jolly-Club 88
Stage 7: Olaf Ludwig (Ger), Panasonic
Stage 8: Phil Anderson (Aus), Motorola
Stage 9: Rolf Sörensen (Den), Ariostea
Stage 10: Stefano Colage (It), ZG-Bottechia

ORE-IDA WOMEN'S CHALLENGE *page 82*

1	Jeannie Longo (Fr), Weight Watchers	24:12.11
2	Dede Demet (USA), TGI Friday's	at 0:44
3	Daiva Tchepiene (Lit), Powerhouse	at 0:48
4	Sally Zack (USA), Shacklee-Ritchey	at 1:09
5	Maureen Manley (USA), TGI Friday's	at 2:01
6	Tea Vikstedt-Nyman (Fin), Weight Watchers	at 2:24
7	Eve Stephenson (USA), TGI Friday's	at 2:42
8	Linda Brenneman (USA), TGI Friday's	at 2:48
9	Julie Young (USA), Kahlua	at 3:18
10	Jaqui Uttien, Australia	at 4:02

Stage winners
Prologue: Jeannie Longo (Fr), Weight Watchers
Stage 1: Sally Zack (USA), Shacklee-Ritchey
Stage 2: Sally Zack (USA), Shacklee-Ritchey
Stage 3: Sally Zack (USA), Shacklee-Ritchey
Stage 4 (TTT): Lithuania
Stage 5: Dede Demet (USA), TGI Friday's
Stage 6 (TT): Tea Vikstedt-Nyman (Fin), Weight Watchers
Stage 7: Jeannie Longo (Fr), Weight Watchers
Stage 8: Tea Vikstedt-Nyman (Fin), Weight Watchers
Stage 9: Linda Brenneman (USA), TGI Friday's
Stage 10: Jaqui Uttien, Australia
Stage 11: Sally Zack (USA), Shacklee-Ritchey
Team
TGI Friday's
Points
Tea Vikstedt-Nyman (Fin), Weight Watchers
Queen of the Mountains
Jeannie Longo (Fr), Weight Watchers
Hot Spots
Linda Brenneman (USA) TGI Friday's

TOUR DE FRANCE *page 84*

1	Miguel Indurain (Sp), Banesto	101:01.20
2	Gianni Bugno (It), Gatorade	at 3:36.3
3	Claudio Chiappucci (It), Carrera	at 5:56
4	Charly Mottet (Fr), RMO	at 7:37
5	Luc Leblanc (Fr), Castorama	at 10:10
6	Laurent Fignon (Fr), Castorama	at 11:27
7	Greg LeMond (USA), Z	at 13:13
8	Andrew Hampsten (USA), Motorola	at 13:40
9	Pedro Delgado (Sp), Banesto	at 20:10
10	Gérard Rué (Fr), Helvetia	at 20:13
11	Eduardo Chozas (Sp), ONCE	at 21:00
12	Abelardo Rondon (Col), Banesto	at 26:47
13	Gert-Jan Theunisse (Hol), TVM	at 27:10
14	Jean-François Bernard (Fr), Banesto	at 28:57
15	Maurizio Fondriest (It), Panasonic	at 30:09
16	Denis Roux (Fr), Toshiba	at 30:40
17	Eric Caritoux (Fr), RMO	at 32:39
18	Alberto Carmargo (Col), Ryalcao-Postobon	at 32:54
19	Alvaro Mejia (Col), Ryalcao-Postobon	at 33:52
20	Frédéric Vichot (Fr), Castorama	at 36:43
21	Gilles Delion (Fr), Helvetia	at 38:43
22	Javier Murguialday (Sp), Amaya	at 39:11
23	Jérôme Simon (Fr), Z	at 39:14
24	Fabrice Philipot (Fr), Banesto	at 41:56
25	Thierry Bourguignon (Fr), Toshiba	at 42:32
26	Steven Rooks (Hol), Buckler	at 44:49
27	Thierry Claveyrolat (Fr), RMO	st
28	Patrice Esnault (Fr), Amaya	at 46:14
29	Roberto Conti (It), Ariostea	at 46:41
30	Marco Giovannetti (It), Gatorade	at 47:06
31	Luis Herrera (Col), Ryalcao-Postobon	at 47:58
32	Uwe Ampler (Ger), Histor	at 49:11
33	Pello Ruiz-Cabestany (Sp), Clas	at 53:21
34	Gerrit de Vries (Hol), Buckler	at 54:47
35	Johan Bruyneel (B), Lotto	at 57:28
36	Jean-Claude Bagot (Fr), Z	at 59:51
37	Anselmo Fuerte (Sp), ONCE	at 59:20
38	Eric Boyer (Fr), Z	at 59:51
39	Alberto Leanizbarrutia (Sp), Clas	at 1:03.09

40	Alessandro Giannelli (It), Carrera	at 1:03.52
41	Ronan Pensec (Fr), Amaya	at 1:06.04
42	Viatcheslav Ekimov (USSR), Panasonic	at 1:06.17
43	Henry Cardenas (Col), Ryalcao-Postobon	at 1:07.23
44	Philippe Louviot (Fr), Toshiba	at 1:07.31
45	Phil Anderson (Aus), Motorola	at 1:08.13
46	Guiza Moncada (Col), Ryalcao-Postobon	at 1:08.45
47	Mauro Ribeiro (Bra), RMO	at 1:09.45
48	Oscar Vargas (Col), Ryalcao-Postobon	at 1:11.04
49	Pascal Richard (Swi), Helvetia	at 1:11.16
50	Didier Virvaleix (Fr), Histor	at 1:12.05

Stage winners
Prologue (TT): Thierry Marie (Fr), Castorama
Stage 1: Djamolidin Abdujaparov (USSR), Carrera
Stage 2 (TTT): Ariostea
Stage 3: Etienne de Wilde (B), Histor
Stage 4: Djamolidin Abdujaparov (USSR), Carrera
Stage 5: Jelle Nijdam (Hol), Buckler
Stage 6: Thierry Marie (Fr), Castorama
Stage 7: Jean-Paul Van Poppel (Hol), PDM
Stage 8: Miguel Indurain (Sp), Banesto
Stage 9: Mauro Ribeiro (Br), RMO
Stage 10: Phil Anderson (Aus), Motorola
Stage 11: Charly Mottet (Fr), RMO
Stage 12: Charly Mottet (fr), RMO
Stage 13: Claudio Chiappucci (It), Carrera
Stage 14: Bruno Cenghialta (It), Ariostea
Stage 15: Moreno Argentin (It), Ariostea
Stage 16: Marco Lietti (It), Ariostea
Stage 17: Gianni Bugno (It), Gatorade
Stage 18: Thierry Claveyrolat (Fr), RMO
Stage 19: Dmitri Konyshev (USSR), TVM
Stage 20: Viatcheslav Ekimov (USSR), Panasonic
Stage 21 (TT): Miguel Indurain (Sp), Banesto
Stage 22: Dmitri Konyshev (USSR), TVM
Teams classification
Banesto (Spain)
Points
Djamolidin Abdujaparov (USSR), Carrera
Mountains
Claudio Chiappucci (It), Carrera
Best young rider (under 25)
Alvaro Mejia (Col), Postobon

WINCANTON CLASSIC *page 104*

1	Eric Van Lancker (B), Panasonic	6:16.05
2	Rolf Gölz (Ger), Ariostea	at 06:29
3	Jan Goessens (B), Weinmann	at 04:22
4	Gilles Delion (Fr), Helvetia	st
5	Maurizio Fondriest (It), Panasonic	st
6	Steven Rooks (Hol), Buckler	st
7	Marc Madiot (Fr), RMO	st
8	Luc Leblanc (Fr), Castorama	st
9	Claudio Chiappucci (It), Carrera	st
10	Frans Maassen (Hol), Buckler	st

KELLOGG'S TOUR OF BRITAIN *page 106*

1	Phil Anderson (Aus), Motorola	24:59.57
2	Rudy Verdonck (B), Weinmann	at 0:1
3	Heinz Imboden (Swi), Helvetia	st
4	Robert Millar (GB), Z	at 0:17
5	Jens Heppner (Ger), Panasonic	at 0:41
6	Allan Peiper (Aus), Tulip	0:53
7	Scott Sunderland (Aus), TVM	st
8	Rob Holden (GB), Banana-Falcon	st
9	Eddy Bouwmans (Hol), Panasonic	at 0:56
10	Adri Van Der Poel (Hol), Tulip	3:20

Stage winners
Stage1: Phil Anderson (Aus), Motorola
Stage 2: Johan Museeuw (B), Lotto
Stage 3; Phil Anderson (Aus), Motorola
Stage 4a(TT): Gianluca Bortolami (It), Colnago-Lampere
Stage 4b: Rolf Aldag (Ger), Helvetia
Stage 5: Adri Van Der Poel (Hol), Tulip
Team
Panasonic
King of the Mountains
Phil Anderson
Points
Rudy Verdonck
Sprints
Hendrik Redant

CLASICÁ SAN SEBASTIAN *page 110*

1	Gianni Bugno (It), Gatorade	6:04.28
2	Pedro Delgado (Sp), Banesto	at 0:55
3	Maurizio Fondriest (It), Panasonic	at 1:17
4	Laurent Jalabert (Fr), Toshiba	st
5	Iñaki Gaston (Sp), Clas	st
6	Gilles Delion (Fr), Helvetia	st
7	Bruno Cenghialta (It), Ariostea	st
8	Piotr Ugrumov (USSR), Seur	st
9	Andreas Kappes (Ger), Histor	at 1:58
10	Charly Mottet (Fr), RMO	st

CHAMPIONSHIP OF ZÜRICH *page 112*

1	Johan Museeuw (B), Lotto	6:28.13
2	Laurent Jalabert (Fr), Toshiba	st
3	Maximillian Sciandri (It), Carrera	st
4	Maurizio Fondriest (It), Panasonic	st
5	Edwig Van Hooydonck (B), Buckler	st
6	Andrei Tchmile (USSR), SEFB	st
7	Phil Anderson (Aus), Motorola	st
8	Falk Boden (Ger), PDM	st
9	Luc Roosen (B), Tulip	st
10	Dirk De Wolf (B), Tonton Tapis	st

NORBA SERIES *page 114*
Men

1	Ned Overend, Specialized	133pts
2	David Wiens, Diamond Back	113pts
3	John Tomac, Raleigh-Nike	101pts
4	Daryl Price, Specialized	93pts
5	Rishi Grewal, GT Bicycles	92pts
6	Ranjeet Grewal, Scott USA	85pts
7	Tinker Juarez, Klein-Campagnolo	84pts
8	Tim Rutherford, Ritchey USA	77pts
9	Mike Kloser, Alpine Stars USA	71pts
10	Don Myrah, Steelman-Campagnolo	69pts

Women

1	Juli Furtado, Yeti Cycles	96pts
2	Sara Ballantyne, Specialized	76pts
3	Susan DeMattei, Diamond Back	51pts
4	Darcy Dangremont, Fat Chance	42pts
5	Cindy Whitehead, Klein	34pts
6	Susan DiBiase, GT	33pts
7	Ruthie Matthes, Ritchey	29pts
8	Tammy Jacques, Giant	24pts
9	Penny Davidson, Klein	17pts
10	Teresa Williams, Park City	13pts

WORLD ROAD CHAMPIONSHIPS *page 116*
Men's professional road race

1	Gianni Bugno (It)	6:20.23
2	Steven Rooks (Hol)	st
3	Miguel Indurain (Sp)	st
4	Alvaro Mejia (Col)	st
5	Kai Hundertmarck (Ger)	at 0:11
6	Bjarne Riis (Den)	st
7	Dirk De Wolf (B)	st
8	Stephen Hodge (Aus)	st
9	Davide Cassani (It)	st
10	Federico Echave (Sp)	st
11	Maurizio Fondriest (It)	st
12	Franco Ballerini (It)	st
13	Piotr Ugrumov (USSR)	st
14	Rudy Dhaenens (B)	st
15	Bo Hamburger (Den)	st
16	Laurent Fignon (Fr)	st
17	Claudio Chiappucci (It)	st
18	Gert-Jan Theunisse (Hol)	st
19	Heinz Imboden (Swi)	st
20	Miguel Arroyo (Mex)	st
21	Gérard Rué (Fr)	st
22	William Palacio (Col)	st
23	Luc Roosen (B)	st
24	Efrain Rico (Col)	st
25	Marc Madiot (Fr)	st

Men's amateur road race

1	Viktor Riaksinski(USSR)	4:28.04
2	Davide Rebellin (It)	st
3	Beat Zberg (Swi)	st
4	Viatcheslav Djavanian (USSR)	st
5	Jacek Bodyk (Pol)	st
6	Vladimir Belli (It)	st
7	Pascal Hervé (Fr)	st
8	Daniel Lanz (Swi)	st
9	Mirko Gualdi (It)	at 0:23
10	Andrzej Sypytkowski (Pol)	st

Women's road race

1	Leontien Van Moorsel (Hol)	2:09:47
2	Inga Thompson (USA)	at 1:54
3	Alison Sydor (Can)	at 2:46
4	Sally Zack (USA)	st
5	Elena Ogoui (USSR)	st
6	Marie Höljer (Swe)	st
7	Luzia Zberg (Swi)	st
8	Monica Bandini (It)	st
9	Jolanta Polikavitchutee (USSR)	st
10	Heidi Van de Vijver (B)	st

Men's team time trial

1	Italy (Flavio Anastasia, Luca Colombo, Gianfranco Contri, Andrea Peron)	1:54.48
2	Germany (Uwe Berndt, Bernt Dittert, Uwe Peschel, Michael Rich)	1:57.21
3	Norway (Stig Kristiansen, Johnny Saether, Roar Skanne, Björn Stenersen)	1:57.39
4	Poland	
5	Holland	
6	France	

7	USA
8	Switzerland
9	Czechoslovakia
10	Denmark

Women's team time trial

1	France (Marion Clignet, Nathalie Gendron, Cécile Odin, Catherine Marsal)	1:02.14
2	Holland (Monique De Bruin, Monique Knol, Astrid Schop, Cora Westland)	1:02.41
3	USSR (Nina Grinina, Nadejda Kibardina, Valentina Polkhanova, Aiga Zagorska)	1:02.51
4	USA	
5	Italy	
6	Germany	
7	New Zealand	
8	Great Britain	
9	China	
10	Sweden	

WORLD TRACK CHAMPIONSHIPS *page 122*
PROFESSIONALS
Sprint
Quarter-finals: Carey Hall (Aus) *beat*

Michael Hübner	2-0
Stephen Pate (Aus) *beat* Kazuo Namigata (Jap)	2-0
Fabrice Colas (Fr) *beat* Nelson Vails (USA)	2-0
Claudio Golinelli (It) *beat* Patrick Da Rocha (Fr)	2-0
Semi-finals: Hall *beat* Golinelli	2-1
Colas *beat* Pate	2-1

Fifth place: Namigata *beat* Vails, Da Rocha; dns Hübner

Bronze medal: Stephen Pate (Aus) *beat* Claudio Golinelli (It)	2-1
Final: Carey Hall (Aus) *beat* Fabrice Colas (Fr)	2-1

(Hall and Pate disqualified for a positive drugs test; only the silver medal awarded)

5000m pursuit

Quarter-finals: Viatcheslav Ekimov (USSR)	5:40.200
beat Mike McCarthy (USA)	5:40.512
Shaun Wallace (GB)	5:38.063
beat Dean Woods (Aus)	5:45.19
Francis Moreau (Fr)	5:32.224
caught Tony Davis (Aus)	
Colin Sturgess (GB)	5:39.22
beat Peter Pieters (Hol)	5:43.659
Semi-finals: Wallace	5:35.457
beat Sturgess	5:38.563
Moreau	5:33.761
beat Ekimov	5:39.107
Final: Moreau	5:34.444
beat Wallace	5:39.594

Final positions:

1	Francis Moreau (Fr)	
2	Viatcheslav Ekimov (USSR)	
3	Colin Sturgess (GB)	

Keirin

1	Michael Hübner (Ger)	10:79
2	Claudio Golinelli (It)	
3	Fabrice Colas (Fr)	
4	Nelson Vails (USA)	
5	Koichi Nakano (Jap)	
6	Patrick da Rocha (Fr)	

Points race

1	Viatcheslav Ekimov (USSR)	27pts
2	Francis Moreau (Fr)	44pts
3	Peter Pieters (Hol)	44pts
4	Etienne de Wilde (B)	42pts
5	Daniel Wyder (Swi)	32pts
6	Steve Hegg (USA)	29pts
7	Carsten Wolf (Ger)	27pts
8	Silvio Martinello (It)	23pts
9	Juan Curuchet (Arg)	20pts
10	Gary Sutton (Aus)	20pts

Motor-paced

1	Danny Clark (Aus)	59:28.97
2	Peter Steiger (Swi)	
3	Arno Kuttel (Swi)	
4	(at one lap) Luigi Belli (It)	
5	(at two laps) Alexander Romanov (USSR)	
6	(at three laps) Roland Gunther (Ger)	
7	(at seven laps) Andrea Bellati (Swi)	

AMATEUR MEN
Kilometre TT

1	José-Manuel Moreno (Sp)	1:03.827
2	Jens Glücklich (Ger)	1:04.808
3	Gene Samuel (Trin)	1:04.797
4	Frédéric Magné (Fr)	1:04.808
5	Alexander Kiritchenko (USSR)	1:05.030
6	Aldo Capelli (It)	1:05.750
7	Rocco Travella (Swi)	1:05.761
8	Kenneth Ropke (Den)	1:05.830
9	Mika Hämäläinen (Fin)	1:05.930
10	Erin Hartwell (USA)	1:06.119

Sprint
Quarter-finals: Bill Huck (Ger) *beat* Erik Schoefs (B) 2-0

Curt Harnett (Can) *beat* Denis Lemyre (Fr)	2-0
Jens Fiedler (Ger) *beat* Christian Schink (Ger)	2-0
Gary Neiwand (Aus) *beat* Federico Paris (It)	
Semi-finals: Huck *beat* Neiwand	2-1
Fiedler *beat* Harnett	2-0
Final: Fiedler *beat* Huck	2-1

Final positions:

1	Jens Fiedler (Ger)
2	Bill Huck (Ger)
3	Gary Neiwand (Aus)
4	Curt Harnett (Can)
5	Federico Paris (It)
6	Denis Lemyre (Fr)
7	Christian Schink (Ger)
8	Erik Shoefs (B)

Tandem sprint

Semi-finals: Germany (Eyk Pokorney-Emanuel Raasch) *bt* France (Frédéric Lancien-Denis Lemyre)	2-0
Czechoslovakia (Pavel Buran-Lubomir Hargas) *disq bt* Italy (Gianluca Capitano-Federico Paris)	2-1

Third place: France *bt* Italy
Final: Germany *bt* Czechoslovakia

4000m pursuit

Semi-finals: Jens Lehmann (Ger)	4:26.29
beat Valeri Baturo (USSR)	4:31.81
Michael Glöckner (Ger)	4:24.91
beat Jan-Bo Petersen (Den)	4:28.53
Final: Lehmann	4:25.77
beat Glöckner	4:31.46

4000m team pursuit

Quarter-finals: USSR	4:09.079
beat France	4:16.243
Denmark	4:13.567
beat Czechoslovakia	4:15.934
Australia	4:8.134
beat New Zealand	4:13.743
Germany	4:7.707
beat Holland	4:14.562
Semi-finals: USSR	4:09.011
beat Australia	4:10.940
Germany	4:07.707
beat Denmark	4:12.533
Finals: Germany	4:07.003
beat USSR	4:12.259

Final positions:

1 Germany (Michael Glöckner, Jens Lehmann, Stefan Steinweg, Andreas Waltzer)
2 USSR (Eugeni Berzin, Vladislav Bobrik, Vadim Kravtchenko, Dmitri Neljubin)
3 Australia (Brett Aitken, Stephen McGlede, Shaun O'Brien, Stuart O'Grady)

Points race

1	Bruno Risi (Swi)	55pts
2	Stephen McGlede (Aus)	40pts
3	Jan-Bo Petersen (Den)	31pts
4	Leon Van Bon (Hol)	19pts
5	Manuel Youshimatz (Mex)	18pts
6	Hiroshi Daimon (Jap)	10pts
7	Dmitri Nelubin (USSR)	37 (-1 lap)
8	Eric Weispfennig (Ger)	23 (-1 lap)
9	Emanuel Heynemans (B)	23 (-1 lap)
10	Jim Pollack (USA)	22 (-1 lap)

Motor-paced

1	Roland Königshofer (Austria)	42:46.60
2	Davide Solari (It)	
3	(at 2 laps) Carsten Podlesch (Ger)	
4	(at 4 laps) Adriano Tondini (It)	
5	(at 4 laps) Richi Rossi (Swi)	
6	(at 6 laps) Sven Harter (Ger)	
7	(at 7 laps) Mario Van Barle (Hol)	
8	(at 7 laps) Thomas Königshofer (Austria)	

WOMEN
Sprint

Quarter-finals: Ingrid Haringa (Hol) *beat* Xuemei Wang (China)	2-0
Annette Neumann (Ger) *beat* Galina Enukhina (USSR)	2-1
Connie Paraskevin-Young (USA) *beat* Lingmai Zhou (China)	2-1
Felicia Ballanger (Fr) *beat* Renée Duprel (USA)	2-0
Semi-finals: Haringa *beat* Ballanger	2-0
Neumann *beat* Paraskevin-Young	2-0
Third place: Paraskevin-Young *beat* Ballanger	2-0
Final: Haringa *beat* Neumann	2-0

Final positions

1	Haringa
2	Neumann
3	Paraskevin-Young
4	Ballanger
5	Zhou
6	Duprel
7	Enukhina
8	Wang

3000m pursuit

Quarter-final: Kristel Werckx (B)		3:42.703
beat Svetlana Samokhavlova (USSR)		3:44.152
Janie Eickhoff (USA)		3:39.159
beat Barbara Erdin-Ganz (Swi)		3:43.461
Petra Rossner (Ger)		3:40.661
beat Jacqueline Nelson (NZ)		3:42.131
Marion Clignet (Fr)		3:42.008
beat Hanne Malmberg (Den)		3:45.041
Semi-finals: Rossner		3:38.941
beat Clignet		3:39.501
Eickhoff		3:39.885
beat Werckx		3:43.534
Final: Rossner		3:39.884
beat Eickhoff		3:40.379

Final positions
1 Rossner
2 Eickhoff
3 Clignet
4 Werckx

Points race

1	Ingrid Haringa (Hol)	40pts
2	Kristel Werckx (B)	37pts
3	Janie Eickhoff (USA)	37pts
4	Barbara Erdin-Ganz (Swi)	25pts
5	Svetlana Samokhavlova (USSR)	19pts
6	Kathrin Ranger (Ger)	18pts
7	Lucille Hunkler (Swi)	11pts
8	Isabelle Nicoloso (Fr)	9pts
9	Elizabetta Guazzaroni (It)	7pts
10	Lisa Munck (Den)	6pts

GRUNDIG WORLD CUP SERIES *page 126*

Men

1	John Tomac, Raleigh	132pts
2	Gerhard Zadrobilek, Red Bull	131pts
3	Dave Wiens, Diamond Back	126pts
4	Rishi Grewal, GT	117pts
5	Ned Overend, Specialized	114pts
6	Mike Kloser, Alpine Stars	106pts
7	Mike Kluge, Wheeler	95pts
8	Daryl Price, Specialized	84pts
9	Peter Hric, Carrera	81pts
10	Hendrik Djernis, Ritchey	78pts

Women

1	Sara Ballantyne, Specialized	94pts
2	Juli Furtado, Yeti	85pts
3	Regina Steifl, Scott	74pts
4	Silvia Fürst, Mongoose	67pts
5	Susan DeMattei, Diamond Back	54pts
6	Chantal Daucourt, Cilo	51pts
7	Cindy Whitehead, Klein	25pts
8	Susan DiBiase, GT	16pts
9	Cindy Devine, Kona	14pts
10	Nancy Aubrey Walker, Klein	7pts

GRAND PRIX DE LA LIBERATION *page 128*

1	Buckler (Hol) (Gerrit De Vries, Frans Maassen, Jelle Nijdam, Wilco Zuyderwijk, Patrick Eyk, Edwig Van Hooydonck)	1:37.15
2	ONCE (Sp) (Herminio Diaz Zabala, Johnny Weltz, Stephen Hodge, Marino Lejarreta, Juan Llaneras, Melchor Mauri)	at 0:18
3	Panasonic (Hol) (Maurizio Fondriest, Dmitri Zdhanov, Olaf Ludwig, Rudy Dhaenens, Viatcheslav Ekimov)	at 0:42
4	PDM (Hol) (Raúl Alcalá, Sean Kelly, Falk Boden, Eric Breukink, Tom Cordes, Uwe Raab)	at 1:25
5	TVM (Hol)	at 1:33
6	Motorola (USA)	at 2:02
7	Tulip (B)	at 2:34
8	Lotus (Sp)	at 2:46
9	Weinmann (B)	at 2:28
10	Histor (B)	at 2:33

PARIS-BRUSSELS *page 130*

1	Brian Holm (Den), Histor	6:03.10
2	Olaf Ludwig (Ger), Panasonic	at 0:07
3	Johan Museeuw (B), Lotto	st
4	Christophe Capelle (Fr), Z	st
5	Weibren Veenstra (Hol), Buckler	st
6	Andreas Kappes (Ger), Histor	st
7	Benny Van Brabant (B), SEFB	st
8	Christian Chaubet (Fr), Toshiba	st
9	Johan Capiot (B), TVM	st
10	Danny Neskens (B), La William	st

NISSAN CLASSIC *page 132*

1	Sean Kelly (Ire), PDM	21:53.11
2	Sean Yates (GB), Motorola	at 0:04
3	Johan Museeuw (B), Lotto	at 0:38
4	Adri Van Der Poel (Hol), Tulip	at 0:42
5	Eric Van Lancker (B), Panasonic	at 0:45
6	Udo Bölts (Ger), Telekom	at 0:50
7	Dag-Otto Lauritzen (Nor), Motorola	at 0:50
8	Raúl Alcalá (Mex), PDM	at 1:01
9	Viatcheslav Ekimov (USSR), Panasonic	at 1:02
10	Martin Earley (Ire), PDM	at 1:06

Stage winners
Stage 1: Eric Vanderaerden (B), Buckler
Stage 2: Olaf Ludwig (Ger), Panasonic
Stage 3: Johan Museeuw (B), Lotto
Stage 4: Sean Yates (GB), Motorola
Stage 5: Olaf Ludwig (Ger), Panasonic

WORLD MOUNTAIN BIKE CHAMPIONSHIPS *page 138*

Men's cross-country

1	John Tomac (USA)	2:38.56
2	Thomas Frischknecht (Swi)	at 3:04
3	Ned Overend (USA)	at 3:31
4	Don Myrah (USA)	at 6:37
5	Mike Kloser (USA)	at 7:06
6	Tim Gould (GB)	at 7:34
7	Tim Davies (GB)	at 7:34
8	Riccardo De Bertolis (It)	at 9:43
9	Bernt Johansson (Swe)	10:06
10	Daryl Price (USA)	at 10:20

Women's cross-country

1	Ruthie Matthes (USA)	2:20.2
2	Eva Orvosova (Cz)	at 1:48
3	Sylvia Fürst (Swi)	at 4:20
4	Chantal Daucourt (Swi)	at 5:59
5	Alison Sydor (Can)	at 8:17
6	Sara Ballantyne (USA)	at 9:42
7	Nathalie Fiat (Fr)	at 9:53
8	Susan De Mattei (USA)	at 11:32
9	Sophie Eglin (Fr)	at 11:47
10	Susi Buchweiser (Ger)	11:50

Junior men's cross-country

1	John Mutolo (USA)	1:23.09
2	Chris Fox (USA)	at 1:17.3
3	Paul Lasenby (GB)	at 1:34
4	Dario Acquaroli (It)	at 2:58
5	Alberto Balcells (Sp)	at 3:22
6	Matt Smith (USA)	at 3:56
7	Alex Smith (USA)	at 4:02
8	Jens Winterhalder (Ger)	at 4:49
9	Pietro Castellino (It)	at 4:58
10	Filippo Belloni (It)	at 5:23

Junior women's cross-country

1	Karin Romer (Ger)	1:52.29
2	Rita Burgi (Swi)	at 2:05
3	Denise Mueller (USA)	at 5:55
4	Giuliana Lamastra (It)	at 8:43
5	M Lindgren (Swe)	at 13:32
6	Melanie Eberle (Ger)	at 18:16
7	Stephanie Ethoin (Fr)	at 19:51
8	Nicolle Leyton (Hol)	at 19:52
9	Letitia Ronnat (Fr)	at 21:32
10	Antonella Di Meo (It)	at 32:05

Men's downhill

1	Albert Iten (Swi)	7:11.2
2	John Tomac (USA)	at 0:4
3	Glen Adams (USA)	at 0:9
4	Philippe Perakis (Swi)	st
5	Paolo Rosola (It)	at 0:11
6	Philip Meirhaeghe (B)	at 0:12
7	Paul Heryghers (B)	st
8	Dave Cullinan (USA)	at 0:13
9	Andrew Shandro (Can)	at 0:14
10	Christian Taillefer (Fr)	at 0:15

Women's downhill

1	Giovanna Bonazzi (It)	8:4.3
2	Nathalie Fiat (Fr)	at 0:14
3	Cindy Devine (Can)	at 0:16
4	Elladee Brown (Can)	at 0:19
5	Regina Steifl (Ger)	at 0:20
6	Susi Buchweiser (Ger)	at 0:26
7	Linda Spiazzi (It)	at 0:34
8	Juli Furtado (USA)	at 0:36
9	Sophie Kempf (Fr)	at 0:39
10	Deb Murrell (GB)	at 0:46

Junior men's downhill

1	Bruno Zanchi (It)	7:26.8
2	Tomas Misser (Sp)	at 0:02
3	Verner de Cuester (B)	at 0:06
4	Vincent Julliot (Fr)	at 0:11
5	Filippo Belloni (It)	at 0:16
6	Alex Vidal (Sp)	at 0:17
7	Ludovic Dubau (Fr)	at 0:18
8	Alessandro Lajolo (It)	at 0:18
9	Markus Petschenis (Austria)	at 0:19
10	Alex Morgan (USA)	at 0:21

Junior women's downhill

1	Rita Burgi (Swi)	8:44.23
2	Denise Mueller (USA)	at 0:23
3	Melanie Emerle (Ger)	at 0:55
4	Stephanie Ethoin (Fr)	at 1:06
5	Letitia Ronnat (Fr)	at 1:10
6	Giuliana Lamastra (It)	at 1:27
7	Paolo Zucchinali (It)	at 1:28
8	Antonella Di Meo (It)	at 1:57
9	Courtney Reeser (USA)	at 2:57
10	Barbara Alberti (It)	at 6:00

MONTREAL GRAND PRIX *page 140*

1	Eric Van Lancker (B), Panasonic	5:54.15
2	Steven Rooks (Hol), Buckler	st
3	Martin Earley (Ire), PDM	st
4	Mauro Gianetti (Swi), Helvetia	st
5	Robert Millar (GB), Z	st
6	Tony Rominger (Swi), Toshiba	st
7	Maurizio Fondriest (It), Panasonic	st
8	Adri Van Der Poel (Hol), Tulip	at 1:02
9	Edwig Van Hooydonck (B), Buckler	st
10	Marc Madiot (F), RMO	st

PARIS-TOURS *page 142*

1	Johan Capiot (B), TVM	7:26.48
2	Olaf Ludwig (Ger), Panasonic	st
3	Nico Verhoeven (Hol), PDM	st
4	Adri Van Der Poel (Hol), Tulip	st
5	Rolf Sörensen (Den), Ariostea	st
6	Peter Pieters (Hol), Tulip	st
7	Laurent Jalabert (Fr), Toshiba	st
8	Frankie Andreu (USA), Motorola	st
9	Johan Museeuw (B), Lotto	st
10	Rudy Verdonck (B), Tulip	st

TOUR OF LOMBARDY *page 144*

1	Sean Kelly (Ire), PDM	6:10.38
2	Martial Gayant (Fr), Toshiba	st
3	Franco Ballerini (It), Del Tongo	at 0:35
4	Bruno Cornillet (Fr), Z	at 2:09
5	Rolf Sörensen (Den), Ariostea	st
6	Alberto Volpi (It), Gatorade	st
7	Dante Rezze (Fr), RMO	st
8	Laurent Jalabert (Fr), Toshiba	at 2:19
9	Sammie Moreels (B), Lotto	st
10	Marco Vitali (It), Jolly-Club 88	st

GRAND PRIX DES NATIONS *page 150*

1	Tony Rominger (Swi), Toshiba	1:20.40
2	Eric Breukink (Hol), PDM	at 0:58
3	Thomas Wegmüller (Swi), Weinmann	at 2:08
4	Maurizio Fondriest (It), Panasonic	at 2:12
5	Federico Echave (Sp), Clas	at 2:16
6	Frans Maassen (Hol), Buckler	at 2:22
7	Rolf Sörensen (Den), Ariostea	at 2:24
8	Stephen Hodge (Aus), ONCE	at 2:25
9	Melchor Mauri (Sp), ONCE	at 2:44
10	Laurent Jalabert (Fr), Toshiba	at 3:20
11	Edwig Van Hooydonck (B), Buckler	at 3:46
12	Martial Gayant (Fr), Toshiba	at 4:11
13	Adri Van Der Poel (Hol), Tulip	at 4:21
14	Johan Museeuw (B), Lotto	at 5:01
15	Marc Madiot (Fr), RMO	at 5:08
16	Franco Ballerini (It), Del Tongo	at 5:42
17	Phil Anderson (Aus), Motorola	at 6:05
18	Claudio Chiappucci (It), Carrera	at 7:22
19	Johan Capiot (B), TVM	at 7:45
20	Nico Verhoeven (Hol), PDM	Did not start